BRIDGES
OUT OF POVERTY

STRATEGIES
FOR PROFESSIONALS
AND COMMUNITIES

Ruby K. Payne, Ph.D.
Philip DeVol
Terie Dreussi Smith

aha!
Process, Inc.

Bridges Out of Poverty: Strategies for Professionals and Communities. Revised edition.
© 2001 by Ruby K. Payne, Philip DeVol, & Terie Dreussi Smith. Revised 2005, 2006, 2009.

Printed in the United States of America
Book design by Sara Patton

Payne, Ruby K., DeVol, Philip, & Dreussi Smith, Terie.
    Bridges Out of Poverty: Strategies for Professionals and Communities by
    Ruby K. Payne, Philip DeVol, & Terie Dreussi Smith © 2001. 296 pp.
        Bibliography pp. 279–285
        ISBN 978-1-934583-35-7
    1. Education   2. Sociology   3. Title

Grateful acknowledgment is made to the following copyright holders for permission to use their copyrighted material:

Bantam Books, for quotations from pp. x–xi, 8, 11, 16–18, 108, and 202 of *Convicted in the Womb* by Carl Upchurch. © 1996 by Carl Upchurch. Used by permission of Bantam Books, a division of Random House, Inc.

Bantam Books, for quotations from pp. 64, 114–115, and 160 of *The Spirituality of Imperfection* by Ernest Kurtz and Katherine Ketcham. © 1992 by Ernest Kurtz and Katherine Ketcham. Used by permission of Bantam Books, a division of Random House, Inc.

Basic Books, for quotations from pp. 66, 68, 70, 82–83, 85, 93, 100, 104–105, 107, 116–117, 119, and 122 of *The War Against the Poor* by Herbert J. Gans. © 1995 by Herbert J. Gans. Reprinted by permission of Basic Books, a member of Perseus Books, L.L.C.

HarperCollins Publishers, for quotations from pp. 157–158 of *Data Smog* by David Shenk. © 1997 by David Shenk. Reprinted by permission of HarperCollins Publishers, Inc.

Contents

Acknowledgments

■ ■ ■ ■ ■ ■ ■ ■ ■ ■ ■ ■ ■ ■

Thanks to Erma Morgan for pointing the way; Julie Miller and my wife, Susan, for their commitment to the project; and the members of the Life Skills Provider Network and Carol Curl for letting me experiment with my ideas. Thanks also to the many people who shared their stories with me. The staff of the Ashley Wornstaff Memorial Library was a great help in locating articles and books.

– Philip DeVol

Thank you to the fine women who spent hours sharing their stories during our interviews. Your contributions truly enrich our understanding of how bridges out of poverty are built and traversed. Many thanks to Ben for his unfailing humor and continual encouragement—and to my parents for providing an exceptionally "resourceful" home and family.

– Terie Dreussi Smith

Ruby Payne's book *A Framework for Understanding of Poverty* clicked with us as it does with most people, particularly those who work closely with people who live at the bottom of the socioeconomic ladder. Ruby offered insight and encouragement to us as we worked on ways to apply her framework to the organizations that work with people in poverty. She continually offered us books and research from a variety of disciplines, always pushing us to a broader understanding of our topic and turning this project into a wonderful learning experience.

– Phil DeVol, Terie Dreussi Smith

BRIDGES
OUT
OF
POVERTY

STRATEGIES
FOR PROFESSIONALS
AND COMMUNITIES

I sit on the splintery front porch of my cheesy Oregonian love shack and watch these people struggle to escape their ugliness, only to be recaptured by it again and again. Once you go trash, you never come back. The current climate offers me nothing but self-denial, so I'm comfortable living in the past. It's like coming out of the closet— I've come out of the trailer. I embrace the shame.

— Jim Goad, *The Redneck Manifesto*

Makes me wanna holler.

— Marvin Gaye, Singer

Anyone could tell it, anyone who had a momma who went eighteen years without a new dress so that her sons could have school clothes, who picked cotton in other people's fields and ironed other people's clothes and cleaned the mess in other people's houses, so that her children didn't have to live on welfare alone, so that one of them could climb up her backbone and escape the poverty and hopeless-ness that ringed them, free and clean.

— Rick Bragg, *All Over but the Shoutin'*

Introduction

■ ■ ■ ■ ■ ■ ■ ■ ■ ■

Much has changed since this book was first published in 1999.
At that time the U.S. Welfare Reform Act of 1996 appeared to be
producing impressive results. TANF (Temporary Assistance to Needy
Families) caseloads had been cut in half, poverty and unemployment rates
were at record lows, and there were substantial increases in the income levels
of single-mother families. When the technology-driven economic boom
ended in early 2000 it became apparent to poverty watchers, if not the media
or the general public, that the gains were more a function of a strong
economy than the welfare reform policy. When the attention of the nation
shifted to terrorism and wars, people in poverty became invisible again,
almost as invisible as they were in the 1950s.

Now, with a dubious debt of gratitude to Hurricane Katrina in 2005,
poverty in the United States became visible again. Katrina blew away the
generally held belief that welfare reform was a success and the U.S. economy
was working for everyone. Even the popular media began raising questions
about race and class.

But Katrina did more than make poverty visible again; it also has served
as a metaphor for poverty itself. The storm threw communities into chaos,
forcing community organizations, as well as individuals, into survival mode.
Basic community resources such as housing, health care, education, police,
transportation, and utilities were wiped out or severely disrupted. Community
structures and budgets were overwhelmed. Similar language can be used to
describe the impact of poverty on families. Poverty itself throws families into
chaos, forcing them into survival mode. Basic resources are wiped out or
severely disrupted. Family structures and budgets are inadequate and overwhelmed. Furthermore, the Katrina metaphor can be used to describe some

cities and rural communities. The difference between a natural disaster and the poverty disaster is this: For people and communities in poverty, the crisis tends to creep along in obscurity rather than front and center, day after day, in the news.

So what were the results of welfare reform, and what has happened since 2000 when the economic boom ended? Even though the minimum wage was raised four times during the 1990s, the arithmetic of life was still not working for people at the bottom of the ladder. In 1999 about 42% of persons considered poor *worked* and were still living in poverty. Poverty rates are up. From 2000 to 2005 the number of people in poverty in the United States rose 17%. In 2004 an additional 1.1 million people fell into poverty; it was the fourth year in a row that poverty numbers had grown. In 2004 there were 37 million people in poverty. The U.S Bureau of Labor Statistics reported in December 2004 that 25% of all the jobs in the U.S. economy did not pay enough to lift a family above the poverty line. In some states 30% of all jobs did not pay a living wage. This country has become a nation where people can work full time and still be in poverty. Amy Glasmeier, in *An Atlas of Poverty in America*, sums up the current situation: ". . . [T]he experiment of the 1990s . . . has resulted in a growth in income poverty [as opposed to net-worth poverty] that leaves the nation's must vulnerable members unprotected from economic uncertainty and insecurity."

The Katrina metaphor can be used to illustrate how people respond to disasters and to poverty. To survive Katrina, people used reactive and sensory skills to solve immediate and concrete problems. There's nothing abstract about keeping your head above water or finding food or shelter. Solving problems minute-by-minute, day-by-day with limited resources is a valuable survival skill that people in poverty possess. In a crisis of a relatively short duration—such as hurricanes, tsunamis, and earthquakes—concrete, reactive problem solving is eventually replaced by abstract, proactive strategies that are based on future ramifications. This is the experience of many middle-class and wealthy people caught in the upheaval and chaos of natural disasters. For folks in poverty, on the other hand, natural disasters create a double whammy. First, there is the disaster itself, after which the unrelenting and unending crisis, as experienced in poverty, forces people into the tyranny of the moment. This is where the future is lost, where people get stuck solving the same problems over and over, and where proactive planning is difficult to do.

Individuals in poverty aren't alone in this trap; many communities across the U.S. are so busy responding to crises that they too are using reactive strategies to survive. The same can be said of nations where poverty rates are extremely high.

People at the very bottom of the economic ladder aren't the only ones in trouble. For the first time in U.S. history, the middle class is shrinking. The median household income has been flat for five straight years, and only the top 5% of households experienced real income gains in 2004. The structures that created the middle class—well-paying jobs, the 40-hour workweek, assistance with college loans and home mortgages, and employer-provided health care and pensions—are falling away.

The economic insecurity of low-wage workers and the middle class threatens the viability of our communities. When members of the middle class flee the cities, taking the tax base and spending power with them . . . when Main Street empties of viable businesses and refills with pawn shops, used clothing stories, social service storefronts, and payday lenders . . . when people can't afford to stay in the community to raise their children because of the lack of well-paying jobs . . . and when the free and reduced-price lunch rate at the schools hits 50%, our communities are becoming unsustainable.

Our work is to improve the lives of people in poverty and, by extension, to help make sustainable communities in which everyone can do well. In this edition of *Bridges Out of Poverty* you will find an essay titled "The Additive Model: the aha! Process Approach to Developing Sustainable Communities." It expands on the ideas introduced here and lays out the philosophy behind our work. In it you will read about:

- Using the knowledge of people in poverty to build an accurate mental model of poverty.

- Studying poverty research in order to develop a continuum of strategies for building prosperous and healthy communities.

- Theories of change.

- The additive model and how it applies to aha! Process constructs.

- Sharing aha! Process constructs with people in poverty.

- Creating sustainable communities.

Bridges Out of Poverty is a starting point where one can develop accurate mental models of poverty, middle class, and wealth. It is a new lens through which readers can view themselves, their clients, and the community. Readers can begin to work on front-line staff skills and to develop new program designs in order to improve relationships and outcomes. The purpose is to give community leaders from all disciplines a start on that path. Hundreds of thousands of professionals in education, social services, health care, law enforcement, corrections, business, and government already have been exposed to and inspired by Dr. Ruby K. Payne's understanding of economic diversity. Many towns, cities, and counties—and some states—have begun making changes that come from her ideas, techniques, and approaches to change.

We hope this book will contribute to the good work you are doing.

SOME KEY POINTS TO REMEMBER

1. *Poverty is relative.* If everyone around you has similar circumstances, the notion of poverty and wealth is vague. Poverty or wealth exists only in relationship to known quantities or expectations.

2. *Poverty occurs in all races and in all countries.* The notion of middle class as a large segment of society is a phenomenon of the 20th and 21st centuries. The percentage of the population that is poor is subject to definition and circumstance.

3. *Economic class is a continuous line, not a clear-cut distinction.*
    In 2004, the poverty line in the United States was considered
    $18,850 for a family of four. According to census data from 2003,
    the median household income was $43,318, and 15% of U.S.
    households earned more than $100,000 per year. Individuals are
    stationed all along the continuum of income; they sometimes
    move on that continuum as well.

4. *Generational poverty and situational poverty are different.* Genera-
    tional poverty is defined as being in poverty for two generations
    or longer. Situational poverty is a shorter time and is caused by
    circumstance (i.e., death, illness, divorce, etc.).

5. *This work is based on patterns. All patterns have exceptions.*

6. *An individual brings with him/her the hidden rules of the class in
    which he/she was raised.* Even though the income of the individual
    may rise significantly, many of the patterns of thought, social
    interaction, cognitive strategies, etc., remain with the individual.

7. *Schools and businesses operate from middle-class norms and use the
    hidden rules of middle class.* These norms and hidden rules are not
    directly taught in schools or in businesses.

8. *For our clients to be successful, we must understand their hidden
    rules and teach them the rules that will make them successful at
    school, at work, and in the community.*

9. *We can neither excuse persons from poverty nor scold them for not
    knowing; as professionals we must teach them and provide support,
    insistence, and expectations.*

10. *In order to move from poverty to middle class or middle class to wealth, an individual must give up relationships for achievement (at least for some period of time).*

11. *We cannot blame the victims of poverty for being in poverty.* Economic systems are far beyond the reach of most people to control. Factories close, small farms fold, racism persists, and the economy fails to provide enough well-paying jobs. What we offer is a way for individuals to do better.

12. *We cannot continue to support stereotypes and prejudices about the poor.* There are many forms of welfare, but the poor are the only ones who are labeled "undeserving." Others who receive welfare are students with government fellowships, homeowners with federal-tax and mortgage-interest deductions, corporations with government subsidies, and military bases that are kept open to prevent job losses.

When children grow up together in poverty, a bond is formed that is stronger than most anything. It's this same bond that causes so much pain. Adolph and Arnold reminded each other of their childhood, how they hid crackers in their shared bedroom so they would have something to eat.

– Sherman Alexie, *The Lone Ranger and Tonto Fistfight in Heaven*

It still broke Rico's heart to see poor families out for walks, the kids (thanks to television with its commercial overloads) with the "gimme" expressions on their faces. Or the mothers who had no business having so many kids dragging their children along, rage in their faces and the kind of anger that, to Rico's way of thinking, amounted to a craving to both take and destroy at the same time, like the kids he knew who started out breaking windows, gashing car finishes with broken beer bottles and knives, graduating to armed robbery and sometimes murder. . . .

– Oscar Hijuelos, *Empress of the Splendid Season*

The only thing poverty does is grind down your nerve endings to a point that you can work harder and stoop lower than most people are willing to. It chips away a person's dreams to the point that the hopelessness shows through, and the dreamer accepts that hard work and borrowed houses are all this life will ever be. While my mother will stare you in the eye and say she never thought of herself as poor, do not believe for one second that she did not see the rest of the world, the better world, spinning around her, out of reach.

– Rick Bragg, *All Over but the Shoutin'*

Sometimes, despite all her boundless "dignity"—that wondrous pride-saving province of the poor and working class—she got up in the morning and vomited, not from morning sickness or from something she'd eaten, but out of a kind of despair, the "bad nerves" that come from getting down on one's knees to wipe clean a stranger's toilet; from swallowing one's pride, out of necessity.

– Oscar Hijuelos, *Empress of the Splendid Season*

Definitions and Resources

To better understand people from poverty, the definition of poverty will be the "extent to which an individual does without resources." The resources are the following:

FINANCIAL: Having the money to purchase goods and services.

EMOTIONAL: Being able to choose and control emotional responses, particularly to negative situations, without engaging in self-destructive behavior. This is an internal resource and shows itself through stamina, perseverance, and choices.

MENTAL: Having the mental abilities and acquired skills (reading, writing, computing) to deal with daily life.

SPIRITUAL: Believing in divine purpose and guidance.

PHYSICAL: Having physical health and mobility.

SUPPORT SYSTEMS: Having friends, family, and backup resources available to access in times of need. These are external resources.

RELATIONSHIPS/ROLE MODELS: Having frequent access to adult(s) who are appropriate, who are *nurturing* to the child, and who do not engage in self-destructive behavior.

KNOWLEDGE OF HIDDEN RULES: Knowing the unspoken cues and habits of a group.

COPING STRATEGIES: Being able to engage in procedural self-talk and the mindsets that allow issues to be moved from the concrete to the abstract. It is the ability to translate from the personal to the issue.

Typically, poverty is thought of in terms of financial resources only. However the reality is that *financial resources,* while extremely important, do not explain the differences in the success with which some individuals leave poverty nor the reasons that many stay in poverty. The ability to leave poverty is more dependent upon other resources than it is upon financial resources. Each of these resources plays a vital role in the success of an individual.

Emotional resources provide the stamina to withstand difficult and uncomfortable emotional situations and feelings. Emotional resources are the most important of all resources because, when present, they allow the individual not to return to old habit patterns. In order to move from poverty to middle class or middle class to wealth, an individual must suspend his/her "emotional memory bank" because the situations and hidden rules are so unlike what he/she has experienced previously. Therefore, a certain level of persistence and an ability to stay with the situation until it can be learned (and therefore feel comfortable) are necessary. This persistence (i.e., staying with the situation) is proof that emotional resources are present. Emotional resources come, at least in part, from role models.

Mental resources are simply being able to process information and use it in daily living. If an individual can read, write, and compute, he/she has a decided advantage. That person can access information from many different free sources, as well as be somewhat self-sufficient at the least.

Spiritual resources are the belief that help can be obtained from a higher power, that there is a purpose for living, and that worth and love are gifts from God. This is a powerful resource because the individual does not see him/herself as hopeless and useless, but rather as capable and having worth and value.

Physical resources are having a body that works, that is capable and mobile. Such an individual can be self-sufficient.

Support systems are resources. To whom does one go when help is needed? Those individuals available and who will help are resources. When the child is sick and you have to be at work—who takes care of the child? Where do you go when money is short and the baby needs medicine?

Support systems are not just about meeting financial or emotional needs. They are about knowledge bases as well. How do you get into college? Who sits and listens when you get rejected? Who helps you negotiate the mountains of paper? Who assists you with your algebra homework when you don't know how to do it? Those people are all support systems. They may also be role models.

Relationships/role models are resources. All individuals have role models. The question is the extent to which the role model is nurturing or appropriate. Can the role model parent? Work successfully? Provide a gender role for the individual? It is largely from role models that the person learns how to live life emotionally.

Knowledge of hidden rules is crucial to whatever class in which the individual wishes to live. Hidden rules exist in poverty, in middle class, and in wealth, as well as in ethnic groups and other units of people. Hidden rules are about the unspoken understandings that cue the members of the group that this individual does or does not fit. For example, three of the hidden rules in poverty are the following: The noise level is high (the TV is always on, and everyone may talk at once), the most important information is non-verbal, and one of the main values of an individual to the group is an ability to entertain. And in all classes there are hidden rules about food, dress, decorum, etc. Generally, in order to successfully move from one class to the next, it is important to have a spouse or mentor from the class to which you wish to move to model and teach you the hidden rules.

Coping strategies are the mindsets, approaches and techniques (including procedural self-talk) that allow issues to be moved from the concrete to the abstract. It is the ability to translate from the personal to the issue.

SCENARIO #1: SALLY AND HER SUPERVISOR

Background

Sally recently graduated with an LPN from a community college 20 miles from her home. Her education was paid for by the Home Health Aides Program at the local Department of Human Services. Because of her complex home life it took Sally twice as long as usual to get through the course. The head of the Nursing Department took a special interest in Sally and supported her determination to make it. Sally made friends with others in the nursing program, but none of them lives in her county. She was hired at the rural community hospital three months ago. While going through school she lived with her mother who looked after her children. Since getting a job she has moved in with her boyfriend who insulted Sally's mother, and now Sally and her mother aren't talking. Sally depends on her boyfriend to provide her with rides. He works construction and is laid off in the winter. He has agreed to look after her three children. Sally and her boyfriend fight often over his drinking, and she suspects that he is fooling around with another woman. Sally has gotten into trouble with her supervisor for taking and making a lot of personal phone calls to resolve family crises that occur almost on a daily basis. In the last three months she has used all of her sick days and has been late several times.

Current Situation

You've just gotten a call from your kids. Your boyfriend was meant to pick them up after your son's basketball practice, but he didn't show up. The two girls went to the gym to wait like you told them. You've talked to the coach but he can't take them home today like he has done in the past. The other two LPNs on the unit have agreed to cover for you, but your supervisor has said you can't leave. She says there are three hours left on your shift, and you have been missing too much work over family problems. You can't understand what the problem is if the others are willing to cover for you. You thought that when you got a degree you would be treated with more respect, not like at the factory and fast-food places where you've worked for short periods of time in the past.

What resources does Sally have? Mark 1 if resources are very low, 3 if there are some but not enough resources, and 5 if there are enough resources to function in a middle-class environment. Use a question mark if there isn't enough information to make a determination.

RESOURCES — SCENARIO #1	VERY LOW ➤ ENOUGH					?
	1	2	3	4	5	
Financial						
Emotional						
Mental						
Spiritual						
Physical						
Support systems						
Knowledge of middle-class hidden rules						
Role models						

SCENARIO #2: BERTHA

Background

Bertha is a 23-year-old Caucasian woman with three children. She just got off probation for beating up a woman. Until ninth grade she did well in school, but in high school others teased her about her name, her looks, and her clothes. Her brother taught her how to fight to get respect and to stop the teasing. It worked, but she was angry a lot, and her grades kept dropping. Bertha dated older men and would take them home with her. Her parents were in their 70s and unable to control her. Several of the older boyfriends lived with her and her parents. The father of her first child took off before the baby was born.

Bertha has been on and off welfare since her first child was born. She has been to mental-health counseling twice—once as part of her probation and earlier when she was suspected of child abuse and encouraged to get counseling by Children's Services.

Current Situation

You are married to a man who makes minimum wage. He is very supportive of you and tries hard with your kids. You are on food stamps. You have been attending a technical school and are one quarter away from completing a secretarial course. Things are now going well for you, and you want to help others to make up for your past. One way would be to take in a 16-year-old foster child. You've just heard through the grapevine that the people who make the foster placements don't think you are a good candidate. You are angry because the counseling you've done and the classes you've taken don't seem to count for anything. You plan to go to the department first thing on Monday to tell them how you feel.

What resources does Bertha have? Mark 1 if resources are very low, 3 if there are some but not enough resources, and 5 if there are enough resources to function in a middle-class environment. Use a question mark if there isn't enough information to make a determination.

RESOURCES — SCENARIO #2	VERY LOW ➤ ENOUGH					?
	1	2	3	4	5	
Financial						
Emotional						
Mental						
Spiritual						
Physical						
Support systems						
Knowledge of middle-class hidden rules						
Role models						

SCENARIO #3: OPIE AND OPRAH

Background

Opie is a 12-year-old African-American girl and the oldest of five children. She runs the household because her mother, Oprah, works long hours as a domestic. Grandmother, who is 80, is senile and lives with them, as well as an out-of-work uncle.

You are Opie's mother, Oprah. You are 32 years old. You were married for 10 years to your husband, and then he was killed in a car accident on the way to work two years ago. You work 60 hours a week as a domestic for a doctor. You go to the Missionary Baptist Church every Sunday where you lead the choir. Your employer treats you well, and you take home about $300 every week. You ride public transportation to work and the church bus on Sunday. You want your children to go to college, even though you only finished 10th grade.

Current Situation

Your employer gives you a $400 Christmas bonus. You thank the Lord at church for the gift. After church, three different people approach you privately. One asks for $50 to have the electricity turned on; one asks for $100 to feed her brother's family; one asks for $60 to replace a pair of broken glasses. You were hoping to save some money for an emergency.

Opie has the opportunity to be in a state-sponsored competition that requires after-school practices. You want her to do that, but you must have her at home after school every day.

What resources do Opie and Oprah have? Mark 1 if resources are very low, 3 if there are some but not enough resources, and 5 if there are enough resources to function in a middle-class environment. Use a question mark if there isn't enough information to make a determination.

RESOURCES — SCENARIO #3	VERY LOW → ENOUGH					?
	1	2	3	4	5	
Financial						
Emotional						
Mental						
Spiritual						
Physical						
Support systems						
Knowledge of middle-class hidden rules						
Role models						

SCENARIO #4: JERRY

Background

Jerry just completed a substance-abuse treatment program while serving time in the county jail. He sees an outpatient counselor once a week and attends two AA meetings a week. Most of his family members are heavy drinkers, and several use drugs as well. Jerry is in his second marriage. His wife, who threatened to leave him because of his drinking, is now saying that he is spending too much time at AA meetings. She isn't sure about the AA talk she hears, and she distrusts the AA people. His brothers and mother think that he has been brainwashed by the treatment program into thinking that he is alcoholic. His mother fixes him dinner and tells him to come live with them. She doesn't believe that he has a drinking problem either. She thinks that all of his problems stem from his wife.

Meanwhile, Jerry's ex-wife has let him know that she is interested in him again. His daughter, who lives with his ex-wife, wants him back too, and he doesn't get along well with the two children of his current wife. Both of Jerry's wives have been on and off welfare, and for short periods of time they have held jobs. He has made his money by fixing people's cars, selling scrap, and shoplifting. He has been in the county jail a number of times for disorderly conduct and resisting arrest, but he has never been caught for shoplifting and doesn't see it to be a problem. In fact, he is so accomplished that his wife and other family members usually give him a list of what they want for birthdays and Christmas, and he will get them what they want.

Current Situation

You've been told by your counselor and the guys in AA that you need to be with dry people in dry places and get honest (which means giving up stealing)—and that you shouldn't make any major relationship decisions during the first year of your sobriety. You know you're an alcoholic, and you want to quit drinking, but they're asking you to give up your family. You're thinking of taking your mom up on her offer to live with her. That way you could start over and forget about the headaches everyone is giving you.

What resources does Jerry have? Mark 1 if resources are very low, 3 if there are some but not enough resources, and 5 if there are enough resources to function in a middle-class environment. Use a question mark if there isn't enough information to make a determination.

RESOURCES — SCENARIO #4	VERY LOW → ENOUGH					?
	1	2	3	4	5	
Financial						
Emotional						
Mental						
Spiritual						
Physical						
Support systems						
Knowledge of middle-class hidden rules						
Role models						

SCENARIO #5: LARRY AND THE TRUST FUND

Background

Larry is a low-functioning 35-year-old man. He went to the Mental Retardation/Developmental Disabilities school as a child and to the workshop as an adult. With the help of the agency he found a job in a pallet factory where he has been earning minimum wage for two years. He sees less of his job coach now and relies on the boss to give him work he can handle. Larry lives with his father in a mobile home in an old trailer park on the edge of town. His father is a manual laborer also. They have no phone and an old beat-up car. Larry wants a new bicycle, but his father reminds him that they can't afford one, so Larry rides his old bike around town. To save money, Larry's father keeps the trailer cool in winter and turns on the hot water only once a week. On Saturdays Larry takes his weekly bath. Larry's mother died when he was 20. He and his father go to church most Sundays. Larry gives his check to his father, and his father gives him a little pocket money.

Larry's boss has taken a lot of time to teach Larry his job, and he puts up with Larry's occasional outbursts. His boss and wife include Larry in activities of the company's bicycle club and, even though he doesn't really ride "with" the others, Larry does join in some of the social events. A social worker in the group has instructed Larry on how to wash his hands after going to the bathroom.

Current Situation

Your father has just died, and you learn that he had been investing money in the stock market for years. He left you one million dollars! The first thing you did was buy a new bicycle, a phone, an electric blanket, and cable TV. Now you are going to quit your job.

What resources does Larry have? Mark 1 if resources are very low, 3 if there are some but not enough resources, and 5 if there are enough resources to function in a middle-class environment. Use a question mark if there isn't enough information to make a determination.

RESOURCES — SCENARIO #5	VERY LOW → ENOUGH					?
	1	2	3	4	5	
Financial						
Emotional						
Mental						
Spiritual						
Physical						
Support systems						
Knowledge of middle-class hidden rules						
Role models						

SCENARIO #6: JUAN AND RAMON

Background

Juan is a 6-year-old Hispanic boy who lives with his uncle Ramón. Juan's father was murdered in a gang-related killing. His uncle is angry about the death of Juan's father. When his uncle is not around, Juan stays with his grandmother, who speaks no English. The uncle makes his living selling drugs but is very respectful toward his mother.

You are Juan's uncle, Ramón, age 25. You doubt that you will live many more years because you know that most of the people like you are either dead or in jail. You are angry. Your brother, Juan's father, was killed by a rival gang two years ago when Juan was 4. Juan is your godchild, and you will defend him with your blood. Juan's mother was a piece of white trash and wouldn't take care of Juan like a good mother should. She is in jail now for gang-related activities. You leave Juan with your mother often because the activities you're involved in are too dangerous to have Juan along. You are a leader in your gang and sell drugs as well. Your mother speaks only Spanish, but you have taught Juan to be very respectful towards her. She goes to Mass every Sunday and takes Juan with her when she can. You make $1,000 a week on the average.

Current Situation

Juan comes home with a notice about a parent-teacher conference. You are away, hiding from the police. Grandmother cannot read Spanish or English.

The rival gang has killed another one of your gang members. This has forced you to be away from Juan more than you would like. Plans are that you will kill the leader of the rival gang, but then you will need to go to Mexico for some time to hide. You are thinking about taking Juan with you because he is all in the world that you love. You are stockpiling money. You don't want to take him out of school, but he is only 6; he can catch up. You don't think you'll live past 30, and you want to have time with him.

What resources do Juan and Ramón have? Mark 1 if resources are very low, 3 if there are some but not enough resources, and 5 if there are enough resources to function in a middle-class environment. Use a question mark if there isn't enough information to make a determination.

RESOURCES — SCENARIO #6	VERY LOW ➤ ENOUGH					?
	1	2	3	4	5	
Financial						
Emotional						
Mental						
Spiritual						
Physical						
Support systems						
Knowledge of middle-class hidden rules						
Role models						

SCENARIO #7: JOHN AND ADELE

Background

John is an 8-year-old Caucasian boy. His father is a doctor and remarried but does not see his children. He pays minimal child support. The mother, Adele, works part time and is an alcoholic. One younger sibling, a girl who is mentally and physically handicapped, lives with the mother and John.

You are Adele, John's mother. You are 29 years old. You quit college your sophomore year so that you could go to work to support John's father as he went through medical school. You were both elated when John was born. During the time your husband was an intern, you found that a drink or two or three in the evening calmed you down, especially since your husband was gone so much. When your second child was born, she was severely handicapped. Both of you were in shock. A year later your husband finished his residency, announced that he was in love with another woman, and divorced you. Last you heard your husband is driving a Porsche, and he and his new wife spent their most recent vacation in Cancún. Your parents are dead. You have a sister who lives 50 miles away. Your weekly income, including child support, is $300 before taxes. Your handicapped child is 3 years old and is in day care provided by the school district.

Current Situation

You have been late to work for the third time this month. Your car broke down, and it will take $400 to fix it. Your boss told you that you will be docked a day's pay—and that if you're late again you will be fired. You don't know how you're going to get to work tomorrow. You consider several choices: (1) You can go car shopping, (2) you can put the car in the garage and worry about the money later, (3) you can invite the mechanic over for dinner, (4) you can get mad and quit, (5) you can call your ex and threaten to take him back to court unless he pays for the car, (6) you can get a second job, or (7) you can get drunk.

Your daughter has had another seizure, and you took her to the doctor (one of the reasons you were late for work). The new medicine will cost you $45 every month.

John comes home from school and states that the school is going to have a reading contest. Every book you read with him will earn points for him. Each book is one point, and he wants to earn 100 points. You must do physical therapy with your daughter each evening for 30 minutes, as well as get dinner. For John to get his books, he needs you to go to the library with him. You have only enough gas to go to work and back for the rest of the week, maybe not that. He also tells you that the school is having an open house, and he will get a pencil if you come. But John is not old enough to watch your daughter. Your ex has already threatened to bring up in court that you are an unfit mother if you try to get more money from him.

The mechanic calls and invites you out to dinner. He tells you that you might be able to work something out in terms of payment. It has been a long time since you have been out, and he is good-looking and seems like a nice man.

What resources do John and Adele have? Mark 1 if resources are very low, 3 if there are some but not enough resources, and 5 if there are enough resources to function in a middle-class environment. Use a question mark if there isn't enough information to make a determination.

RESOURCES — SCENARIO #7	VERY LOW → ENOUGH					?
	1	2	3	4	5	
Financial						
Emotional						
Mental						
Spiritual						
Physical						
Support systems						
Knowledge of middle-class hidden rules						
Role models						

DISCUSSION OF SCENARIOS

Each scenario illustrates a situation that arises for people with limited resources. The poor act for understandable reasons in direct response to circumstances they face. The scenarios offer a variance in the amount and kinds of resources available, as well as a variation on the theme of poverty. Use the table below to assess resources and focus thinking on the complexities of poverty.

Rank the resources on a scale of 1 to 5—1 for not having any resources at all, 5 for having an abundance of the particular resource.

RESOURCES	SCENARIO						
	#1	#2	#3	#4	#5	#6	#7
Financial							
Emotional							
Mental							
Spiritual							
Physical							
Support systems							
Knowledge of middle-class hidden rules							
Role models							

Like many individuals who live in poverty, Sally doesn't know the middle-class rules about not missing work or being late. She has brought her poverty-culture rules to work. They include relying on others to cover her workload while she takes care of her kids. The supervisor, operating from a middle-class orientation, is baffled by Sally's chaotic lifestyle, a boyfriend whom Sally cannot rely upon, and the failure of Sally to find some consistent way to solve her child-care needs. Sally has held a number of jobs but not the quality of this one. She never kept any of them very long.

According to a 1997 study by the Urban Institute of Washington, DC, this is a common pattern for people working their way out of poverty. It takes two to four years to work into a job that pays well and has medical benefits.

Bertha is also in the process of change, which can take time. Any major life change is done in plateaus of learning and consolidation of gains. Each step is marked by the loss of some relationships, the grieving over the loss, a change in self-image, the learning of new skills, and the practicing of new skills. There is no guarantee that others will recognize the changes Bertha has made. Reputations are hard to change. In this scenario Bertha has learned some middle-class rules and has made significant progress. The way in which she handles this crisis will say a lot about how well she can use middle-class rules.

Another example of a poverty characteristic is the incident with Oprah at church where she receives the extra money and immediately is besieged with requests. One of the hidden rules of poverty is that any extra money is shared. Middle class puts a great deal of emphasis on being self-sufficient. In poverty, the clear understanding is that one will never get ahead, so when extra money is available, it is either shared or quickly spent. There are always emergencies and needs; one might as well enjoy the moment. Oprah will share the money; she has no choice. If she doesn't, the next time she is in need she will be left out in the cold. It is the hidden rule of the support system. In poverty, people are possessions, and people can rely only on each other. It is absolutely imperative that the needs of the individual come first. After all, that is all you have—people.

The scenario about Jerry is included to illustrate the poverty culture's attitude about jail and discipline. For many individuals who live in poverty, jail is a part of life. Chemical dependency and its attendant consequences often lead to problems with the police. An individual in generational poverty views organized society with distrust and distaste. The line between what is legal and illegal is thin and frequently crossed. A lack of resources means that the individual will spend periods of time in jail for crossing that line because he/she doesn't have the resources to avoid it. The reality is that middle class and upper class also cross the line—but not with the frequency of those in poverty. In addition, the upper and middle classes generally have the resources to avoid jail. The poor see jail simply as a part of life and not necessarily always bad.

Jerry's scenario also illustrates the role of the matriarchal household and the view that those in generational poverty have of discipline. Negative consequences and discipline are about penance and forgiveness, not about change. The mother is the most powerful figure in generational poverty. Not only does she control the limited resources, she is also the "keeper of the soul." She dispenses penance and forgiveness. The typical pattern in poverty for discipline is to verbally chastise the child or physically beat the child, then offer forgiveness to him/her. The hidden rule about food in poverty is that food is equated with love. As indicated previously, in the final analysis all you have are people. How do you show people that you love them? You give them food so they can continue to live. One of the mistakes society makes is to misunderstand the role of punishment in generational poverty. Punishment is not about change; individuals in poverty believe in fate and destiny. Punishment is about penance and forgiveness. Therefore, to expect changed behavior after a jail term is usually a false hope.

In Jerry's case his role as a fighter/lover, his family's attitude toward drinking, and his role as the supplier of stolen items illustrates how the poverty culture can undermine efforts an individual makes to remain sober. Achievement in any area means giving up some relationships. In order to remain sober, Jerry will have to give up some contact with his family.

The Larry scenario illustrates that some people in poverty have cognitive deficiencies. Those who qualify for services from MR/DD agencies may be blended into the workforce with training and the help of a job coach. Larry's life of financial poverty was reversed in part by the sudden acquisition of $1 million, but there is the danger that Larry will cut himself off from the people who have served as mentors and a support system for him. Who will mediate experiences to Larry if he cuts himself off from the people who care about him and help him?

The Juan/Ramón scenario is included to make some points about the role of violence and gangs in poverty. Gangs are a type of support system. They provide virtually all of the resources needed for survival. Fighting and physical violence are a part of poverty. People living in poverty need to be able to defend themselves physically, or they need someone to be their protector.

Middle class uses space to deal with conflict and disagreement—i.e., they go to a different room and cool off; they purchase enough land so they are not encroached upon; they live in neighborhoods where people keep their distance. But in poverty, separation is not an option. The only way to defend turf is physically. Also, individuals in poverty are seldom going to call the police, for two reasons: First, the police may be looking for them; second, the police are going to be slow to respond. So why bother calling?

The John/Adele scenario highlights the number of children who are in situational poverty because of divorce. Adele is making the slide from middle class to poverty, and she doesn't know the rules of poverty. Adele is an example of what happens when an individual allows her difficulties to erode her emotional resources. Because of her alcoholism, she is emotionally weak. (The reverse also is true—i.e., her emotional weakness leads to her dependence on alcohol.) Of all the resources, emotional resources seem to be paramount in maintaining a lifestyle with some semblance of order. When emotional resources are absent, the slide into poverty is almost guaranteed. But because her financial resources are limited, she must learn the rules of generational poverty. And one of the rules in generational poverty for women is this: You may need to use your body for survival. After all, that is all that is truly yours. Sex will bring in money and favors. Values are important, but they don't put food on the table—or bring relief from intense pressure. So Adele will probably go out with the mechanic, for two reasons: (1) She can get her car fixed, and (2) she can have an evening out on the town.

WHAT IMPLICATIONS DOES THIS INFORMATION HAVE FOR THE SOCIAL SERVICE, HEALTH CARE, OR WORK SETTING?

Once it has been determined that the problems being faced by clients or employees are not systems issues, the resources of the individual should be analyzed. We want to avoid blaming individuals and yet seek to understand and be aware of their strengths and weaknesses. What may seem to be workable suggestions from a middle-class point of view may be virtually impossible given the resources available to someone who is in poverty.

Staff members who do intakes and assessments should be trained in gathering data on the resources that are available to clients. The intention to identify and adequately serve people from the poverty culture should be formalized by gathering the necessary data on intake and assessment forms.

The following form can be added to the client file as a way to focus attention on economic resources. Filling out the form can serve as a reminder to staff members that economic resources determine behavior and must be taken into account when doing planning with clients.

Resources

RESOURCES	VERY LOW → ENOUGH					?	COMMENTS, PLANNING/ TREATMENT ISSUES
	1	2	3	4	5		
Financial							
Emotional							
Mental							
Spiritual							
Physical							
Support systems							
Knowledge of middle-class hidden rules							
Role models							

Now suddenly I was expected to sit in a room and communicate with a bunch of strangers in an entirely new way. Compared with South Street, school was artificial and pointless. I had received no preparation to help me adjust to it or do what was expected of me.

– Carl Upchurch, Convicted in the Womb

Rico found his way and grew accustomed to the coded diction and syntax of his instructors. (In Catholic school his teachers always talked about life and school as a communal experience, as in "We must pray," or, "We must study." In public school the teachers were more tentative about their relationships to the students: "Which of you can answer that question? Anyone? You there . . . Anyone?" In this school the teachers spoke in a detached but certain manner: "One must be prepared. One must study. One must be resilient.") He worked hard, and not for one moment, for all his misgivings, did he forget that, among the sons of investment bankers, advertising executives, lawyers, doctors, psychologists, corporate presidents, he was the son of a waiter and a cleaning woman.

– Oscar Hijuelos, Empress of the Splendid Season

The nearly uniform advantages received by the children of the college-educated professionals suggest the evolution of an increasingly distinct subculture in American society, one in which adults routinely transmit to their offspring the symbolic thinking and confident problem solving that mark the adults' economic activities and that are so difficult for outsiders to acquire in mid-life. A trend toward separation into subcultures jeopardizes the upward mobility that has given this nation greatness and presages the tragedy of downward mobility that produces increasing numbers of working poor. If this trend is to be reversed, a beginning must be made now. The issue is no longer one of eradicating poverty or of putting welfare recipients to work but of reversing a trend, the downward drift of the working class.

– Betty Hart and Todd R. Risley (1995). Meaningful Differences in the Everyday Experience of Young American Children. (p. 204).
Baltimore: Paul H. Brookes.

The Role of Language and Story

To better understand poverty, one must understand three aspects of language: registers of language, discourse patterns, and story structure. Many of the key issues for agencies, schools, and businesses are related to these three patterns that often are different in poverty from middle class.

REGISTERS OF LANGUAGE

Every language in the world has five registers (Joos, 1967). These registers are the following:

REGISTER	EXPLANATION
FROZEN	Language that is always the same. For example: Lord's Prayer, wedding vows, etc.
FORMAL	The standard sentence syntax and word choice of work and school. Has complete sentences and specific word choice.
CONSULTATIVE	Formal register when used in conversation. Discourse pattern not quite as direct as formal register.
CASUAL	Language between friends and is characterized by a 400- to 800-word vocabulary. Word choice general and not specific. Conversation dependent upon non-verbal assists. Sentence syntax often incomplete.
INTIMATE	Language between lovers or twins. Language of sexual harassment.

RULE: Joos found that one can go one register down in the same conversation, and that is socially accepted. However, to drop two registers or more in the same conversation is to be socially offensive.

How then does this register impact individuals from poverty? First of all, the work of Dr. Maria Montano-Harmon (1991) found that the majority of minority students and poor students in her research do not have access to formal register at home. As a matter of fact, these students cannot use formal register. The problem is that all the state tests—SAT, ACT, etc.—are in formal register. It is further complicated by the fact that to get a well-paying job it is expected that one will be able to use formal register. Ability to use formal register is a hidden rule of the middle class. The inability to use it will knock one out of an interview in two or three minutes. The use of formal register, on the other hand, allows one to score well on tests and do well in school and higher education.

This use of formal register is further complicated by the fact that these individuals don't have the vocabulary or the knowledge of sentence structure and syntax to use formal register. When conversations in the casual register are observed, much of the meaning comes, not from the word choices, but from the non-verbal assists. To be asked to communicate in writing without the non-verbal assists is an overwhelming and formidable task, which most of them try to avoid. It has very little meaning for them.

DISCOURSE PATTERNS IN FORMAL AND CASUAL REGISTER

This pattern of registers is connected to the second issue: the patterns of discourse. Discourse will be discussed here with two different meanings. The first meaning is the manner in which the information is organized. In the formal register of English, the pattern is to get straight to the point. In casual register, the pattern is to go around and around and finally get to the point. For clients who have no access to formal register, social service workers and law enforcement officers often become frustrated with the tendency of these clients to meander almost endlessly through a topic. It is simply the manner in which information is organized in casual register.

LANGUAGE ACQUISITION IN PRIMARY AND SECONDARY DISCOURSE

The other meaning associated with discourse is the notion of primary and secondary discourse issues (Gee, 1987). Primary discourse is the language an individual first acquired. Secondary discourse is the language of the larger society that the individual must be able to use to function in the larger society. For example, if a student has as his/her primary discourse casual register of Spanish, then he/she must also learn formal register of English in order to fully negotiate and participate in the larger American society. Gee points out that students do much better in school when their primary discourse is the same as their secondary discourse.

RAMIFICATIONS

Gee proceeds to make a distinction between acquisition and learning. Acquisition is the best and most natural way to learn a language and is simply the immersion in, and constant interaction with, that language. Learning is the direct teaching of a language and usually is at a more metacognitive level. However, what Gee does not talk about is the following: Acquisition of language only occurs when there is a significant relationship. That then leads to the next question: To what extent can a formal institution create significant relationships? Just think . . . would you learn to use sign language well if there were no significant relationship that called for that usage? Would you learn to speak Chinese well if there were no significant relationship?

Therefore, when we ask students to move from casual to formal register, we almost need to direct-teach it. Natural acquisition of formal register would require a significant relationship.

Montano-Harmon (1991) found that for students to move from casual-register English to formal-register English required them to translate because the word choice, sentence syntax, and discourse pattern are different. This translation becomes much more meaningful if there is a significant relationship. However, if there is not a significant relationship, then the instruction must be more direct.

PATTERNS OF DISCOURSE

In the oral-language tradition in which the casual register operates, the pattern of discourse is quite different. Discourse is defined as the organizational pattern of information (see graphic representations below).

Formal-Register Discourse Pattern

Speaker or writer gets straight to the point.

Casual-Register Discourse Pattern

Writer or speaker goes around the issue before finally coming to the point.

How does this make a difference for police officers, counselors, welfare department workers, social workers, and health care providers? First of all, exchanges between clients and the workers tend to be misunderstood on both sides. Workers want to get right to the point; clients, particularly those from poverty, need to beat around the bush first. When workers cut the conversation and get to the point, clients view that as being rude and non-caring. Second, writing becomes particularly difficult for clients because they tend to circle the mulberry bush and not meet the standard organizational pattern of getting to the point. This discourse pattern is coupled with a third pattern; that of story structure.

STORY STRUCTURE

Formal-Register Story Structure

The formal-register story structure starts at the beginning of the story and goes to the end in a chronological or accepted narrative pattern. The most important part of the story is the plot.

Casual-Register Story Structure

The casual-register story structure begins with the end of the story first or the part with the greatest emotional intensity. The story is told in vignettes, with audience participation in between. The story ends with a comment about the character and his/her value. The most important part of the story is the characterization.

WHAT CAN ORGANIZATIONS DO TO ADDRESS CASUAL REGISTER, DISCOURSE PATTERNS, AND STORY STRUCTURE?

There is a direct link between achievement and language, so the matter must be addressed. For clients who need the services of social service, health care, and law enforcement agencies, communication begins with data gathering. Professionals in these agencies begin by gathering the usual demographics and from there move quickly to requesting a description of the presenting problem and histories of past medical, legal, and employment problems, and so on. As the relationship continues, more information may be needed so that a diagnosis can be made or a treatment plan developed. The following suggestions are not exhaustive, but rather a place to begin.

1. During the data-gathering phase, professionals should be skilled in communicating with people who use the casual register and circular story structures. For example, Darla White, a school counselor in Ohio, draws the story as it is told to her, using symbols and making brief notes on dates, ages, and so on. Divorce, for example, is drawn as a line between the husband and wife with a short mark crossing the connecting line. Dates and timelines are added as the story unfolds. The students usually contribute to the drawing and, when the session is over, White has a complete history on one page from which she can make her notes. The circular story structure can be straightened into a linear report later.

2. Have clients/customers write in casual register and translate to the formal register.

3. Make it a rule that clients learn how to express their displeasure in the formal register, thereby avoiding reprimands.

4. Use graphic organizers to show patterns of discourse.

THE ROLE OF LANGUAGE AND STORY

5. In the treatment setting, tell the story both ways. Tell the story using the formal-register story structure; then tell the story with the casual-register structure. Talk about the stories: how they stay the same and how they're different.

6. Allow for participation in the writing and telling of stories.

7. Use stories to educate and to process experiences. Twelve-step programs such as Alcoholics Anonymous utilize stories in this way.

8. Make up stories with the clients that can be used to guide behavior.

WHAT IMPLICATIONS DOES THIS INFORMATION HAVE FOR THE SOCIAL SERVICE, HEALTH CARE, OR WORK SETTING?

■ Formal register needs to be directly taught.

■ Casual register needs to be recognized as the primary discourse for many clients.

■ Discourse patterns need to be directly taught.

■ Both story structures need to be used as a part of instruction.

■ Correction that occurs when a client uses the inappropriate register should be a time for instruction in the appropriate register.

■ Clients need to be told how much their use of formal register affects their ability to get a well-paying job.

■ Social service agencies and child care providers that work with children who are just learning to speak need to focus a great deal of energy on language development skills so as to enrich the language experience of children.

The sheltered, pampered, weakened, atrophied, protected kids who never HAD to work hard to survive won't have the remotest clue what I'm blathering about. To them, working-class anger always seems dumb, violent, and—beyond all else— groundless. The kids who perch mosquitolike atop their parents' wealth, the "nice" kids with nice teeth from the nice side of town, have no solid explanation for white trash's existence beyond the purely behavioral. They just shake their heads until dandruff flakes flutter gently to the marble floor, wondering how anyone could ACT that way. They seem to think that if rednecks just showered, dressed nice, and kept their noses to the grindstone for a few weeks, they'd all blossom into investment bankers.

– Jim Goad, *The Redneck Manifesto*

In the welfare families, the lesser amount of talk with its more frequent parent-initiated topics, imperatives, and prohibitions suggested a culture concerned with established customs. To teach socially acceptable behavior language rich in nouns and modifiers was not called for; obedience, politeness, and conformity were more likely to be the keys to survival. Rather than attempting to prepare their children with the knowledge and skills required in a technological world with which the parents had had little experience, parents seemed to be preparing their children realistically for the jobs likely to be open to them, jobs in which success and advancement would be determined by attitude, how well the children presented themselves, and whether they could prove themselves through their performance.

– Betty Hart and Todd R. Risley (1995). *Meaningful Differences in the Everyday Experience of Young American Children.* (p. 204). Baltimore: Paul H. Brookes.

Out on the streets I got a sense of power that I didn't have at home. I went where I wanted, did what I wanted, and took what I wanted. South Street and its surroundings were colorful and lively, and I couldn't get enough of the sights and sounds. From the time I could get down the stairs, I roamed—first with my eyes, later with my feet, watching adult interactions and acquiring wisdom far beyond my years, despite the absence of the love and nurturing that all young children need. By the time I was old enough to go to school, I had life as I knew it all figured out.

– Carl Upchurch, *Convicted in the Womb*

■ ■ ■ ■ ■ ■

Hidden Rules Among Classes

Hidden rules are the unspoken cues and habits of a group. Distinct cueing systems exist between and among groups and economic classes. Generally, in America, that notion is recognized for racial and ethnic groups, but not particularly for economic groups. There are many hidden rules to examine. The ones examined here are those that have the most impact on achievement in schools and success in the workplace.

But first . . .

A LITTLE QUIZ

Take the quiz on the next three pages, putting a check mark by all the things you know how to do.

Could You Survive in Poverty?

Put a check by each item you know how to do.

❑ 1. I know which churches and sections of town have the best rummage sales.

❑ 2. I know which rummage sales have "bag sales" and when.

❑ 3. I know which grocery stores' garbage bins can be accessed for thrown-away food.

❑ 4. I know how to get someone out of jail.

❑ 5. I know how to physically fight and defend myself physically.

❑ 6. I know how to get a gun, even if I have a police record.

❑ 7. I know how to keep my clothes from being stolen at the Laundromat.

❑ 8. I know what problems to look for in a used car.

❑ 9. I know how to live without a checking account.

❑ 10. I know how to live without electricity and a phone.

❑ 11. I know how to use a knife as scissors.

❑ 12. I can entertain a group of friends with my personality and my stories.

❑ 13. I know what to do when I don't have money to pay the bills.

❑ 14. I know how to move in half a day.

❑ 15. I know how to get and use food stamps or an electronic card for benefits.

❑ 16. I know where the free medical clinics are.

❑ 17. I am very good at trading and bartering.

❑ 18. I can get by without a car.

Could You Survive in Middle Class?

Put a check by each item you know how to do.

❑   1.   I know how to get my children into Little League, piano lessons, soccer, etc.

❑   2.   I know how to set a table properly.

❑   3.   I know which stores are most likely to carry the clothing brands my family wears.

❑   4.   My children know the best name brands in clothing.

❑   5.   I know how to order in a nice restaurant.

❑   6.   I know how to use a credit card, checking account, and savings account—and I understand an annuity. I understand term life insurance, disability insurance, and 20/80 medical insurance policy, as well as house insurance, flood insurance, and replacement insurance.

❑   7.   I talk to my children about going to college.

❑   8.   I know how to get one of the best interest rates on my new-car loan.

❑   9.   I understand the difference among the principal, interest, and escrow statements on my house payment.

❑ 10. I know how to help my children with their homework and do not hesitate to call the school if I need additional information.

❑ 11. I know how to decorate the house for the different holidays.

❑ 12. I know how to get a library card.

❑ 13. I know how to use most of the tools in the garage.

❑ 14. I repair items in my house almost immediately when they break— or know a repair service and call it.

Could You Survive in Wealth?

Put a check by each item you know how to do.

❏ 1. I can read a menu in French, English, and another language.

❏ 2. I have several favorite restaurants in different countries of the world.

❏ 3. During the holidays, I know how to hire a decorator to identify the appropriate themes and items with which to decorate the house.

❏ 4. I know who my preferred financial advisor, legal service, designer, domestic-employment service, and hairdresser are.

❏ 5. I have at least two residences that are staffed and maintained.

❏ 6. I know how to ensure confidentiality and loyalty from my domestic staff.

❏ 7. I have at least two or three "screens" that keep people whom I do not wish to see away from me.

❏ 8. I fly in my own plane or the company plane.

❏ 9. I know how to enroll my children in the preferred private schools.

❏ 10. I know how to host the parties that "key" people attend.

❏ 11. I am on the boards of at least two charities.

❏ 12. I know the hidden rules of the Junior League.

❏ 13. I support or buy the work of a particular artist.

❏ 14. I know how to read a corporate financial statement and analyze my own financial statements.

The first point about this exercise is that if you fall mostly in the middle class, the assumption is that everyone knows these things. However, if you did not know many of the items for the other classes, the exercise points out how many of the hidden rules are taken for granted by a particular class, which assumes they are a given for everyone. What, then, are the hidden rules? The chart on pages 44–45 gives an overview of some of the major hidden rules among the classes of poverty, middle class, and wealth.

Several explanations and stories may help explain parts of the quiz and the chart on the next two pages. The bottom line or driving force against which decisions are made is important to note. For example, in one school district, the faculty had gone together to buy a refrigerator for a family who did not have one. About three weeks later, the children in the family were gone for a week. When the students returned, the teachers asked where they had been. The answer was that the family had gone camping because they were so stressed. What had they used for money to go camping? Proceeds from the sale of the refrigerator, of course. The bottom line in generational poverty is entertainment and relationships. In middle class, the criteria against which most decisions are made relate to work and achievement. In wealth, it is the ramifications of the financial, social, and political connections that have the weight.

Being able physically to fight or have someone who is willing to fight for you is important to survival in poverty. Yet, in middle class, being able to use words as tools to negotiate conflict is crucial. Many times the fists are used in poverty because the words are neither available nor respected.

One of the biggest difficulties in getting out of poverty is managing money and just the general information base around money. How can you manage something you've never had? Money is seen in poverty as an expression of personality and is used for entertainment and relationships. The notion of using money for security is truly grounded in the middle and wealthy classes.

Hidden Rules Among Classes

	POVERTY
POSSESSIONS	People.
MONEY	To be used, spent.
PERSONALITY	Is for entertainment. Sense of humor is highly valued.
SOCIAL EMPHASIS	Social inclusion of people he/she likes.
FOOD	Key question: Did you have enough? Quantity important.
CLOTHING	Clothing valued for individual style and expression of personality.
TIME	Present most important. Decisions made for moment based on feelings or survival.
EDUCATION	Valued and revered as abstract but not as reality.
DESTINY	Believes in fate. Cannot do much to mitigate chance.
LANGUAGE	Casual register. Language is about survival.
FAMILY STRUCTURE	Tends to be matriarchal.
WORLD VIEW	Sees world in terms of local setting.
LOVE	Love and acceptance conditional, based upon whether individual is liked.
DRIVING FORCES	Survival, relationships, entertainment.
HUMOR	About people and sex.

MIDDLE CLASS	WEALTH
Things.	One-of-a-kind objects, legacies, pedigrees.
To be managed.	To be conserved, invested.
Is for acquisition and stability. Achievement is highly valued.	Is for connections. Financial, political, social connections are highly valued.
Emphasis is on self-governance and self-sufficiency.	Emphasis is on social exclusion.
Key question: Did you like it? Quality important.	Key question: Was it presented well? Presentation important.
Clothing valued for its quality and acceptance into norm of middle class. Label important.	Clothing valued for its artistic sense and expression. Designer important.
Future most important. Decisions made against future ramifications.	Traditions and history most important. Decisions made partially on basis of tradition and decorum.
Crucial for climbing success ladder and making money.	Necessary tradition for making and maintaining connections.
Believes in choice. Can change future with good choices now.	Noblesse oblige.
Formal register. Language is about negotiation.	Formal register. Language is about networking.
Tends to be patriarchal.	Depends on who has money.
Sees world in terms of national setting.	Sees world in terms of international view.
Love and acceptance conditional and based largely upon achievement.	Love and acceptance conditional and related to social standing and connections.
Work, achievement.	Financial, political, social connections.
About situations.	About social faux pas.

The question in the quiz about using a knife as scissors was put there to illustrate the lack of tools available to those in poverty. Tools in many ways are one of the identifiers of middle class—from the kitchen to the garage. Therefore, the notion of maintaining property and repairing items is dependent upon having tools. When they are not available, things are not repaired or maintained. Students often do not have access to scissors, pens, paper, pencils, rulers, etc., which may be part of an assignment.

One of the biggest differences among the classes is how "the world" is defined for them. Wealthy individuals view the international scene as their world. As one told me, "My favorite restaurant is in Brazil." Middle class tends to see the world in terms of a national picture, while poverty sees the world in its immediate locale. Several fourth-grade poor students told us when they were writing to the prompt, *How is life in Houston different from life in Baytown?* (Baytown is 20 minutes from Houston): "They don't have TVs in Houston."

In wealth, to be introduced or accepted, one must have an individual already approved by that group make the introductions. Yet to stand back and not introduce yourself in a middle-class setting is not the accepted norm. And in poverty it is not unusual to have a comment made about the individual before he/she is ever introduced.

The discussion could continue about hidden rules. The key point is that hidden rules govern so much of our immediate assessment of an individual and his/her capabilities. These are often the factors that keep an individual from moving upward in a career—or even getting the position in the first place.

WHAT IMPLICATIONS DOES THIS INFORMATION HAVE FOR THE SOCIAL SERVICE, HEALTH CARE, OR WORK SETTING?

- Assumptions made about individuals' intelligence and approaches to life and/or the work setting may relate more to their understanding of hidden rules.

- Clients and program participants need to be taught the hidden rules of middle class—not in denigration of their own but rather as another set of rules that can be used if they so choose.

- Many of the attitudes that clients and participants bring with them are an integral part of their culture and belief systems. Middle-class solutions should not be imposed when other, more workable, solutions might be found.

- An understanding of poverty will lessen the anger and frustration (and prejudice?) that social workers, health care workers, and employers may feel when working with people in poverty.

- Most of the individuals I have talked to in poverty don't believe they are poor, even when they are on welfare. Most of the wealthy adults I have talked to don't believe they are wealthy; they will usually cite someone who has more than they do.

The parties were fun, with everyone laughing. And despite all the violence,
I never felt that any of them were bad people. I never felt afraid of them. What
I did feel, though, even at the age of three, four, or five, was a kind of emptiness
that shadowed the stretches between the parties. Later I figured out that they felt
it too and partied so hard to avoid its stark reality.

– Carl Upchurch, *Convicted in the Womb*

If someone were to devise a machine that could measure hatred—a Hateno-
meter®—I'd bet all my wooden nickels that more hatred exists between bosses
and employees than between blacks and whites. . . . Of all the hating I've done in
my life—and I've done my share—ninety-nine percent of it was directed at rich
white people, most of them my bosses. . . . I had been born into a class where I was
on the RECEIVING end of decisions. I flippin' had no CONTROL over anyone else's
life, and mastery of my own was compromised by the need to work a full-time job.

– Jim Goad, *The Redneck Manifesto*

When he finally goes to bed he still doesn't rest, but has a dream about his dead
wife. She is standing in the kitchen of their little crooked house in the woods,
cutting up a hen for soup. "How come you won't turn around and face me?"
he asks. "You turned loose of family," she says. "I have to turn my back on you."
"Why even talk to me, then?" he asks. "I'm cooking for you, aren't I?" "Yes.
But I'm afraid you hate me." "Why would I cook for you, then?" "I don't know,"
he says. "Pay attention to who takes care of you." . . . "There's a hundred ways to
love someone," her voice tells Cash. "All that matters is that you stay here in the
same room."

– Barbara Kingsolver, *Pigs in Heaven*

"Goddamn it, Thomas," Junior yelled. "How come your fridge is always f------
empty?" Thomas walked over to the refrigerator, saw it was empty, and then sat
down inside. "There," Thomas said. "It ain't empty no more." Everybody in
the kitchen laughed their asses off. It was the second-largest party in reservation
history and Thomas Builds-the-Fire was the host. He was the host because he
was the one buying the beer. And he was buying all the beer because he had just
got a ton of money from Washington Water Power.

– Sherman Alexie, *The Lone Ranger and Tonto Fistfight in Heaven*

Patterns in Generational Poverty

Generational poverty is defined as having been in poverty for at least two generations; however, the patterns begin to surface much sooner than two generations if the family lives with others who are from generational poverty.

Situational poverty is defined as a lack of resources due to a particular event (i.e., a death, chronic illness, divorce, etc.).

Generational poverty has its own culture, hidden rules, and belief systems. One of the key indicators of whether it is generational or situational poverty is the prevailing attitude. Often the attitude in generational poverty is that society owes one a living. In situational poverty the attitude is often one of pride and a refusal to accept charity. Individuals in situational poverty often bring more resources with them to the situation than those in generational poverty. Of particular importance is the use of formal register.

What, then, makes generational poverty so different from the middle class? How is it that work is such an unsatisfactory experience for many students from poverty? Several of these differences were mentioned in the last chapter on hidden rules. To examine the differences, a case study will be used.

CASE STUDY: WALTER (Caucasian male)

Italicized type indicates the narrator; plain type indicates comments from various listeners. Names have been changed to protect the girl.

**AS THE STORY WOULD BE TOLD IN POVERTY . . .
PROBABLY BY A RELATIVE OR NEIGHBOR:**

Well, you know Walter got put away for 37 years. Him being 48 and all. He'll probably die in jail. Just couldn't leave his hands off that 12-year-old Susie.

Dirty old man. Bodding's gonna whup his tail.

Already did. You know Bodding was waiting for him in jail and beat the living daylights out of him.

In jail?

Yeah, Bodding got caught for possession. Had $12,000 on him when they arrested him.

Golly, wish I had been there to cash in!!!! (laughter) A man's gotta make a living!

Susie being blind and all—I can see why Bodding beat the daylights out of Walter. Lucky he didn't get killed, old Walter is.

Too bad her momma is no good.

She started the whole thing! Susie's momma goes over there and argues with Bodding.

Ain't they divorced?

Yeah, and she's got Walter working for her, repairing her house or something.

Or something, I bet. What's she got in her house that's worth fixing?

Anyway, she goes over to Bodding's house to take the lawnmower . . .

I reckon so as Walter can mow the yard?? I bet that's the first time old Walter has ever broken a sweat! Reminds me of the time I saw Walter thinking about taking a job. All that thinking and he had to get drunk. He went to jail that time, too—a felony, I think it was. So many of those DWIs. Judge told him he was egregious. Walter said he wasn't greasy—he took a bath last week!!! (laughter)

Bodding and Susie's momma got in a fight, so she tells Walter to take Susie with him.

Lordy, her elevator must not go all the way to the top!! Didn't she know about him getting arrested for enticing a minor???

With Susie blind and all. And she sends Susie with Walter?

She sure don't care about her babies.

Well, Walter's momma was there 'cause Walter lives with his momma, seeing as how he can't keep no job.

Ain't his other brother there?

Yeah, and him 41 years old. That poor momma sure has her burdens to bear. And then her 30-year-old daughter, Susie's momma, at home, too. You know Susie's momma lost custody of her kids. Walter gets these videos, you know. Those adult videos. Heavy breathing! (laughter)

Some of them are more fun to listen to than look at! (laughter) Those people in the videos are des-per-ate!!

Anyway, he puts those on and then carries Susie to his room and tells her she wants him—and describes all his sex-u-al exploits!!

Golly, he must be a loooooooooover. (laughter) He should be shot. I'd kill him if he did that to my kid!!

Then he lets his fingers do the walking.

Kinda like the Yellow Pages! (laughter)

I guess he didn't do anything with his "thang," according to Miss Rosie who went to that trial every day. And Susie begging him to stop so many times.

Probably couldn't do anything with it; that's why he needs to listen to that heavy breathing! Pant! Pant! (laughter) What a no-count, low-down creep. I'll pay Bodding to kill him!!

Bodding says the only way Walter is coming out of jail is in a pine box.

Don't blame him myself.

Yeah, Miss Rosie said Walter's momma said at the trial that the door to Walter's room was open and there ain't no way Walter could have done that. That she is a good Christian momma and she don't put up with that.

Oh Lordy, did God strike her dead on the spot, or is she still alive??? I'd be afraid of ending up in eternal damnation for telling a story like that!

Miss Rosie said her 12-year-old nephew testified that the door was closed and his grandma told him to say it was open!!!!

Ooo! Ooo! Oooo! That poor baby tells the truth? His grandma's gonna make him mis-er-a-ble!!!

And then Walter's momma tells that jury that she never allows those adult videos in her house, leastways not that she pays for them!! (lots of laughter)

I bet the judge bit on that one!! How is Walter gonna get videos except for her money? Mowing yards? (more laughter) No, I bet he saves his pennies!! (laughter)

All these years she has covered for Walter. Guess she just couldn't cover no more.

Remember that time Walter got drunk and wrecked her car, and she said she was driving? And she was at the hospital at the time with a broken leg. And the judge asked her how she could be driving and in the hospital "simultaneously." And she said that's just how it was—simultaneously—she had never felt so excited in her life. (laughter) Who turned Walter in?

Well, it wasn't Susie's momma. She was busy with Skeeter, her new boyfriend. I hear he's something.

Remember that one boyfriend she had? Thought he was so smart?

Speaking of smart, that Susie sure is. Her blind and all, and she won the district spelling bee for the seventh grade this year. I hear she's in National Honor Society, whatever that is.

Wonder if it's kinda like the country club. Instead of playing golf, you just spell!!! (laughter)

Susie calls this friend of hers who tells her mother and they come and get her and take her to the police and hospital.

Some rich lady, not minding her own business, that's for sure.

Well, it was a good thing for Susie, 'cause that momma of hers sure ain't good for Susie. She don't deserve a kid like Susie. SHE oughta be the one who's blind.

Ain't that the truth. Way I see it, she already is. Just look at Skeeter!! (gales of laughter)

(The preceding was an actual court case heard in Houston, Texas, during March 1995. Italicized print indicates what came out in the trial; plain print indicates the kinds of comments that might be made by others in generational poverty.)

■　■　■　■　■　■

Using this case, check which of the following patterns in generational poverty are present . . .

- ❑ *Background "noise":* Almost always the TV is on, no matter what the circumstance. Conversation is participatory, often with more than one person talking at a time.

- ❑ *Importance of personality:* Individual personality is what one brings to the setting—because money is not brought. The ability to entertain, tell stories, and have a sense of humor is highly valued.

- ❑ *Significance of entertainment:* When one can merely survive, then the respite from the survival is important. In fact, entertainment brings respite.

- ❑ *Importance of relationships:* One only has people upon whom to rely, and those relationships are important to survival. One often has favorites.

- ❑ *Matriarchal structure:* The mother has the most powerful position in the society if she functions as a caretaker.

- ❑ *Oral-language tradition:* Casual register is used for everything.

❑ *Survival orientation:* Discussion of academic topics is generally not prized. There is little room for the abstract. Discussions center around people and relationships. A job is about making enough money to survive. A job is not about a career (e.g., "I was looking for a job when I found this one").

❑ *Identity tied to lover/fighter role for men:* The key issue for males is to be a "man." The rules are rigid and a man is expected to work hard physically—and be a lover and a fighter.

❑ *Identity tied to rescuer/martyr role for women:* A "good" woman is expected to take care of and rescue her man and her children as needed.

❑ *Importance of non-verbal/kinesthetic communication:* Touch is used to communicate, as are space and non-verbal emotional information.

❑ *Ownership of people:* People are possessions. There is a great deal of fear and comment about leaving the culture and "getting above your raisings."

❑ *Negative orientation:* Failure at anything is the source of stories and numerous belittling comments.

❑ *Discipline:* Punishment is about penance and forgiveness, not change.

❑ *Belief in fate:* Destiny and fate are the major tenets of the belief system. Choice is seldom considered.

❑ *Polarized thinking:* Options are hardly ever examined. Everything is polarized; it is one way or the other. These kinds of statements are common: "I quit" and "I can't do it."

❑ *Mating dance:* The mating dance is about using the body in a sexual way and verbally and subverbally complimenting body parts. If you have few financial resources, the way you sexually attract someone is with your body.

❑ *Time:* Time occurs only in the present. The future does not exist except as a word. Time is flexible and not measured. Time is often assigned on the basis of the emotional significance and not the actual measured time.

❑ *Sense of humor:* A sense of humor is highly valued, as entertainment is one of the key aspects of poverty. Humor is almost always about people—either situations that people encounter or things people do to other people.

❑ *Lack of order/organization:* Many of the homes/apartments of people in poverty are unkempt and cluttered. Devices for organization (files, planners, etc.) don't exist.

❑ *Lives in the moment—does not consider future ramifications:* Being proactive, setting goals, and planning ahead are not a part of generational poverty. Most of what occurs is reactive and in the moment. Future implications of present actions are seldom considered.

DEBRIEFING THE WALTER CASE STUDY

The Walter case study is an example of many of the issues in generational poverty. The family members all live together. Momma is still the most powerful position and these children are nearly 50. Momma will always make excuses for her children. After all, they are *her* children. The matriarchal structure and possession of people are there. She decides their guilt and punishment, not some outside authority. She leans on the self-righteous defense of being moral and Christian, but not in the middle-class sense of Christianity. For her it is simply one of unconditional love. Reality is the present—what can be persuaded and convinced in the present. Future ramifications are not considered by anyone. Entertainment is key, whether it is moral or not.

The neighbors' view of the situation gives more insight into the reality of generational poverty. While there is a deep distaste for sexual abuse of children, the story is really to make fun of Walter and his family, as well as spread the news. Humor is used to cast aspersions on the character of Walter and his family. In many of these stories, aspersions would also be cast on the legal system and "rich lawyers." But there is an attitude of fate or fatalism; what are you going to do about it? That's the way it is.

FAMILY PATTERNS IN GENERATIONAL POVERTY

One of the most confusing things about understanding generational poverty is the family patterns. In the middle-class family, even with divorce, lineage is fairly easy to trace because of the legal documents. In generational poverty, on the other hand, many marital arrangements are common-law. Marriage and divorce in a legal court are only important if there is property to distribute or custody of children. When you were never legally married to begin with and you have no property, why pay a lawyer for something you don't have, don't need, and don't have the money to purchase?

In the middle class, family diagrams tend to be drawn as shown at the top of page 57. The notion is that lineage is traceable and that a linear pattern can be found.

In generational poverty, the mother is the center of the organization, and the family radiates from that center. Although it can happen that the mother is uncertain of the biological father, most of the time the father of the child is known. The second diagram on page 57 is based on a real situation. (Names have been changed.)

In this pattern, Jolyn has been legally married three times. Jolyn and Husband #1 had no children. Jolyn and Husband #2 had one child, Willy.

DIAGRAM OF MIDDLE-CLASS FAMILY

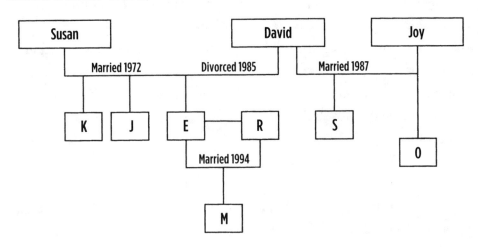

DIAGRAM OF FAMILY FROM GENERATIONAL POVERTY

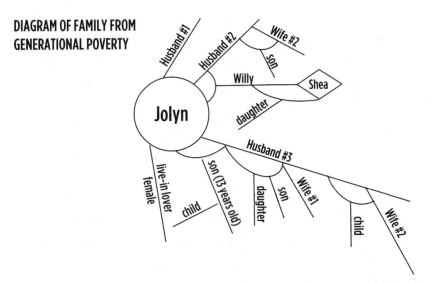

They divorced. Husband #2 eventually married the woman he lived with for several years, and they had a child together. She also had a son from a previous marriage. Willy has a common-law wife, Shea; Shea and Willy have a daughter. Jolyn and Husband #3 lived together several years before they were married, and they have a son named M.J. When M.J. was 13 he had a child with a 13-year-old girl, but that child lives with the girl's mother. Husband #3 and Jolyn divorced; Jolyn is now living with a woman in a lesbian relationship. Husband #3 is living with a younger woman who is pregnant with his child.

The mother is always at the center, though she may have multiple sexual relationships. Many of her children also will have multiple relationships, which may or may not produce children. The basic pattern is the mother at the heart of things, with nearly everyone having multiple relationships, some legal and some not. Eventually the relationships become intertwined. It wouldn't be out of the question for your sister's third husband to become your brother's ex-wife's live-in boyfriend. Also in this pattern are babies born out of wedlock to children in their early teens; these youngsters are often raised by the grandmother as her own children. For example, the oldest daughter has a child at 14. This infant becomes the youngest child in the existing family. The oldest daughter, who is actually the mother of the child, is referred to as her sister—and the relationship is a sibling one, not a mother-daughter one.

But the mother or maternal grandmother tends to keep her biological children. Because of the violence in poverty, death tends to be a prominent part of the family history. But it is also part of the family present because the deceased plays such a role in the memories of the family. It is important to note when dealing with the family patterns who is alive and who is dead—because in the discussions they are often still living (unless you, the listener, know differently).

Frequently, in the stories that are brought to caseworkers or employers, the individual will tell the story in the episodic, random manner of the casual-register story structure. Key individuals are usually not referred to during the story because making reference to them isn't part of the story structure. *The most important keys to understanding the story are often the omissions.* For example, when someone says, "He left," you can pretty much predict who "he" will go stay with when there is trouble. If he is having trouble with his mother, he will go stay with an ex-wife or a girlfriend. If he is having trouble with his current wife, he will go stay with his mother. Women tend to go stay with their sisters and sometimes their mothers. Whether or not a mother or ex-wife is mentioned in the story, if the family is in generational poverty, you can be fairly certain that these are key players. You can also be fairly sure that the males are in and out—sometimes present, sometimes not, but not in any predictable pattern. Furthermore, you can know that as the male temporarily or permanently changes residences, the allegiances will change also.

Additionally within these families there tend to be multiple internal feuds. Allegiances may change overnight; favoritism is a way of life. *Who children go to stay with after school, who stays with whom when there is trouble, and who is available to deal with school issues are dependent on the current alliances and relationships at that moment.* For example, Ned comes home drunk and beats up his wife, Susan. She calls the police and escapes with the three kids to her mother's house. He goes to his mother's because she arranges to get him out of jail. His mother is not speaking to Susan because she called the cops on him and put him in jail. But Ned's mother usually keeps his kids after school until Susan gets home. Now it's Monday, and Susan doesn't have any place to send the kids. So she tells them to go to her mother's house after school, which means they must go on a different bus because she doesn't know if Ned will show up at the house and be waiting for her. On Tuesday the kids again go to Susan's mom's house. But on Wednesday Ned's mom calls Susan and tells her that that no-good Ned got drunk last night, and she kicked him out of her house. So now Susan and Ned's mother are good friends, and Ned is on the hot seat. So Ned goes to the apartment of his ex-wife, Jackie, because last week she decided she'd had enough of Jerry, and she was very glad to see Ned . . . And so the story continues.

The key roles in these families are fighter/lover, caretaker/rescuer, worker, storyteller, and "keeper of the soul" (i.e., dispenser of penance and forgiveness). The family patterns in generational poverty are different from the middle class. *In poverty the roles, the multiple relationships, the nature of the male identity, the ever-changing allegiances, the favoritism, and the matriarchal structure result in a different pattern.*

HOW THESE PATTERNS SURFACE AT WORK OR IN SOCIAL SERVICE SETTINGS

Place a check mark in front of the items that describe workers/clients with whom you regularly interact. They . . .

❑ get mad and quit their job/work. If they don't like the boss/teacher, they will quit. The emphasis is on the current feeling, not the long-term ramifications.

❑ will work hard if they like you.

❑ do not use conflict-resolution skills, preferring to settle issues in verbal or physical assaults.

❑ use survival language, tending to operate out of casual register.

❑ are not emotionally reserved when angry, usually saying exactly what is on their mind.

❑ have an extreme freedom of speech, enjoy a sense of humor, use the personality to entertain, have a love of stories about people.

❑ are very independent. They won't take kindly to the "parent" voice. If their full cooperation is sought, the boss/employer needs to use the "adult" voice.

❑ often need time off or arrive late due to family emergencies.

❑ need emotional warmth from colleagues/boss/teacher(s) in order to feel comfortable.

❑ require a level of integrity from management, actively distrusting organizations and the people who represent the organizations. They see organizations as basically dishonest.

❑ exhibit a possessiveness about the people they really like.

❑ need a greater amount of "space" to allow for the uniqueness of their personalities.

❑ show favoritism for certain people and give them preferential treatment.

❑ are very disorganized, frequently lose papers, don't have signatures, etc.

❑ bring many reasons why something is missing, or the paper is gone, etc.

❑ only see part of what is on the page.

❑ only do part of the job.

❑ can't seem to get started (no procedural self-talk).

❑ cannot monitor their own behavior.

❑ tell stories in the casual-register structure.

❑ don't know or use middle-class courtesies.

❑ dislike authority.

❑ talk back and are extremely participatory.

Also . . .

■ Men socialize with men and women with women. Men tend to have two social outlets: bars and work. Women with children tend to stay at home and have only other female relatives as friends, unless they work outside the home. Men tend to be loners in any other social setting and avoid those social settings. When a man and a woman are together, it is usually about a private relationship.

- A real man is ruggedly good-looking, is a lover, can physically fight, works hard, takes no crap.

- A real woman takes care of her man by feeding him and downplaying his shortcomings.

NOTE: In generational poverty, the primary role of a real man is to physically work hard, to be a fighter, and to be a lover. In middle class, a real man is a provider. If one follows the implications of a male identity as one who is a fighter and a lover, then one can understand why the male who takes this identity (of fighter and lover as his own) cannot have a stable life. Of the three responses to life—to flee, flow, or fight—he can only fight or flee. So when the stress gets high, he fights, then flees from the law and the people closest to him, leaving his home. Either way he is gone. When the heat dies down, he returns—to an initial welcome, then more fights. The cycle begins again.

GENERATIONAL POVERTY

One of the reasons it is getting more and more difficult to work as we have in the past is that the workers who bring the middle-class culture with them are decreasing in numbers, and the workers who bring the poverty culture with them are increasing in numbers. As in any demographic switch, the prevailing rules and policies eventually give way to the group with the largest numbers.

In order to better serve these workers, the next several chapters have ideas about ways in which we can do our work more effectively. But to do so, we must rethink the notions we have traditionally assigned to relationships and achievement.

WHAT IMPLICATIONS DOES THIS INFORMATION HAVE FOR THE SOCIAL SERVICE, HEALTH CARE, OR WORK SETTING?

- Individuals leave poverty for one of four reasons: a goal or vision of something they want to be or have; a situation that is so painful that anything would be better; someone who "sponsors" them (i.e., an educator or spouse or mentor or role model who shows them a different way or convinces them that they could live differently); or a specific talent or ability that provides an opportunity for them.

- Being in poverty is rarely about a lack of intelligence or ability.

- Many individuals stay in poverty because they don't know there is a choice—and if they do know, they have no one to teach them hidden rules or provide resources.

- Schools, welfare-to-work organizations, and other social-sector organizations are places where people can learn the rules of the middle class.

- Each agency or discipline will, upon examining these patterns, find some that impact their work more than others. For example, workers who make home visits report that background noise had a negative impact on their work until they learned how to adjust for it. Those who work in domestic violence shelters say that the gender roles impact their outcomes, and those in the criminal justice system point to the cycle of penance and forgiveness as a pattern that contributes to recidivism.

A broad spectrum of African-Americans have used education . . .
Malcolm X, Martin Luther King, Jr., Maya Angelou, Carter G. Woodson,
W.E.B. DuBois, Cornel West, and many others. All these men and women
hold the road map for change. They tell us in every way that education is
essential to any movement toward freedom. Even in our most desperate
hours—during slavery—we understood one fundamental truth: that we
must become educated to make progress in this culture.

– Carl Upchurch, Convicted in the Womb

Survival = Anger × Imagination. Imagination is the only weapon on the
reservation.

– Sherman Alexie, The Lone Ranger and Tonto Fistfight in Heaven

We saw that in the working-class families about half of all feedback was
affirmative among family members when the child was 13 to 18 months old
. . . In the professional families . . . more than 80% of the feedback to the
13- to 18-month-old child was affirmative. . . . Almost 80% of the welfare
parents' feedback to their 13- to 18-month-old children was negative. . . .
A consistent and pervasive negative Feedback Tone was the model for
the children of how families work together. Given the strong relationships
shown in the longitudinal data between the prevalence of prohibitions in
the first years of life and lowered child accomplishments, lasting still at
age 9, the prospects for the next generation of welfare children seem bleak.

– Betty Hart and Todd R. Risley (1995). Meaningful Differences in
the Everyday Experience of Young American Children. (p. 204).
Baltimore: Paul H. Brookes.

Role Models and Emotional Resources

To understand the importance of role models and their part in the development of emotional resources, one must first briefly look at the notion of functional and dysfunctional systems. The following definitions will be used:

> **A SYSTEM is a group in which individuals have rules, roles, and relationships.**
>
> **DYSFUNCTIONAL is the extent to which an individual cannot get his/her needs met within a system.**

All systems are, to some extent, dysfunctional. A system is not equally functional or dysfunctional for each individual within a given system. The extent to which an individual must give up meeting his/her needs in order to meet the needs of another person is the extent to which the situation is dysfunctional.

Michael Dumont (1994) gives a case study of a girl named Ellie.

ELLIE

Ellie's mother, Victoria, is bedridden with multiple sclerosis and her father, Larry, is a small storekeeper. Victoria, in her rage at the disease and her distrust of Larry, attempts suicide when Ellie is 9 years old. It is Ellie's job each day when she comes home from school to count her mother's pills to make certain they are all there—and to check to see if her mother is alive. Ellie tells Mr. Dumont that the worst part of her day is when she comes home from school and must check on her mother's well-being. When he tells Ellie that she is smart and asks her what she wants to be, she tells him she would like to be a secretary. At 13 Ellie becomes pregnant and drops out of school.

The situation is *dysfunctional* for Ellie because she must sublimate her needs to address the needs of her mother. In order for Ellie to have an appropriate developmental process emotionally, she needs to be a child, then an adolescent, then an adult. By being forced to take on an adult role earlier, she must in essence put her emotional development on hold while she functions in an adult role. Therefore, for the rest of her life, Ellie will seek to have her emotional needs met that were not met during her childhood. She almost certainly will not have the emotional resources and stamina necessary to function as an interdependent adult.

DEPENDENCE
INDEPENDENCE
INTERDEPENDENCE

To become a fully functioning adult, one moves developmentally from being dependent to being independent to being interdependent. Stephen Covey (1989) calls it *the maturity continuum*, and John Bradshaw (1988) refers to it as *becoming whole*. Regardless of the terminology, it basically means moving from being dependent on others to being able to work together with other adults, each independent of the other, but jointly, as equal partners.

Simply put, an individual operating in a dysfunctional setting is often forced to take an adult role early—and then as an adult is literally caught between being dependent and independent. So one will see this fierce independence coupled with a crippling dependence that weakens the person to the point that he/she has few emotional resources. This roller-coaster ride up and down between dependence and independence takes a heavy toll.

Bradshaw and others refer to this constant fluctuation between dependence and independence as *co-dependency*.

As Ellie's case study illustrates, the emotional resources come in part from the role models who are present for the child. When the appropriate role models are present, the child can go through the developmental stages at appropriate times and build emotional resources. Emotional resources are built in this fashion: The child watches the adult for emotional responses to a given situation and notes the continuum of behaviors that go with those responses. In Ellie's situation, her mother's response to her husband's infidelity was to create an even greater level of dependence—and to use the emotional ploy of guilt to manipulate Ellie. So what does Ellie do when she gets old enough? She creates a level of dependence on others as well (i.e., through pregnancy and going on welfare).

A child may decide that the role-model responses are not appropriate. Often what occurs then is that the child selects the opposite extreme from which to operate. What is problematic for the child is simply what is "normal"; an appropriate adult response is rarely observable. The child, therefore, is forced to guess at what "normal" or appropriate is.

> Question: Why would emotional resouces have such importance in the social service setting and at work?
>
> Answer: Emotional responses dictate behavior and, eventually, determine achievement.

Furthermore, in order to move from poverty to middle class or from middle class to wealth, one must trade off some relationships for achievement at least for a period of time. To do this, one needs emotional resources and stamina.

An *emotional memory bank* is defined as the emotions that are accessed habitually and "feel right." When a relationship is traded off for achievement, the emotional memory bank must be held in abeyance until the new "feel right" feeling can be obtained. That process sometimes takes years. The driving force behind an individual holding the emotional memory bank in abeyance is usually one of four things: (1) The current situation is too painful for the individual to stay, (2) a compelling goal or vision of the future drives the individual, (3) a talent or skill takes the individual into new surroundings, or (4) a spouse or mentor provides an emotional comfort level while the individual learns the new skills/knowledge.

Emotional resources and stamina allow the individual to live with feelings other than those in the emotional memory bank. This allowance provides the individual the opportunity to seek options and examine other possibilities. As the case study shows, Ellie stays with her emotional memory bank and creates situations that "feel right."

HOW DO YOU PROVIDE EMOTIONAL RESOURCES WHEN THE CLIENT HAS NOT HAD ACCESS TO APPROPRIATE ROLE MODELS?

1. Through support systems. Two support systems can be utilized: the one that clients bring with them, the other that is created with the help of professionals.

2. By using appropriate discipline strategies and approaches.

3. By establishing long-term relationships (apprenticeships, mentorships) with adults who are appropriate.

4. By teaching the hidden rules.

5. By identifying options.

6. By increasing individuals' achievement levels through appropriate instruction and treatment.

7. By teaching goal-setting.

WHAT IMPLICATIONS DOES THIS INFORMATION HAVE FOR THE SOCIAL SERVICE, HEALTH CARE, OR WORK SETTING?

■ Social service agencies, behavioral health care facilities, and other organizations need to establish schedules and instructional arrangements that allow clients to stay with the same case worker, case manager, or therapist for as long as possible.

■ Administrators, managers, and support staff are much more important as role models than has previously been addressed.

■ The development of emotional resources is crucial to success. Mental health facilities, substance abuse treatment centers, JOBS clubs, and other organizations that have contact with clients for some time can all teach emotional management skills.

■ Families who live with chronic crisis often come to rely on survival strategies that in the long term become destructive. Those who work with such families must remember that the individuals in the families are doing the best they can with what they know and have.

There was only so much trouble we could get into in those early days. Cavalier Manor was a neighborhood filled with surrogate parents, people who would punish you like your momma and daddy if they caught you doing wrong. . . . School was part of the surrogate system. . . . Some of the parents even took it upon themselves to patrol the neighborhood on school days to make sure we were where we were supposed to be. We kids hated that surrogate system. . . . It was only years later, when black communities as we knew them started falling apart, that I came to understand the system for the hidden blessings it contained: It had built-in mechanisms for reinforcing values and trying to prevent us from becoming the hellions some of us turned out to be.

– Nathan McCall, *Makes Me Wanna Holler*

Welfare recipients can get hung up on the same everyday needs that draw from our momentum and focus: childcare, parenting, relationships, housing. But in the absence of financial or family backup, bumps can become insurmountable obstacles: reasons to miss work, or worse, quit.

– Linda Hall Whitman, "Welfare-to-Work Management"

Support Systems

Support systems are the friends, family, and backup resources that can be accessed in times of need. These systems of support tend to fall into seven general categories.

1. Coping Strategies

Coping strategies are the ways in which one copes with daily living: the disappointments, the tragedies, and the triumphs. Coping strategies are ways to think about things, attitudes, self-talk, strategies for resolving conflicts, problem-solving techniques, and the avoidance of needless conflicts. Coping strategies are also ways of approaching tasks, setting priorities, and determining what one can live with and what one can live without.

2. Options During Problem-Solving

Options are all the ways to solve a problem. Even very capable adults often talk over a problem with another adult just in order to see other options they haven't considered.

3. Information and Know-How

This is a key aspect of a support system. When a child has homework, who in the support system knows enough math to help the child? Who knows the research process? Who knows the ropes for going to college or getting a new-car loan? Who knows how to talk to the insurance agent so the situation can be clarified? Who knows how to negotiate difficult situations with a teacher and come to a resolution? Who understands the court system, the school system? Information and know-how are crucial to success.

4. Temporary Relief from Emotional, Mental, Financial, and/or Time Constraints

When you are upset, who provides relief for you? When you aren't sure how you will get everything finished, who helps you? Who takes your children when you are desperate for a break? These people are all part of a support system.

5. Connections to Other People and Resources

When you don't have the information and know-how, who are the people you turn to for assistance? Those people are your connections. Connections to people and resources are an integral part of a healthy support system.

6. Positive Self-Talk

Everyone has a little voice inside his/her head that talks to him/her all the time. This little voice gives encouraging messages. These encouraging messages help one finish tasks, complete projects, and get through difficult situations. If an individual does not listen to this encouraging little voice, the success rate is much lower.

7. Procedural Self-Talk

Procedural self-talk is the voice that talks an individual through a task. It is key to success. Many individuals in poverty have a very limited support system—and particularly missing is procedural self-talk. Many tasks are never finished. In numerous dealings with clients, social workers and employers often find that self-talk is simply not available to the client.

The following case study identifies the nature of the support system for a young single mother who just started back to work. Her support system consists of her internal strengths and weaknesses, her home situation, and the services available in the workplace.

ANITA

You are a Human Resources specialist in a mid-sized plastics company. Ron, a line supervisor, comes to your office, bringing Anita, a new employee, with him. He explains that Anita is a good machine operator who is on the verge of quitting. If she stays another month, she will be hired with full benefits. He doesn't want to lose her and hopes that you can help her so that she can stay on the job. Having broken the ice, the supervisor leaves.

Anita tells you that she wouldn't have come in at all, but she likes Ron and doesn't want to let him down. Also, Ron told her that you could be trusted. As Anita's story unfolds you learn that she has worked for the company for two months. She has already missed work once and been late to work twice. She knows that she is about to get fired, so she thinks she might as well quit and start looking for another job. She tells you that it's easy to find a job. You also learn that her child has been sick and the woman that she used to rely on has been spreading tales about her, so Anita isn't talking to her and has to rely on her boyfriend and his mother to care for her baby. She hasn't used the company's child care providers because she doesn't know them; she doesn't want just anybody looking after her baby. A male co-worker has been assigned to her machine, and people on the floor are beginning to talk about them. She is sure this will get back to her boyfriend, and she is expecting trouble, big time. There is just too much coming at her at once, so she figures that a clean break and starting over is her best option.

What support systems can be brought to bear on Anita's situation to help her stay on the job?

What follows is a sample list of support systems and strategies used by a cross-section of employers, community organizations, and governmental agencies.

SUPPORT SYSTEMS USED BY SOCIAL SERVICE AGENCIES AND LAW ENFORCEMENT, BEHAVIORAL HEALTH CARE, HEALTH CARE, AND OTHER AGENCIES

1. Providing an integrated system of care across agency lines—by considering the client's life cycle through all of the serving agencies. Collaborating agencies can ensure that clients don't fall through the cracks in the system at the point where they leave one agency to go to another.

2. Keeping clients and therapists, caseworkers, and case managers together for long periods can be a positive strategy. This allows time to develop supportive relationships. One welfare-to-work collaborative assigns caseworkers to program participants according to where the strongest personal relationships are developed, regardless of where the professional works.

3. Teaching coping strategies can be done in several ways. One is to address each issue as a client needs assistance. Individual, family, and group counseling are ways to address coping strategies.

4. Scheduling events so that people from the poverty culture can attend them will support their achievement. Until clients learn the rules of the middle-class work world they operate under the rules of their own culture. Scheduling events over a span of a few hours so that people can drop in—or making arrangements for children to be present—will increase involvement.

5. Parent training supports change for all members of the family. One man who attended parenting classes while in a county jail sent parenting materials to his daughter so that she could improve her skills. His intention was to become a better grandparent.

6. Using videos is common in the poor community because of the value placed on entertainment. Social service agencies may consider making videos to send home with clients to support their education and achievements. The topics, of course, will vary with the mission of the organization.

7. Direct-teaching the survival skills for work and the organization. What are the hidden rules of that particular workplace? Every workplace has rules (hidden and otherwise) about attendance, sick time, vacations, how to get things done, who to go to when you have a problem, and so on. One employer who hires people from poverty assigns a mentor to all new employees in order to "teach them the ropes."

   What are the rules at your organization, and how do the clients learn them? The clients' success at any organization can be tied to their understanding of what is expected of them and what they can expect of the organization. This can be done at the time of client orientation. Videos can ensure consistent orientations where the information, tone, and methods are carefully presented. The information in the orientation video can be discussed with staff and supported with written material.

8. Requiring daily goal-setting and procedural self-talk. In the beginning, goal-setting would focus on what a client wants to accomplish by the end of each day and by the end of a week. Goals would be in writing. At the end of the day the goals should be reviewed. Procedural self-talk would begin in the written form first and would need to be assisted. Procedural self-talk has value when tied to a specific task, as procedures vary with tasks.

9. Using team interventions is a way to provide support to clients. This happens when staff members from the agencies involved with

a client meet with the client to make a plan for helping him/her. Behavioral health care agencies are doing more cooperative work with each other by providing wraparound and home-based support services.

10. Utilizing the "middle people." These are the people who know the ropes, who have "been there," those who are natural helpers or mentors. They are the people whom others go to for advice and to talk things over. They are also the ones who can be the bridge between people in poverty and the institutions they don't yet trust. They are the ones who can say, "You can trust this person. This person will help you; talk to him (or her)." The "middle people" can be trained in peer listening skills, so that they can skillfully mediate situations, teach hidden rules, and form an informal support system for their co-workers.

11. In order to improve retention rates, front-loading relationship-building activities and rewards for hew hires from poverty. Some companies use job coaches (in-house or provided by outside organizations), hold frequent informal meetings to keep communications open and clear, avoid a bureaucratic tone, celebrate short-term gains, and make certain they don't make promises to new hires they cannot keep.

12. Developing contracts with child-care providers who will care for sick children because this is a problem for employees from all economic groups, but particularly for former welfare recipients. On-site child care is becoming a more common practice.

13. Setting up toll-free phone lines to help troubled employees talk through personal and work-related problems with professionals.

14. Arranging for outside organizations to provide immediate mediation services between new hires and themselves when problems arise.

WHAT IMPLICATIONS DOES THIS INFORMATION HAVE FOR THE SOCIAL SERVICE, HEALTH CARE, OR WORK SETTING?

- By reorganizing the work day and schedule, and often by making minor adjustments, social workers and health care professionals can build support systems into the agency day without significant additional cost.

- Organizations that are built on the machine metaphor where each person represents a replaceable and separate part (and roles are compartmentalized) will find it difficult to provide support to clients and/or employees. In these organizations the emphasis is on control. On the other hand, organizations with metaphors that recognize interdependence, connectedness, flexibility, process, and relationships will be positioned to work most effectively with people in and from poverty. More appropriate metaphors may well be webs, weaving, sailing, cyberspace, rivers, and holograms.

- It must be acknowledged that it takes a lot of "emotional labor" from both sides for people to make the transition from poverty to middle class. This is where one takes an attitude that it is "better to give than to receive." Remember that leaving poverty is a process, not an event. It is a long series of steps.

- While managers remain empathetic, boundaries must be maintained; supervisors do not want to play the role of social worker. That is when outside resources are used, and carefully thought-out programs are implemented.

Despite fantasies of becoming a movie or sports star and get rich fast schemes, the two most successful means of class-climbing among poor whites, like other poor groups, is marrying up and/or education. Marrying out and up is probably more possible for women than men and is certainly something my mother preached to my sister and me.

– Roxanne A. Dunbar, *White Trash*, Matt Wray and Annalee Newitz (Eds.)

Carl Upchurch, author of Convicted in the Womb, *was in "solitary" at Lewisburg, Ohio, when he found a collection of Shakespeare's sonnets wedged under the short leg of a table. "I won't pretend that Shakespeare and I immediately connected," writes Upchurch. "I must have read those damn sonnets twenty times before they started to make sense. Even then, comprehension came slowly—first a word, then a phrase, and finally a whole poem. Those sonnets began to take hold of me, transported me out of the gray world into a world I had never, ever imagined."*

Mentoring and Bridging

Mentoring Adults and Youths from Generational Poverty

*The wise . . . mentor knows that being aware of what is not known is
important in order to begin to learn. To attain true knowledge and wisdom,
we must remain open and empty, allowing ideas from other people to rush
in. To be empty, to recognize how little we know, is to be abundant.*

– Chungliang Al Huang and Jerry Lynch, *Mentoring:
The TAO of Giving and Receiving Wisdom*

Imagine you are embarking on a great journey. You have been allowed to take
only a limited amount of luggage; much of what has been meaningful to you
is being left behind. You're also leaving behind many of the people on whom
you've depended for love, support, and friendship. They cannot or do not
want to go on this journey with you. You feel alone. You have heard that the
"old ways" do not work as well in the place where you are going—and that
you must learn the new ways. In fact, you don't even know the language of
the New World! You're not sure that you can do this. You think you may be
making a mistake by leaving what you know for something that is foreign.
But this new place is said to be better.

NOTE: Most of the quotations in this chapter are paraphrases of statements stemming
from interviews that author Dreussi Smith did with six women who were in the process
of moving out of poverty toward middle class. The illustrations from the women's lives
are true. In order to ensure confidentiality, their names are not included.

The most significant mentor in my early years was a widow who lived next door. We called her Grandma Sheila, though now I suppose she was only about 50 years old. Grandma Sheila's son had graduated from college, and she believed in getting an education. On report card days, all the neighborhood children would make a stop at Grandma Sheila's house on the way home. In third grade I got an "F" in math. Grandma Sheila announced that I needed to bring this grade up. "You can do it," she said.

In fact, my first "job" was given to me by Grandma Sheila. Grandma Sheila paid me 50¢ a day to go to the grocery store for her. She always needed something: a loaf of bread, some hot dogs; at least, she always made sure she needed something. She gave me 25¢ before going to the store; that way I could spend it on candy or do whatever I liked with it. Mostly, I spent it on candy. When I returned with the groceries, Grandma Sheila took me over to the piggy bank in the living room. I would put the other quarter in the piggy bank. In this way, Grandma Sheila hoped to teach me not to spend everything I earned. At the end of the month, Grandma Sheila helped me open a savings account at a local bank. When the account earned $60 (and I had eaten almost $60 worth of candy), my mom took me to the bank to take out the money to pay the electric bill. After that, Grandma Sheila gave me that 50¢ a day up front. I guess she wanted the money to be just for me.

– Interview excerpt

Cultural journeys were commonplace as a result of the mass emigration to the United States at the beginning of the 20th century. One such immigrant was Angelo Dreussi. Repeatedly, he had been forced to leave his wife and children for months at a time in northern Italy so that he could find employment in Austria. His family was sorely dissatisfied with his absence and still poor. Now he was boarding a boat, which would take him to America. Again he was to be separated from his wife and sons. But this time Angelo hoped that he could establish himself and send for them. The hope of a better life was the impetus for change.

One thing made a great difference to Angelo as he boarded the French Line *La Lorraine* as a third-class passenger. He was secure in knowing that his relatives who had already made the journey and established themselves in America were awaiting him. He could count on them to teach him "the ropes," help him get a job, teach him English. These were people with whom he had a *relationship*. When Angelo sent for his wife and small sons several years later, she knew (as she began her journey) that Angelo was awaiting her. He would help her learn the new language and ways. And they would finally be together with their children.

This journey ended happily for the Dreussis. The family eventually prospered, primarily due to a belief in their religion, ethnic culture, family, and hard work. The children of Angelo and Lydia learned both Italian and English, but the older children dropped out of school by eighth grade to help support the family. Today the family boasts at least 20 grandchildren who are upper-middle-class, college-educated professionals. The remaining grand-children are productive members of the middle class, holding professional or skilled-labor professions.

Why did this family succeed in achieving middle class? Not all descen-dants of the Great Immigration did so. Was it luck? Pluck? Perhaps a sole mentor's influence can greatly change the flow of "circumstances." When Angelo's 38-year-old daughter Florence, a cashier at an IGA, decided to go to college to become a teacher, the course of Dreussi history was altered. Aunt Florence, with no children of her own, became an award-winning elementary teacher in a public school system in the Midwest. "Florencie" took seriously the task of mentoring her many nieces and nephews. This woman and her sister Annie spent much time and energy taking the little ones to art muse-ums, plays, musical events. Florence took the children to her school and showed them what it meant to be a professional, explaining the importance of getting an education. She consciously played the part of middle-class role model to her young protégés, which probably included not only her relatives but a percentage of her students. Could it be that the mentoring touch of these women made the difference in the next generation?

My fifth-grade art teacher let me be "helper," setting the stage for what occurred with the next art teacher. He would let me spend time in the art room, doing various jobs. This attention made me feel useful and special, really increasing my self-image. I remember that he mailed me a postcard from Alaska and brought me a polished rock from his vacation. The most important thing was that he always treated me with respect. But he kept a certain distance because of the gender difference. . . .

When he moved on to another job, my next art teacher was female and was more nurturing. She also let me spend time in the art room as her helper, but she gave me my first view of a middle-class home and family life. I had the opportunity to meet my teacher's husband and little 3-year-old girl, who was simply charming. Mrs. Craig told me how she had become an art teacher by attending the University of Maryland. I was impressed with the beautiful original artwork in the teacher's home, with how the furniture matched, with little extras such as candles and ceramic pieces. That's when I decided I wanted to be an art teacher.

– Interview excerpt

Over generations, the Dreussi family has moved across social, ethnic, and economic lines. The harsh realities of the original journey have acquired a romantic blush over time. Today the family views the immigrant great-grandparents as heroic.

What remains constant in moving across class barriers is the benefit of the mentor/protégé relationship. The barriers of language and "hidden rules" of ethnic and socioeconomic culture are learned more quickly *through the use of mentors*. As Angelo and Lydia realized that their mentors awaited them, they were strengthened and encouraged through relationships with those who had come to America earlier. These mentors had struggled and continued to face cultural barriers. The task that towered above them, and which other relatives in Italy told them was a crazy venture, was now perceived as being within grasp. The same has held true for those bridging purely economic chasms (i.e., moving from generational poverty to middle class).

When I graduated from college, I rented a stretch limo. In the limo were the people that had helped me to get through school—my husband, my friend Pam, and my kids. I wouldn't let my mom in that limo. She was always saying, "Why are you wasting your time with this school stuff now? Why didn't you do this when you were supposed to? Now you got kids to raise!" I am the first child on my mom's side (she had 12 siblings; I have 100 cousins) to graduate from college! To even go to college!

– Interview excerpt

Due to welfare reform, in the next five years there are many who will stand in the shoes of the young Angelo Dreussi, boarding *La Lorraine*. There are no seas to cross, but the journey is equally daunting. The movement from one class to another is fraught with perils, misunderstanding, language barriers, and mental-model adjustments. Who will mentor those of the poverty culture who want and/or need to move toward middle-class structures and values?

DOES MENTORING WORK?

Big Brothers/Big Sisters volunteers meet with their protégés an average of three times a month, creating relationships that span many years. The Big Brothers/Big Sisters organization of Santa Clara County, California, reports that 98% of youths affiliated with the program remain in school, graduate, and don't have "run-ins" with the law. The organization points to its recruitment program, which matches youths to appropriate mentors, then offers additional support through the use of case counselors during the mentoring relationship.

A study of 2,400 life insurance agents shows a correlation between success and the presence of mentors. The survival rate of new agents with in-house mentors was 74% compared with a 64% rate among the control group. The percentage difference translates into 240 agents who failed from lack of mentoring. Many successful and even famous people attribute their success to early mentor experiences and attest to the time saved by learning through mentoring experiences. Some corporations currently encourage mentoring as a means of contributing to the community and as an effective process for recruiting valuable employees.

In a 1993 study among Belgian business graduates, a correlation was established between work satisfaction and career achievement and early professional mentoring relationships. Those who were mentored received significantly more promotions than those who were not. If mentoring has proved beneficial to middle-class workers with higher education and developed language skills, is it not even more crucial to those in poverty who may not yet have all the tools needed for "upward" movement?

WHAT IS MENTORING?

Mentoring has been around since ancient times when King Odysseus, leaving for war, asked his friend, Mentor, to look after his young son. A mentor is someone who helps another learn the ways of the world—or specific tasks.

More and more, this form of "coaching" is taking place in today's business and educational settings. Professionals are seeking mentors in order to speed the process of "climbing the ladder of success." Many successful people are open to sharing with a protégé what they have learned. The protégé benefits from the mentor's career and life experiences.

WHO WILL MENTOR?

In the case of those who will assist individuals from the poverty culture, the mentors can be anyone with the knowledge of hidden rules and values of middle class. The mentor is someone willing to give some time and energy in helping someone else succeed. This someone could be a relative, neighbor, teacher, income-maintenance worker, counselor, law enforcement officer, receptionist, agency van driver, or peer/co-worker. Mentors are those who can use the process to help others—usually one on one—avoid sabotaging themselves by repeating learned, but ineffective or destructive, behaviors.

Successful mentors are willing to share their own mistakes and how they were resolved. Mentoring is a gift from the heart.

Some mentoring programs recruit intermediary mentors. Intermediary mentors are individuals selected from the population being served. One of the most successful of these (in Mansfield, Ohio) is the Community Health Access Project (CHAP), which utilizes Community Health Advisors (CHA). The CHAP program was initiated by Dr. Mark Redding to improve birth weights and reduce infant mortality in Alaska. There it is called the Community Health Aide Program. In 1988, the number of Alaskan babies with low birth weights was among the highest in the United States. CHAP was designed to reach the village women who are most at risk. In order to bridge the distrust of doctors and "outsiders," CHAP organizers contact villages to assist in selecting the Community Health Aide for their region. Community groups select a woman who would be trusted by her peers and who would be able to meet the training requirements. The CHA does not diagnose or treat but serves as a medical intermediary within her community to improve health outcomes through preventive medicine. The Community Health Aide is supervised by a doctor in the region. The success of this program in terms of reaching women to increase birth weights and other health issues has been remarkable. After just one year of program implementation, the fetal and infant mortality rate in the pilot region dropped from 10 a year in 1988 to only one in 1990. The CHAP model has been replicated in urban and rural communities with equivalent success.

The use of intermediaries also is successful in youth mentoring programs. One of the most distinguished is *Natural Helpers (NH)*, a school-based program that also has been successfully adapted to adult populations, especially in corporate settings. What makes *Natural Helpers* stand out is the mentor selection process, in which students identify students who already are doing the helping or listening. The actual selection of the mentors is done by the faculty or advisors, using the helpers identified. The advisors look for helpers in each peer group within the school, in order to ensure that the entire student body is represented. The *Natural Helpers* program is extremely low-profile.

Students simply continue to help their friends, but with a support system in place to deal with serious issues that may need referral, such as violence, abuse, or suicide. According to a *New York Times* article, Long Island schools have found the program to be beneficial in violence prevention. The article notes further that the student helpers created so many referrals of serious problems to the mental health workers in the school system that their caseload increased significantly.

Both CHAP and *Natural Helpers* are examples of successful programs that use intermediaries. The key is that the intermediaries are given considerable training and support—and learn to trust the organization as a support system. The relationship between the intermediary and the supervisor (CHAP) or advisor *(NH)* is significant because this sets the stage for helping and mentoring to occur in a safe and confidential environment. Both strategies invest a great deal of time and money in building and maintaining relationships, as well as providing support via the intermediary. The key difference between these two programs is that CHAP uses formal mentoring strategies, while *Natural Helpers* are informal mentors and are intentionally kept in this setting in order to minimize alienation from the peer group. *Natural Helpers* are not "mini-counselors"; there are no scheduled times for helping their peers, nor are there formal mentoring sessions. Student helpers continue to talk to their friends in informal situations as the need arises.

Note: CHAP (Community Health Access Project) of Ohio can be contacted at P.O. Box 1986, Mansfield, OH 44903.

Natural Helpers is a peer helper program owned by CHEF (Comprehensive Health Education Foundation), Seattle, WA, and disseminated by AGC, 1560 Sherman Ave., Suite 100, Evanston, IL 60201.

MENTORING MODELS

Floyd Wickman and Terri Sjodin, co-authors of *Mentoring: A Success Guide for Mentors and Protégés*, promote mentoring as building relationships that can enhance the success for both parties. Mentoring can be an informal or a formal process; it can take place in short, casual segments or can be as structured and involved as deemed appropriate by both partners. Often, mentoring occurs in employer/employee relationships—or with co-workers. It's obvious that caseworkers, other social workers, and counselors are actually being paid to mentor. Most types of mentoring can be long- or short-term. Some forms are even momentary!

The Primary Mentor

This mentor will focus on a broad variety of issues and questions with the protégé. Family, friends, work, hidden rules, problems with co-workers . . . all of these are part of the primary mentor's realm. The amount of time a protégé spends with his/her primary mentor varies, but the relationship tends to be more extensive than that of secondary mentoring.

The Secondary Mentor

Secondary mentors offer expertise in a specific area, such as those listed below. An individual may consult with many secondary mentors simultaneously, as well as maintain the primary mentoring relationship. Each heading as presented by Wickman and Sjodin lists the following topics as possible areas for secondary mentoring experiences: professional development and employment issues, health and fitness, education, social protocol, philanthropy, and finances. Ideas for mentoring in several of these areas are discussed below.

Formal (Structured) vs. Informal

Formal mentoring usually involves setting regular mentor meetings that include goal-setting, assignments (reading, written, experiential), and some form of reporting. The formal mentoring process requires more commitment from the protégé. Protégés are encouraged to keep notes on the sessions. Formal mentoring may take place as a result of corporate or non-profit mentor programs. In some cases a protégé will contact someone with/from whom he/she desires to learn and ask the mentor to enter into a structured mentoring relationship.

Informal mentoring is sometimes described as offering a "pearl of wisdom here and there." This relationship may not involve designated appointments or meetings, and the goals need not be concrete. Things are considerably more casual. It is likely that, initially, most persons from the poverty culture will prefer informal mentoring situations. Learning can take place in a comfortable, relaxed atmosphere during shorter encounters—often over coffee or a snack in a neutral place. In the long term the structure of formal mentoring serves as the ultimate tool for learning organization, goal-setting, and other abstract concepts needed to survive or thrive in middle-class settings.

Active vs. Passive

Active mentors are just that . . . actively involved in the relationship with the protégé. They maintain an awareness of topics that may be of interest to their protégé(s), usually initiate appointments, and intentionally participate in the protégé's learning process. The active mentor expects to be asked for strategies and consultation. Active mentoring can be formal or informal.

Passive mentors make themselves available only as an informal and possibly momentary mentor. They may offer brief suggestions, guidance, and support in mini-modules on a sporadic basis. The important thing about passive mentoring is the willingness or openness to be available when needed. Receptionists, van drivers, community educators, teachers, nurses, and administrators—as well as caseworkers and counselors—need to be aware of their potential as persons who can share the hidden rules of middle class, offer support and encouragement, and help a protégé process language-structure barriers and family issues. A passive mentor may also be a *momentary mentor*—someone who pops into a life, sheds some light, and then disappears. All this can be done informally if the mentor is looking for the "mentor-able moment"!

While interviewing women who had moved from the poverty culture toward middle class, I first spoke with Sally. We met at the public library and discussed her journey from a public housing development in England to her present success working as a preschool teacher. What was most impressive, and confirmed my sense that Sally was truly seeking a better way of life, was her constant presence at the library! On at least five other occasions, when I was conducting other interviews, I encountered Sally at the library. It seemed she was always there, and so were her two boys. Browsing together through Children's Literature, Periodicals, Adult Non-Fiction; researching for Science Fair; signing up for the Internet . . . absolutely making the best possible use of the facilities. I thought, perhaps Sally does not feel she has achieved middle-class status, but no doubt her children will!

BENEFITS TO THE MENTOR

Mentoring relationships can be of equal benefit to both parties. Successful people benefit from sharing their "secrets" with select individuals. Most people have a need to share their experiences in order to help others. Erik Erickson described this need as the generativity vs. stagnation process: the need to pass along one's learnings, one's success to someone who will benefit, thereby rendering a form of "immortality" to the mentor. In fact, mentor/author Floyd Wickman claims that he earned an extra $100,000 in two years due to following the advice he was giving in response to his protégé's questions. Yes, mentoring is a two-way street! According to Wickman, "It is part of a person's vision of his or her life to be able to pass on what they have learned over the years. Mentoring someone can be pivotal in various stages of a person's career and give individuals a chance for introspection and reassessment."

Indeed, the mentoring relationship, by its very nature, offers the mentor time to review and re-evaluate personal and career goals and priorities. The protégé also may offer a fresh approach or insights that will be of benefit to the mentor.

Karen is an income-maintenance worker who sees many clients struggling with the welfare-reform requirements. Karen is willing to serve as an informal mentor to many individuals, perhaps helping the client process difficulties in a new workplace, or by gently reframing or offering new perspective regarding family or work issues. The reframing is sometimes in question form, and never in the parent voice. Karen's efforts are ineffective in motivating some of her clients. But there are others who greatly benefit from this form of encouragement and relationship. The clients who offer Karen positive feedback on issues they have discussed increase her desire to share more ideas and to give more time and effort to that protégé. The mentoring relationship becomes stronger.

BENEFITS TO THE PROTÉGÉ

Potential protégés in middle-class work settings are wise to seek out a successful person and approach him/her regarding a possible mentoring relationship. Within the poverty culture, there will be some individuals who are willing and able to do this. It may also be that a mentor will choose to begin the relationship by sharing information with a person from the poverty culture. Eventually, a mentoring relationship may be established. In either case, there is a "natural selection" process that matches compatible mentors and protégés. An individual's internal and external resources will affect his/her success as a protégé, as will level of determination and self-discipline. Not everyone is a potential protégé, and the same is true of mentors. The qualities of a good protégé include a willingness to respect the mentor and the mentor's time, as well as determination to follow his/her advice. Some mentoring programs use a survey in which protégés identify individuals who already are coaching or helping others.

> *I never had a teacher who made a positive difference in my life until I was in college. There was this teacher, the one who asked us to evaluate ourselves in a paper in our first social work class. . . . That woman made me think for myself . . . helped to open my eyes. She had us turn in this project,*

and then she kept it until we graduated. When I read it at the time I graduated, I couldn't believe the way I had thought about myself. I had really grown a lot! And then this other teacher . . . I never met a man like him. He's fair. I've never seen him put a male above a female. He'll change his mind during a class discussion! He's a great father. He's changed his share of diapers and everything.

– Interview excerpt

PROFESSIONAL DEVELOPMENT AND EMPLOYMENT ISSUES

Given that patterns emerge from living within generational poverty, there always will be deviations in mental models and values concerning work and other issues. One reason for this is the wonderfully infinite variation in parental (and other) influences upon the individual. Any implication that people from generational poverty are lazy or irresponsible is not intended. The issue remains that persons from the poverty culture may need to be cued to the common basic and hidden rules of the workplace. Furthermore, just as the mission of this book is to give middle-class professionals insight into the reasons and motivations of people from the poverty culture, the protégé needs to know the employer's perspective in order to maintain employment and possibly move upward.

What the Protégé Needs to Decide

In middle-class culture, the lower an employee is on the economic ladder, the fewer options he/she has in finding desirable employment. Limited resources and support systems minimize social connections and restrict choices. The education necessary to enhance one's ability to think, write, and talk in formal register is paramount to increasing opportunity. To live and work merely to survive allows less time and energy for the "pursuit of happiness." The protégé may be unskilled at seeing options and making choices today that have a positive impact *in the future*.

Education, increasing professional skills, and earning money can translate into resources that impact personal freedom and quality of life. Not every protégé will be ready to grasp the baton and run this particular race. For some, it is too late. Others will not have the emotional or intellectual capabilities to compete.

For those protégés who have ability and are ready to learn, a mentor is needed to listen, explain, tell stories, increase perspective, identify resources, target options and consequences, and provide encouragement. Progress will occur in small steps over time.

> *There are only four ways to make money: through the business communities, through government communities, through social communities (non-profit) or through the outlaw community.*
>
> – Jeremy Rifkin, *The Biotech Century*

Basic Workplace Rules

All employees are expected to be prompt and reliable, dress and behave appropriately, exhibit flexibility and independence, "get the job done" on time, and remain trustworthy and reliable. They must follow safety rules, dress appropriately, use appropriate language registers and be able and willing to follow instructions. For the most part, these rules are not "hidden," and many are posted or included in job descriptions. There are some subtle deviations, such as what dress is appropriate, what language register is acceptable in various situations. If the protégé experiences difficulty with the basic rules of employment, it may be that his/her mental models for work, family, and entertainment conflict with the employer's interests.

Hidden Rules of the Workplace

The subtle rules of the workplace, social service agency, or school are often based on middle-class social norms. An entire book could be written on this subject, and the mentor will need to assess the protégé's needs and the circumstances in this area. However, here are some examples:

- Do not ask for loans from co-workers, or pay advances.

- If in a clerical position, don't make or take personal phone calls. In some offices, some personal calls are acceptable, if kept to a minimum.

- Conflict happens. If it's possible to let go and move on, do so. Know and follow the company/agency table of organization or chain of command if experiencing a problem with a co-worker or supervisor. Serious problems should follow the grievance procedure. Do not gossip or complain about others to co-workers (especially if that "other" is a supervisor). Rudeness, verbal fighting, physical fighting and passive-aggressive behaviors (including ignoring the offending party for long periods of time) are counter-productive. Avoid arguing.

- Maintain professional relationships only. Particularly in the school or office setting, romances are often fatal to successful employment. Even in manufacturing, these are discouraged, especially if a clerical worker becomes involved with someone in the field or factory. Office workers are trusted with time sheets, sick-leave forms, and other confidential matters. Naturally, supervisors will question the integrity of clerical staff who is overly friendly with laborers. The protégés also may need education regarding sexual-harassment issues—and what to do if they feel that someone is infringing on their personal rights.

STRATEGIES FOR INCREASING PROFESSIONALISM—AND OTHER TOPICS

Story: The metaphor story, scenario, and asking the protégé to create questions based on these stories increase the perception of the mental models of middle class. If the syntax of the questions is not intact, this indicates a possible deficiency in reading ability. For example, a question such as "She doesn't go to work because she has a hangover?" is really a sentence with a question mark. "Did she miss work because she had a hangover?" is the correct syntax.

Rubrics: Ask the protégé to draw a picture of his/her mental model for time. If the model has no organized symbol for past, present, and future, it is likely that the capability of decision-making processes and other abstract thinking is impaired. Introduce new models that clearly show the progression of time. Remember that there are several processes involving memory functions: sorting, storing, and retrieving. Rubrics are a valuable tool in organizing thoughts, feelings, events, and learning experiences.

Goal-setting and procedural self-talk: Work with the protégés on a series of short-term goals that will help them achieve long-term goals. Ask them to keep a journal of their thoughts and feelings to share with you at intervals. Remember that drawing pictures can show feelings and mental models; pictures can be used to represent abstract concepts while the journal can be used to measure progress toward the short-term goals.

Support and encouragement: Researching local training opportunities for job-skills training, as well as encouraging the protégé to attend, will complement the learning taking place within the mentoring relationship. Job fairs and other events offer inexpensive or free workshops in most communities. Local agencies offer such training as part of their regular agenda for moving individuals into the job market. The mentor can encourage the protégé to take notes and bring back new learning. New goals, metaphor stories, and other strategies used by the mentor can solidify or clarify new information and perceptions.

HEALTH AND FITNESS ISSUES

"Health and fitness" is about goal-setting and making lifestyle changes to prevent health problems, improve appearance, and increase physical and emotional well-being. In addition, appearance influences employment issues.

Why Might the Protégé Have Difficulty with Health and Fitness Issues?

The patterns evolving from years of poverty are in direct conflict with the concept of changing oneself. People are accepted for what and who they are. Unconditional acceptance of self and others is the result of many factors, but it primarily centers around the concepts of penance/forgiveness (rather than choices and consequences, cause and effect) and living in the present. If Mary would lose 50 pounds and keep the weight off, she would decrease her risk of a heart attack in the future. If Jim would stop smoking today, he likely could avoid lung cancer 10 years from now. Lifestyle changes with long-term benefits are difficult to comprehend if the emphasis is on living in the present.

Time and money impact health and fitness. Weight loss and fitness are big business. The middle class flocks to the gym (an ongoing expense of $25 to $80/month), purchases treadmills, abdominal machines, weight machines. Having the right shoes, the right gear, the right outfit . . . all enhance the motivation for what is truly hard work. It is not easy to eat less, so frustrated dieters enroll in costly private-sector programs where food is purchased in little frozen boxes. The "quicker fixes" are prescription diet pills and plastic surgery, which may be riskier than the diseases that fitness devotees seek to avoid. Frankly, without money, fitness is not as much fun!

Losing weight and exercising take discipline and time. Single parents or individuals working long hours have difficulty finding time to work out. It takes organizational skills and nutritional knowledge to plan well-balanced meals and avoid triggering binges related to stress and other emotions. Healthful foods, including fresh fruits and vegetables, can be more expensive and can take more time to prepare than hot dogs, a can of baked beans, and a bag of chips. Fast foods and convenience foods are a dietician's nightmare, full of hidden fat and lower in nutritional value than "real" food.

In terms of preventive health care, the pattern of distrusting professional institutions deters regular check-ups, even when funded by insurance or Medicaid. The rule is: "If it ain't broke, don't fix it." The middle class is appalled at this reactive approach to health, and intervention programs at the local and state level seek to target children and adults with potential health risks by offering incentives for attendance at health-screening events. According to experts in the field, Medicaid recipients avoid the dentist's office even more than the doctor's office.

Strategies for Increasing Health and Fitness

Health and fitness can be improved even on a limited budget. If the protégé varies the type of workout (jogging, walking, fitness videos borrowed from the library) and connects with others with similar goals, the process will remain fresh and, ideally, fun.

The area of health and fitness is a prime example of assisting the protégé to link up with existing community programs. YMCA organizations have a sliding fee scale for individuals and families. Often child care is available at low cost. Free activities such as lock-ins, fun nights, and parties are available periodically for children. Local extension offices and other agencies offer low-cost or no-charge nutrition workshops, local churches are establishing no-cost weight-loss groups, and community agencies are collaborating to provide services to Jobs First participants. A little local research can result in a more interesting and successful health program for the protégé, who may simply need some information and encouragement to become involved— and some assistance in working through scheduling and other issues to provide the time for such activities.

The strategies discussed in the previous section can be modified for health-and-fitness information. Journals can include eating logs and new short-term and long-term goals. For example, protégés can record how many minutes they spent working out or how many miles they walked. It's probably wise to discourage a certain number of pounds to be lost by a certain date, because individuals lose weight at various rates, and some dieticians claim that fitness is "more than a number." Feelings about emotions, food-binge triggers, and positive emotions about the process can be recorded in the journal.

PHILANTHROPY

The Search Institute of Minneapolis reports that youths who are involved in service projects decrease their own risks regarding use of alcohol and other drugs, along with other offenses. Apparently, helping someone else is an effective way to increase self-image. Volunteering serves as evidence of one's value to others, therefore to self. This applies to young people, as well as adults.

Why Might the Protégé Have Difficulty with Philanthropy Issues?

Each economic group holds its own hidden rules regarding philanthropy.

- *Poverty:* To work for nothing is a "ripoff." You help a friend, someone you know, but to work for a "cause" or an institution is viewed with distrust. Court sentences requiring community service have modified the perception of volunteerism; in recent years volunteering has begun to take on punitive aspects.

- *Middle class:* Service is a way to give back and make the world a better place to live. The preference is often to give time over money, but both are done. Usually this accompanies having at least the basic needs and resources met for oneself—and the desire to share with someone else.

- *Wealth:* Fund-raising is a social activity, a way to enhance connections and a tax write-off. Volunteerism is vital because it's a worthwhile way to use time and maintain social contacts.

Strategies for Increasing Volunteer Service

Asking someone to volunteer his/her time for someone else need not be raking leaves or picking up trash. If the volunteer activity involves relationship, the protégé from the poverty culture will experience greater inner gratification. Schools, retirement homes, and hospitals have programs to which relationship is key. Commitment to some activity outside self is essential to healthy emotional balance and has been linked with longer life spans.

SUMMARY OF THE 16 LAWS OF MENTORING

These "laws" were developed by Wickman and Sjodin because the laws ensure that long-term, formal mentoring is stable and beneficial to both parties. However, some of the laws are applicable to all mentoring forms. *Italics indicate direct quotes.*

The Law of:

1.   **Positive environment:** There needs to be sufficient time and environment to encourage honest, open discussion.

2.   **Developing character:** The primary mentor, especially, will want to deal with more than rules and regulations of middle-class family and work environments. Rather, meaningful spiritual, ethical, and other issues of impact will be part of the process. In training sessions involving people from generational poverty, they were not lacking the values that develop good character. Like all of us, however, they might sometimes need help in translating those values into real action. Everyone experiences times when an inner conflict occurs because our actions and values are at odds.

3.   **Independence:** The boundaries between the mentor and protégé should be well established. In some mentoring relationships, such as that of the AA sponsor/mentor to his/her "pigeon"/protégé, the boundaries are intentionally more lax than in other relationships. In some relationships, protégés may be permitted to call their mentor at all hours of the day or night if they need to talk or feel they need alcohol. Chances are that the sponsor was once a

"pigeon" as well—and knows that such flexibility is necessary to maintaining sobriety in the early months of the recovery process.

Most mentors outside of such circumstances may want to set more rigid boundaries when it comes to their time, energy, and personal assets. One of the characteristics of generational poverty is the view that people are resources. People in poverty need to share, lend, and offer hospitality in ways different from the middle-class system. The mentor should begin by stating what the boundaries will be, if the relationship is to be long term.

4. **Limited responsibility:** *Be responsible to them, not for them.* Mentors need to set their own boundaries regarding their protégés. The mentor is not the protégé's "savior" or "mother." Protégés need the latitude to choose their own course and make their own mistakes. The mentor's job is to share what he/she knows and respect the rights of the protégé. If the mentoring relationship is not working for both parties, despite repeated efforts, it should be terminated in a friendly manner, at least for the present time.

    Your protégé may not be motivated to move out of his/her class or culture into another. Yet he/she may value the knowledge of how to successfully work in the middle-class culture. The protégé may linger somewhere between cultures for extended periods. The mentor must be patient and respect the protégé's choices.

5. **Shared mistakes:** *Share your failures, as well as your successes.*

6. **Planned objectives:** *Prepare specific goals for your relationship.* If the mentoring relationship is to be long term—even if the parties are not meeting frequently—goals can be specific, measurable, and linked to a timetable. Organization skills and goal-setting are areas in which people from the poverty culture can benefit.

7. **Inspection:** *Monitor, review, critique, and discuss potential actions. Do not just expect performance without inspection.* The true value of the mentoring relationship is its interactive nature. A "library" mentor—one who learns much from books and other sources—can give advice and wisdom without knowing the protégé's thoughts, ideas, plans, choices. The live mentor will listen, share, process, and be open to learning while teaching.

8. **Tough love:** Know when to intervene (possibly punitively) and when to let go.

9. **Small successes:** Remember the Italian immigrant Angelo Dreussi? He had a huge goal to accomplish. He could take only one step at a time. Mentors can help the poverty-culture protégé with a series of small successes that may develop into a truly significant success. Moving into the world of another economic class is a huge undertaking.

10. **Direction:** Mentors are advised to use the adult voice. Make "I statements" when sharing, and ask questions regarding options and consequences. There is usually more than one way to accomplish something. The mentor is a resource.

11. **Risk:** *A mentor should be aware that a protégé's failure may reflect back on him/her. A protégé should realize that a mentor's advice will not always work.* It is better to offer possible solutions than to give direct advice. A mentor who gives advice such as "If I were you I would move on" or "Go in tomorrow and tell your boss you deserve a raise" is setting up an environment in which he/she may "own" the protégé's problem. What the protégé needs is someone who is adept at questioning techniques and can offer personal

experience and/or assists in helping reframe potential power struggles. Leading the protégé in a discussion of options and potential consequences is the optimal strategy.

12. **Mutual protection:** *Maintain privacy. The mentor will need to set boundaries to protect privacy. Both parties must feel comfortable with the mentor/protégé relationship.*

13. **Communication:** *Listening is the best way to gather information about the needs of the protégé. A certain balance should be established so that both parties share and respond.*

14. **Extended commitment:** Wickman and Sjodin state that being accessible is part of mentoring. However, when working with individuals from a different class culture, each party must feel comfortable with such extended commitment. This law in particular is not written in stone.

15. **Life transition:** The results on one study showed that individuals who experienced a sense of helping future generations did not "stagnate" but continued to move on to the next stages in life. Successful mentoring can give the mentor a new sense of direction and energy.

16. **Fun/laughter:** Humor enhances relationships. It is a shared response. Enjoy!

WHAT IMPLICATIONS DOES THIS INFORMATION HAVE FOR THE SOCIAL SERVICE, HEALTH CARE, OR WORK SETTING?

▧ Mentoring practices range from structured and formal to momentary and impromptu.

▧ Taking the time to build relationships and mediate individuals to middle class may result in less frustration for the mentor/teacher in the long run.

▧ Employees, clients, and students from poverty need mediation in defining middle-class resources.

▧ The mentor (employer, teacher, supervisor, caseworker, etc.) should use resource assessment to determine if a mentoring relationship would benefit both parties.

▧ Because relationships are key to individuals from poverty, it is practical to use mentoring to increase achievement outcomes.

The most important thing that Mo Battle taught me was that chess was a game of consequences. He said that, just as in life, there are consequences for every move you make in chess. "Don't make a move without first weighing the potential consequences," he said, "because if you don't, you have no control over the outcome." . . .

– Nathan McCall, *Makes Me Wanna Holler*

You sat on the burner, baby. . . . You sit on the blisters.

– Dick Schaefer, *Choices & Consequences*

Discipline, Choices, and Consequences

DISCIPLINE

Structure and Choice

The two anchors of any effective discipline program that moves individuals to self-governance are structure and choice. The organization must clearly delineate the expected behaviors and the probable consequences of not choosing those behaviors. The organization must also emphasize that the individual always has a choice—to follow or not to follow the expected behaviors. With each choice then comes a consequence—either desirable or undesirable.

The key here is to help individuals gain self-governance. There are some instances, particularly in law enforcement, when the goal of discipline and sanctions is security and safety. In the long term, even for law enforcement and corrections, the goal must be to move individuals to self-governance.

When the focus is "I'll tell you what to do and when to do it," as it is in safety and security situations, the individual is unable to move from dependence to independence, thereby remaining at the level of dependence.

In poverty, discipline is about penance and forgiveness, not necessarily change. Because love is unconditional and because the time frame is the present, the notion that discipline should be instructive and change behavior is not part of the culture in generational poverty. In matriarchal, generational poverty, the mother has the most powerful position and is, in some ways, "keeper of the soul." So she dispenses the after judgments, determines the amount and price of penance, and offers forgiveness. After forgiveness has been granted, behaviors and activities return to the way they were before the incident.

It is important to note that the approach to discipline advocated in this book is to teach a separate set of behaviors. Many of the behaviors that clients bring to work are necessary to help them survive outside of work. If clients from poverty don't know how to fight physically, they may be in danger on the streets. But if fighting is the only method for resolving problems, then they will not be successful at work.

The culture of poverty does not provide for success in middle class because middle class to a large extent requires the self-governance of behavior. To be successful outside of poverty requires self-control of behavior. What, then, do employers and agencies need to do to teach appropriate behavior?

Outside of situations where life and limb are threatened, giving orders as opposed to giving choices carries with it two disadvantages. First, the persons carrying out the order may not feel accountable for the outcome. They don't perceive the behavior as their own; it hasn't arisen out of their thinking, intentions, desires, or motivation, so why should they carry it out? Second, orders and demands are not respectful and, as we know, respect is a cornerstone of relationships, and relationships constitute the cornerstone of change.

Sometimes it calls for considerable thought, but each situation can be framed as a choice, then regardless of how unsavory the choices may be, at least the person being disciplined can own the results.

The skill of framing choices and delivering on consequences is finely tuned by those who treat addicted adolescents, the population we would most like to "order" to stop self-destructing. If treatment professionals can help young people who suffer two conditions, addiction and adolescence, and sometimes a third, the penance/forgiveness cycle, to become responsible for their own behavior, then the rest of us can take hope and learn the basics of skillful discipline.

Designing Structure

Each organization will have its own rules and regulations. Each workplace will be different, each office or shop its distinct rules. The rules of a domestic-violence shelter, for example, will be much different from the rules of a manufacturing company. So what elements must the structure have to be successful at encouraging people to become independent?

1. Rules and behavioral expectations are clearly stated. Written handbooks may not be enough. Videos are useful because they give a consistent message to each person and can be carefully written for tone and content. One manufacturer clarified sexual-harassment rules by creating a video using local actors in role plays.

2. Avoid bureaucratic language and tone and write to the appropriate level of the readers.

3. State the consequences for each choice up front. People will then know that consequences are not arbitrary.

4. Train supervisors in how to present choices and consequences. Too often, consequences are not delivered because managers and supervisors want to be nice, are confused, or have been manipulated.

5. Use incorrect choices and resulting consequences as a learning opportunity. If this is done successfully, the clients/employees stay and improve their performance; if not, they quit.

6. When explaining the choices and consequences, describe the "why" (i.e., mediate the situation).

7. When delivering on the consequence, provide a safe setting in which learning can take place. Say, for instance, that John has been making remarks to Carolyn about her body, how she dresses, and so on. Carolyn has objected and told you about it. The rules call for a written reprimand, the first step in a process that can lead to dismissal.

- *Explain the process:* "John, I need to talk with you about your remarks to Carolyn, so let's go into my office, get some coffee, and sit down. This isn't as bad as you may think; I know we can work it out."

- *Agree on a plan:* "Will you agree to hear me out? I want to lay the cards on the table, and then I want to hear what you have to say. I expect we can work out a solution"

- *Have a private backup plan:* People are unpredictable, so you can't expect every disciplinary session to go as you would like it to. Plan A could be to discuss the situation with John, give him the consequence, set up his choices, and create a plan of action. Plan B could be that, if John refuses to cooperate, you give him either an hour to cool off or some time to talk the situation over with his coach before coming back to finish the discussion.

- *Deliver the consequence* (after presenting the information and hearing his point of view and feelings): "Your choice to talk to Carolyn the way you did was really a choice to enter the disciplinary process. The first step is a written reprimand, so I will be writing that to you soon and putting it in your file."

- *Set up choices and future consequences:* "We need to work out a plan of action, so let's discuss your options . . . If you choose not to follow the plan you've created and you break the harassment rule again, the next step in the disciplinary process is a suspension without pay. Do you understand what that means?"

- *Closure:* "I appreciate the way you handled this, John. Your plan looks like a good one to me. Let me know if you need anything else from me."

BEHAVIOR ANALYSIS

Prior to an analysis of behavior we should check with the client or employee to learn his/her reason for the behavior. It could well be that there is a systems issue or situation that should be addressed. Having asked those questions and resolved those issues, we can turn to the following steps to analyze behavior.

BEHAVIOR ANALYSIS

1. What kinds of behaviors does a client or worker need to be successful?

2. Does the client or worker have the resources to develop those behaviors?

3. Will it help to contact families?
   Are resources available through them?
   What resources are available through the community?

4. How will behaviors be taught?

5. What are other choices the individual could make?

6. What will help the individual repeat the successful behavior?

When these questions are answered, they lead to the strategies that will most help the client or worker.

The chart on the next page indicates possible explanations of behaviors, along with suggested interventions.

BEHAVIOR RELATED TO POVERTY	INTERVENTION
LAUGH WHEN DISCIPLINED: A way to save face in matriarchal poverty, as well as a middle-class world where there are few choices and little real power.	Understand the reason for the behavior. Tell the client other behaviors that would be more appropriate.
ARGUE LOUDLY WITH THE STAFF: Poverty is participatory, and the culture has a distrust of authority. See the system as inherently dishonest and unfair.	Don't argue with the individual. Detach by understanding the individual's point of view. Model respect for individuals. Identify the options.
ANGRY RESPONSE: Anger is based on fear. Question what the fear is: loss of face?	Respond in the adult voice. When the clients cool down, discuss other responses they could have used.
INAPPROPRIATE OR VULGAR COMMENTS: Reliance on casual register; may not know formal register.	Have the individual generate (or teach the individual) other phrases that could be used to say the same thing.
PHYSICALLY FIGHT: Necessary to survive in poverty. Only know the language of survival. Do not have language or belief system to use conflict resolution. See themselves as less than a man or woman if they don't fight.	Apply natural consequences for fighting. Examine options that individuals could live with other than fighting.
CANNOT FOLLOW DIRECTIONS: Little procedural memory used in poverty. Sequence not used or valued.	Have clients or workers write the steps needed to finish the project. Have them practice procedural self-talk.
EXTREMELY DISORGANIZED: Lack of planning, scheduling, or prioritizing skills. Not taught in poverty.	Teach planning skills and use of tools and instruments.
COMPLETE ONLY PART OF A TASK: No procedural self-talk. Do not "see" the whole task.	Write out all parts of the task. Check them off as they go.

USING THE LANGUAGE OF NEGOTIATION

One of the biggest issues with individuals from poverty is the fact that many children in poverty must function as their own parents. They parent themselves and others—often younger siblings. In many instances they also act as parent to the adult in the household.

Inside virtually everyone's head are three internal voices that guide the individual. These voices are the child voice, the adult voice, and the parent voice. Individuals who have become their own parent quite young often do not have an internal adult voice. They have a child voice and a parent voice, but not an adult voice.

An internal adult voice allows for negotiation. This voice provides the language of negotiation and allows issues to be examined in a non-threatening way.

Staff members or supervisors often make the mistake of speaking to clients or workers in a parent voice, particularly in discipline situations. To the individual who is already functioning as a parent, this is unbearable. Almost immediately, the situation is exacerbated beyond the original incident. The tendency for staff members to use the parent voice with clients who are poor is based on the assumption that a lack of resources must indicate a lack of intelligence. Clients in poverty are very offended by this.

When the parent voice is used with a young person who is already a parent in many ways, the outcome is anger. The young person is angry because anger is based on fear. What the parent voice forces the young person to do is use either the child voice or the parent voice. If the young person uses the parent voice, which could sound sarcastic in this context, the young person will get in trouble. If the young person uses the child voice, he/she will feel helpless and therefore at the mercy of the adult. Many young people choose to use the parent voice because it is less frightening than memories connected with being helpless.

Part of the reality of poverty is the language of survival. There are simply not enough resources for people in poverty to engage in a discussion of them. For example, if there are five hot dogs and five people, the distribution of the food is fairly clear. The condiments for the hot dogs are going to be limited, so the discussion about their distribution will be fairly limited as well. Contrast that, for example, with a middle-class household where the discussion will be about how many hot dogs, what should go on the hot dog, how much of each ingredient, etc. Thus the ability to see options and to negotiate among those options is not well developed in the culture of poverty.

To teach individuals to use the "language of negotiation" one must first teach them the phrases they can use. Direct-teach the notion of an adult voice, and give them phrases to use. Model the adult voice in interactions with clients and workers.

In addition to these strategies, several staff-development programs are available to teach peer negotiation. It is important that, as part of the negotiation, the culture of origin is not denigrated, but rather the ability to negotiate is seen as a survival tool for the work and agency setting.

THREE VOICES

THE CHILD VOICE *
Defensive, victimized, emotional, whining, losing attitude, strongly negative non-verbal.

- Quit picking on me.
- You don't love me.
- You want me to leave.
- Nobody likes (loves) me.
- I hate you.
- You're ugly.
- You make me sick.
- It's your fault.
- Don't blame me.
- She, he, _____ did it.
- You make me mad.
- You made me do it.

* The child voice is also playful, spontaneous, curious, etc. The phrases listed often occur in conflictual or manipulative situations and impede resolution.

THE PARENT VOICE * **
Authoritative, directive, judgmental, evaluative, win-lose mentality, demanding, punitive, sometimes threatening.

- You shouldn't (should) do that.

- It's wrong (right) to do _____ .

- That's stupid, immature, out of line, ridiculous.

- Life's not fair. Get busy.

- You are good, bad, worthless, beautiful (any judgmental, evaluative comment).

- You do as I say.

- If you weren't so _____ , this wouldn't happen to you.

- Why can't you be like _____ ?

* *The parent voice can also be very loving and supportive. The phrases listed usually occur during conflict and impede resolution.*

** *The internal parent voice can create shame and guilt.*

THE ADULT VOICE
Non-judgmental, free of negative non-verbal, factual, often in question format, attitude of win-win.

- In what ways could this be resolved?

- What factors will be used to determine the effectiveness, quality of _____ ?

- I would like to recommend _____ .

- What are choices in this situation?

- I am comfortable (uncomfortable) with _____ .

- Options that could be considered are _____ .

- For me to be comfortable, I need the following things to occur _____ .

- These are the consequences of that choice/action _____ .

- We agree to disagree.

USING METAPHOR STORIES

Another technique for working with students and adults is to use a metaphor story. A metaphor story will help an individual give voice to issues that affect subsequent actions. A metaphor story does not have any proper names in it and goes like this.

A student keeps going to the nurse's office two or three times a week. There is nothing wrong with her. Yet she keeps going. Adult says to Jennifer, the girl, "Jennifer, I am going to tell a story, and I need you to help me. It's about a fourth-grade girl much like yourself. I need you to help me tell the story because I'm not in fourth grade.

"Once upon a time there was a girl who went to the nurse's office. Why did the girl go to the nurse's office? *(Because she thought there was something wrong with her.)* So the girl went to the nurse's office because she thought there was something wrong with her. Did the nurse find anything wrong with her? *(No, the nurse did not.)* So the nurse did not find anything wrong with her, yet the girl kept going to the nurse. Why did the girl keep going to the nurse? *(Because she thought there was something wrong with her.)* So the girl thought something was wrong with her. Why did the girl think there was something wrong with her? *(She saw a TV show . . .)*"

The story continues until the reason for the behavior is found, and then the story needs to end on a positive note. "So she went to the doctor, and he gave her tests and found that she was OK."

This is an actual case. What came out in the story was that Jennifer had seen a TV show in which a girl her age had died suddenly and had never known she was ill. Jennifer's parents took her to the doctor, he ran tests, and he told her she was fine. So she didn't go to the nurse's office anymore.

A metaphor story is to be used one on one when there is a need to understand the existing behavior and motivate the student to implement the appropriate behavior.

Metaphor stories are powerful instruments for motivation, instruction, and change. First, they are effective because they assist memory. The structure of the story provides a means for the listener to store and later access elements of the story—thus the value of using a predictable structure for stories rather than a circular or scattered presentation. Stories also provide memory cues as information is stored according to the context within which it was experienced. Your memory is cued by who told you the story, where you were, how you felt, what you saw.

In *Data Smog* David Shenk writes, " 'Without metaphor, thought is inert,' explains literacy scholar Frank Smith, likening the power of metaphor to a road map. People are instinctively able to draw inspiration and guidance from simple yet powerful stories—narratives—around which dry information coalesces and begins to make sense."

Shenk warns of the danger of oversimplification: "[W]hat happens when these road maps for the mind feature roads and rivers that do not exist? Perhaps the most famous contemporary abuse of the anecdote was by Ronald Reagan . . . who, in the presidential campaigns of 1976 and 1980, railed against a mythical 'welfare queen' (never publicly named by Reagan), who had allegedly used eighty aliases, thirty addresses, twelve social security cards, and four nonexistent dead husbands to fraudulently collect $150,000. In fact, the closest actual case was a woman in Chicago who had used two false names to improperly collect $8,000." Unfortunately, this untrue story stuck in the memory of the public and lawmakers.

A better use of story can be found in the 12-step programs such as Alcoholics Anonymous where recovering people share their stories. The structure is the same at all "lead" meetings—what was it like, what happened, what is it like now. The many leads heard in the first year of recovery become a metaphor for the life of the individual alcoholic who can identify with the feelings (if not the exact circumstances) of "how it used to be," they can learn new ways of managing their lives from "what happened or what I did" and they can gain inspiration and hope from "what it's like now."

Therapists and social workers should consider using metaphor stories to understand and learn from their clients and add storytelling to their repertoire of skills.

TEACHING HIDDEN RULES

Learning a second set of cultural rules increases an individual's chances for survival and advancement. Immigrants and travelers have a choice between learning the rules of the second culture and becoming self-reliant in the new setting . . . and not learning the rules and relying on others to assist them (if they will).

People in the poverty culture have the same choice. Learning the rules of middle class does not mean that the values or philosophies of middle class have been adopted, but it does mean that the individuals can be more successful where they are. After all, schools, agencies, and the work world operate on the basis of middle-class rules.

Hidden rules can be taught in a straightforward manner: "Look, there are hidden rules on the street and hidden rules at work. What are they?" After the discussion, detail the rules that make individuals successful where they are.

WHAT IMPLICATIONS DOES THIS INFORMATION HAVE FOR THE SOCIAL SERVICE, HEALTH CARE, OR WORK SETTING?

- People from poverty need to have at least two sets of behaviors from which to choose—one for the street and one for the school, agencies, and work settings.

- The purpose of discipline and sanctions should be to promote successful behaviors.

■ Teaching clients, staff members, and employees to use the adult voice (i.e., the language of negotiation) is important for success in and out of school and work settings and can become an alternative to physical aggression.

■ Structure and choice need to be part of treatment approaches, discipline, and sanctions at work and in corrections.

■ Discipline and sanctions should be seen and used as forms of instruction.

. . . the ability to accept the things I cannot change,
the courage to change the things I can, and
the wisdom to know the difference.

– from the Serenity Prayer by Reinhold Niebuhr

Resources and Resiliency: Internal Assets

THE WISDOM TO KNOW THE DIFFERENCE

Why should anyone take the time to help someone from generational poverty move toward increased resources and resiliency? Who will teach people who are adjusting to different language patterns and hidden rules?

A young woman in college was unsure of her career goals but told her mother, "I don't want to teach or sell anything to anyone." Her mother responded, "Let me know if you find a career absent of teaching or selling!" Many professionals are working with populations to whom they sell or teach. Usually some sort of behavior change on the part of their customers, employees, students, parishioners, clients, or co-workers is required. Cultural patterns impact motivation and behavior. Understanding those cultural patterns may result in a bigger sale, a better "mousetrap," a brighter learner, a healthier person.

Throughout this chapter, the term "mentor" signifies the teacher of middle-class "hidden rules and rites." Even the informal mentor needs a process to determine the potential of the protégé—and to evaluate whether the protégé is open/able to change. A car salesman once approached an older man who was shabbily dressed. His colleagues had been systematically ignoring the man for 10 minutes. To the car salesman's delight, that shabbily dressed man purchased a new car "on cash" that morning. Snap judgments regarding a person's potential can be counterproductive.

Knowledge of the resources, hidden rules, characteristics, and patterns of the culture create an assessment tool. In addition to the general information gathered, the mentor also needs to consider the protective factors of the individual. Internal assets, discussed later in this chapter, are micro factors that influence individuals within any culture. Literature relative to asset development and resiliency among adults from generational poverty is explored.

A MATTER OF PERCEPTION

Financial resources are the easiest to measure. After all, they are quantitative, right? The difficulty arises because the client's view of his/her financial resources is a matter of perception. If financial resources are perceived to be adequate, the motivation to change may be limited. The same is true of other resources. The mentor may need to mediate the client/protégé to middle-class definitions of each resource.

A group of seven males incarcerated in a county correctional facility volunteered their participation in focus-group discussions dealing with economic class structures, hidden rules, and resource identification. The group members were diverse in race and age. Most participants identified with the characteristics and hidden rules of generational poverty as one layer of their cultural make-up. Age and education resulted in a variety of responses to activities. One man had successfully completed a four-year college degree. The primary focus of the group was the use of goal-setting and self-awareness strategies to reduce recidivism. Group activities included identification of personal resources and knowledge of middle-class rules.

Group members were asked to read a scenario and instructed to use a "1–10" scale to indicate the character's resources. The facilitator briefly discussed how to complete the worksheet, which stated that a score of "1" was the equivalent of "little or no" money. A score of "10" was meant to be "the largest amount of money imaginable." As clarification, the instructor joked that Bill Gates was a "Perfect 10."

The scenario described a male high school student who had been physically abused by his father and befriended by the school guidance counselor. The father had thrown the boy out of the house, while his weeping mother looked on. This young man went to school daily, got good grades, held a minimum-wage job in the evenings, and shared a low-rent apartment with a friend. His 13-year-old brother, anxious to escape abuse, was requesting shelter.

The facilitator began the discussion: "How did you rate the Financial Resources of this young man in the story?" The instructor shared her score: "3." Most of the group had given the youth a Financial Resources rating of "6," "7," or "8."

"Eight!?!" the shocked facilitator queried. "This kid is working for minimum wage! He has to share a cheap apartment in a low-rent area. He cannot afford a car! Now his younger brother wants to move in with him and his roommate! There will be even less money to go around!" One man responded, "But look, ma'am, he's got enough to eat. He's working. He's got a roof over his head. He's able to make his rent . . . not getting evicted. He's at least an '8'!" The others readily agreed.

For the leader, this experience reinforced the key point that poverty is relative. Throughout the exercise, participants scored meager resources as high, based on their personal experiences. Most of the men had classified the rules of middle class as familiar and felt they could "survive in middle class." Yet only one participant had consistently *experienced* living in middle-class society. For example, while the participants readily agreed that money is important, they showed ambivalence regarding the procedures necessary to improve their resources.

LET'S GET PHYSICAL

In determining physical resources, there may be more involved than "meets the eye." Physical disabilities, racial differences, gender, and personal appearance fall under the category of physical resources. These factors impact the individual who is seeking academic or job-related advancement.

Race: Despite civil-rights legislation, employment quotas, and affirmative action, the potential for race and ethnicity to affect an individual's level of advancement or promotion is still present. The Leslie College Study of

Reinforcements analyzed 100 student teachers of generally equal ability involved in new teaching experiences with supervisors. The study results indicated that African-Americans in the group were 3.5 times more likely to receive negative reinforcement from their instructors than their Euro-American counterparts. White immigrant families have tended to achieve more financial and educational success in less time due to societal factors. It should be noted that the recent studies show that cultures that hold positive attitudes toward education show increased economic mobility.

> *What every black American knows, and whites should try to imagine,*
> *is how it feels to have unfavorable—and unfair—identity imposed on*
> *you every waking hour.*
>
> – Author unknown

Physical disabilities: If one has physical disabilities, extra strength and initiative are required in seeking out resources, thereby providing an additional challenge. Laws governing equal hiring and facility accessibility no doubt improve the situation. The number of individuals with physical disabilities increases in professional circles. Those who are differently abled may experience isolation. In some cases those with special needs have built support systems and community. The deaf, for example, have developed a community defined by its own patterns and characteristics.

Sex/gender: It is still generally acknowledged that women need more education and must work harder in order to achieve the equivalent of their male counterparts. Laws protecting equal rights of all individuals relative to sex, race, and physical disability have improved the achievement levels of many Americans. However, as the Leslie College study indicates, statutes alone will not determine actual practices of individuals making professional decisions in the workplace.

Fitness: The United States is youth-focused. In this culture, survival of the "fittest" takes on new meaning. Professionals are expected to look the part, and that includes discouragement of obesity and other physical characteristics deemed as unhealthy or "aging." TV commercials tout weight loss, age-defying skin creams, and toothpastes that whiten. Physical appearance is a factor that impacts career and social achievement.

Danielle has worked hard for her two-year degree in Human Services. Her instructors were supportive and especially remarked about her ability to write and speak in formal-language structure. She is hard-working and intelligent.

While others in her college classes have moved on to new professional positions, Danielle is working in a hardware store. She is 100 pounds over-weight and needs extensive dental work on her front teeth. Although Danielle attempts to dress professionally, she cannot afford nice clothing. She also cannot afford the dental work she needs because she doesn't earn enough money (she is now making $7/hour) and doesn't receive health- or dental-insurance benefits from her employer. (However, when Danielle was a Medicaid recipient, she made no attempt to get the dental work done.)

Yet Danielle has made some progress. She is no longer on welfare, and now she shares an apartment with a roommate in a middle-class neighbor-hood. She is gaining work experience in her new position. She also has made an effort to increase her emotional stability and modify her family structure.

Danielle could benefit from a mentoring relationship with an individual who has knowledge of middle-class rules, particularly regarding appearance and business etiquette. The mentor might help Danielle see the need to change her diet and exercise habits—and encourage her to see a dentist. Unfortunately, no one has yet offered to be Danielle's mentor. She is not actively seeking such a relationship, perhaps becoming resigned to her circumstances. It is not likely that such a mentor will appear in the small hardware store where she is the only female employee. Danielle has potential. With assistance from one or more mentors, Danielle's intelligence and ability to use formal original language could move her closer to her original pro-fessional goal—a position in a social services agency. The final question is: Even if such a mentor becomes available, does Danielle feel she wants to be a part of a mentor/protégé relationship?

SPIRITUAL RESOURCES: THE FOUNDATION OF SELF-ACTUALIZATION

The Search Institute of Minneapolis and other resiliency researchers subscribe to a broad definition of spirituality. Nan Henderson, editor-in-chief of the newsletter "Resiliency in Action: Bouncing Back from Risk and Adversity," defines spirituality as "personal faith in something greater." Other researchers use a broader definition, simply describing spirituality as an individual's motivation or sense of purpose.

Traditional definition of spirituality: The sense of having a core perspective—the knowledge that you are on a sacred path and are part of a separate and special identity, even as you pass on your religious beliefs and your cultural and personal strengths to the next generation—this is the "stuff" of life. Whether it is a belief in God, a higher power . . . or a sense of sacredness or destiny . . . these resources remain among the most powerful personal tools for anyone experiencing change and/or adversity.

The world is filled with books, stories, and a growing body of research on the importance of faith to a life of success and love. This resource, however, carries a caveat. A mentor may be particularly anxious to share his/her faith with the protégé, who may not share the same faith. In fact, do any two people share exactly the same belief system? Relationship and sharing go hand in hand, and most protégés will probably be willing to share their spiritual needs and thoughts if they trust their mentor. Care should be taken not to force this fragile issue, or the mentor/protégé relationship may suffer.

Cultural identity as spirituality: In Chapter One, ethnic culture is not given a separate resource category because it so closely aligns with the broad definition of spirituality. In fact, ethnicity and religion are intertwined in many cultures. To leave the traditional religion usually is considered a betrayal and can result in conflict.

When discussing key resources with a group of ethnically diverse urban educators, the instructor asked the participants to work in small groups to determine key values surrounding the importance of relationships, education, and other personal goals. Within each group, participants' values were similar and consistent with middle-class values. Indeed, the activity was designed to introduce economic class as separate and viable when interwoven into the large and highly complex cultural tapestry.

Finally, the instructor observed that individuals with a strong identification with an ethnic culture sometimes struggled to align the mental models and characteristics of economic culture with their ethnic-culture structure. Many individuals derive identity, support, and other benefits from participation within the ethnic culture. For them, it is a matter of honor and pride both to come from and grow into the constructs of their ethnicity, thereby helping define self and purpose.

RESOURCES REVISITED: SUPPORT SYSTEMS

Richard Sennett, in his interviews of 150 first-generation Euro-American immigrants, found that support systems were crucial to class mobility. In some cases, individuals never completely resolved the struggle between their old and new cultures. Some families chose to leave the old neighborhood to begin life in the suburbs, away from extended-family ties. Feelings of isolation and guilt continued throughout life for many of these men and women. On the other hand, those striving for middle class who chose to remain in the old neighborhood often felt trapped. They admitted to a feeling of discomfort with friends and relatives who made the transition to the suburbs. Both groups reported deep-seated feelings of inadequacy at some level.

People from generational poverty who desire to function well in middle class usually create new support systems. Considerable skill is necessary to negotiate a positive support system. Those who have these skills increase their chance of middle-class achievement. Since relationships, family, and "people" in general are considered resources within the poverty culture, this cluster of factors may make or break the transition process.

The director of an area volunteer organization was excited about the fundamentals described by Ruby Payne, Ph.D., in *A Framework for Understanding Poverty*. The director contacted the Department of Human Services (DHS) to link DHS clients with agencies looking for volunteers who were enrolled in the Welfare to Work program. She believed that these individuals, whose days on public assistance were numbered, would benefit from the contacts and experience made in volunteer situations. She also was willing to be a reference and assist clients with résumé writing and application-completion skills.

The program was up and running, and she soon had eight women volunteering, mostly within the same office building in which her agency was housed. The director was shocked when the women began dropping out of the program due to negative pressure from friends and family: "The women told me that their families threatened to disown them if they continued, that they were 'gettin' above their raisin'.' One woman told me her boyfriend beat her up so she would miss work and lose her volunteer status." Out of the eight original volunteers, six experienced acute negative reactions from those they loved the most. The volunteer coordinator has decided that in the future she will prepare potential volunteers for the negative reactions they may encounter from their relatives and close friends. Another option would be to ask the volunteers to meet corporately with the coordinator on a weekly basis. The agenda would include problem-solving for both work and home issues, along with a peer-support component.

Most of the women interviewed for this project admitted that they left behind friends and relatives who were non-supportive of their new goals. This is a cost each individual must consider. For some, that cost is too high.

The right relationships offer incredible support for transition. Bobbi, one of the technical-college graduates interviewed, initially moved toward middle-class culture through marriage. Although her husband also claims to be from generational poverty, his family had strong emotional resources. Relationships in his family were stable, and conflict-resolution skills were utilized. Len had a steady job and a willingness to negotiate with his wife on family matters. He even agreed to get his GED with his wife so they could have the experience together. Bobbi sees her relationship with Len as crucial to her development. In fact, Len's stability helped Bobbi finish college despite her parents' scorn and constant negative comments regarding the time she was spending away from her family in order to complete her college program.

In Bobbi's case, the relationship with her husband had a positive impact on her personal growth. Romantic relationships, however, can also be a road-block to upward mobility. In all three socioeconomic classes, traits and patterns interact to create a mental model for relationships, both at home and at work. There are (or should be) well-established boundaries present in the school or workplace that govern and balance relationships. These would be the middle-class hidden rules in which appropriate behavior is determined.

Within the poverty culture, the importance of adult romantic relationships can influence emotional resources and thereby affect work performance. Billy, a man in his 40s, strongly embodies the fighter/lover gender role for males; he also endorses the rescuer/martyr role for females. He has difficulty thinking of women as friends or colleagues, often slipping into familiarity with female co-workers. Billy displays the mental model of the "mating dance," which considers attraction of the opposite sex the norm for male-female interaction. Additionally, he regards people as resources and considers relationships a priority in his life. This combination creates a problem for Billy as he attempts to bridge class cultures.

Billy is fascinated with learning the hidden rules of middle class. He plans someday to achieve middle-class status. Billy has consciously focused several areas of his life toward the goal of "being middle class" and has made strides in planning, organization, and job-related activities. He is almost always prompt and reliable in working situations. However, Billy has difficulty in letting go of the fighter/lover gender role of his class culture. Gender roles are difficult to change, having been ingrained rather early in life (usually around fourth grade). Because of Billy's traditional and cultural gender-role patterns and his limited education, it's difficult for him to develop relationships with middle-class women. Billy repeatedly falls into relationships with women from the poverty culture. As long as he's in these relationships with women from this culture, he isn't likely to move out of generational poverty.

EMOTIONAL RESOURCES: RESILIENT ADULTS

Resiliency means bounding back from problems and stuff with more power and smarts than you started with.

— 15-year-old student quoted by Glenn Richardson, Ph.D.

Coping strategies and protective factors affect an individual's ability to withstand hardship and to use negative experiences for positive emotional development. Autonomy, or the ability to stand on one's own in decision-making and other life skills, may influence the upward movement between classes. Recent studies have determined that the ability to achieve in the midst of adversity is called resiliency.

There are slightly differing definitions of resiliency among researchers. Kimberly Gordon Rouse, Ph.D. (1995), has studied resilient subjects emerging from poverty and stress. She defines resiliency as "a multi-faceted phenomenon that encompasses personal and environmental factors that interact in a synergistic fashion to produce competence despite adversity." Resiliency is "the ability to thrive, mature, and increase competence in the face of adverse circumstances." Gordon Rouse suggests this is done through drawing on resources in three areas: biological, psychological, and environmental.

Norman Garmezy (1991) defines resiliency as "adaptiveness." Garmezy suggests that poverty plays a critical role in the developmental disabilities and maldevelopment of many children, citing a Children's Defense Fund study (1986) that portrayed the overwhelming pattern of risk factors associated with impoverished families. As children grow into adolescence and adulthood, Garmezy reports that "there are hints in the literature that suggest variables which may be operative in stressful life situations." These variables are described as protective factors. Protective factors "neutralize stressors" brought about by temperament, reflectiveness in meeting new situations, cognitive skills, and positive responses to others.

Protective factors are arranged in two categories: internal and external.

The list of internal assets includes the ability to form positive relationships, flexibility, love of learning, self-worth, and creativity. External factors consist of family, school, and neighborhood support systems. The external support systems may be more difficult to manipulate. The lack of these protective factors increases the "at risk" quotient for a given individual.

Gina O'Connell Higgins—psychologist, author, and Harvard professor—has noted patterns of resiliency in her clinical research. O'Connell Higgins, Ph.D., challenges the assumptions that "earlier developmental phases . . . are typically followed by five to seven decades of either minimal change or outright developmental arrest and that trauma necessarily precludes significant growth." The psychologist shares case studies of adults who have grown through the conscious and active process of constructing and organizing meaning from former trauma and chaos.

Relative to poverty, O'Connell Higgins affirms that growing up in abject poverty is indeed traumatizing in itself: "Low income status can be considered intrinsically abusive, as it exposes children and adolescents to many other associated stressors." The list of stressors begins with violence, substandard health conditions, and nutritional deficits and ends with child abuse and parental alcoholism. The individuals on which her case studies are based all shared these early stressors, including abuse, from generational-poverty environments. All of her clients, however, have grown into "faith-full" human beings with the ability to "love well." They have consciously chosen the path opposite from the terrors that were inflicted upon them and are devoted to projects and people outside of themselves.

A 30-year study of 700 children by Emmy Werner and Ruth Smith yielded a 10% resilient subgroup, members of which were working through and beyond their early experiences. The group was insular, low-mobility, and ethnically diverse children from Kauai, Hawaii. Another study of 818 low-income children found 10% to be "exceptionally competent" in their behavior and educational process. It should be noted, however, that in both studies most of the successful subjects had effective parenting and lacked parental psychopathology or abusiveness.

Finally, William Helmreich's 1992 study of 211 Holocaust survivors found 83% of his subjects sustaining successful marriages and other positive outcomes. In contrast, 62% of American Jews of the same ages exhibited these outcomes.

Despite the unusually high levels of the Helmreich study, most research indicates a 10% resiliency rate in those who have faced profound adversity. The question each mentor, teacher, judge, law enforcement officer, counselor, or community must ask is: Is all this worth the 10% who will make the complete transition to middle class?

There is a continuum of resiliency factors, and even though only about 10% will truly reach this long-term goal, many more people can be assisted to improve the resources in their lives. Adults assisting individuals from the culture of survival should not become discouraged if the impact on the majority of their clients and/or protégés seems to miss the mark. Short-term goals, small steps that stretch into larger accomplishments, little celebrations of new insight or mini-successes . . . these are the milestones of the low-income adult who takes on the challenge of transcending economic class. And these must also be the benchmarks for those who assist them. Perhaps the journey is just as important as the destination.

WHAT IMPLICATIONS DOES THIS INFORMATION HAVE FOR THE SOCIAL SERVICE, HEALTH CARE, OR WORK SETTING?

- Resiliency research is being broadened to include adults as well as children.

- Resource assessment should include individual factors in order to determine the potential of the employee, client, or student.

- Given similar risk factors, individuals with internal protective factors are more likely to achieve.

- Adults who increase their resiliency in relation to risk factors are generally those who continue to grow through the active and deliberate process of gathering meaning from former trauma and experiences.

- Mentors, supervisors, co-workers, and teachers will increase achievement in employees, clients, and students by assisting individuals to assign new meaning and perspective to problem situations.

Employers already need to include remedial language classes as part of job training and to hire foreign nationals for work in science and engineering. Declining competitiveness with other nations has become a national concern; it is increasingly unclear whether present intervention programs are commensurate with the complexity of the problem they were designed to help solve.

– Betty Hart and Todd R. Risley (1995). *Meaningful Differences in the Everyday Experience of Young American Children.* (p. 204). Baltimore: Paul H. Brookes.

Manufacturing work takes place in the working-class culture of the shop floor, but offices are run by the rules and social relations practices of middle-class and professional cultures. Many poor people who obtain jobs in offices learn these cultures on their own, but some may need a kind of schooling, not in punctuality and dress codes, but in the subtler cultural practices that are needed for success in the office world, and which the middle class learns almost automatically.

– Herbert J. Gans, *The War Against the Poor*

Improving the Work Performance: Teaching What Is Needed to Do the Job

Survival in poverty is very concrete (sensory dependent) and very non-verbal; survival at work is very abstract and verbal.

One of the reasons so many individuals from poverty make the transition into the world of work through skilled labor is that it is a bridge between the concrete and the abstract. Because the preferred language register in poverty is casual, many individuals never learn enough formal register to have the abstract words needed to do well in work.

To understand why this transition is so important to the world of work, a brief discussion of cognition is needed. To a large extent, teaching is outside the head, and learning is inside the head. When a person has had access to formal register, he/she has abstract words. For example, violence is an abstract word to represent the concrete reality of physically harming someone. People who are successful in an abstract verbal environment have built an abstract replica of reality inside their head. For example, when people are looking for their keys, they go inside their head. We say the keys are lost when individuals cannot find them in the location they thought they were inside their head.

The abstract world is held inside the head in "mental models." Mental models are a two-dimensional drawing, a story, or an analogy (for example, when people talk about building a house). Talk is very abstract. When the house is finally built in three dimensions, in all its concrete reality, there is always something that is used to translate that talk into the concrete reality. That something is blueprints. Blueprints become the mental models that are used to translate the abstract to the concrete.

Formal education is largely about learning the abstract representational systems that are used in the world of work. When an individual drops out of school or doesn't do well in school, often he/she lacks the mental models to do well in the world of work.

This chapter focuses on some of those abstract skills and mental models that need to be taught to adults who haven't yet acquired them.

THE MIND VS. THE BRAIN

Reuven Feuerstein is an Israeli educator who began working in the 1940s with providing individuals the mental models and strategies necessary to do well in the abstract world. He stated that it was "possible to have a brain and not have a mind." What he meant was that part of an individual's capabilities are inherited, and part are developed by the environment. The mind, if you will, is developed by the environment. Cognitive neurologists indicate that it's about a 50-50 deal. About half of who you are is inherited, and about half is developed (for better or for worse) by your environment.

Feuerstein studied under Jean Piaget, and he asked Piaget how he accounted for individual differences. Piaget was a biologist and was much more interested in accommodation and assimilation. Feuerstein concluded that what made a significant difference in learning was whether or not a nurturing, caring individual deliberately made an intervention. He called that intervention mediation, having borrowed the term from Lev Vygotsky, the Russian psychologist.

Mediation, in its simplest form, is when an individual does three things:

Points out the stimulus (WHAT)	Gives it meaning (WHY)	Provides a strategy (HOW)

In other words, the individual doing the teaching tells the person what to pay attention to, why that is important, and how to handle it. For example, we say to a young child, "Do not cross the street (pointing out the stimulus), you could be killed (what is important to pay attention to), and look both ways twice (a strategy to handle it)."

WHY IS MEDIATION SO IMPORTANT?

Mediation gives the ability to identify relationships—the causes and effects of things.

If an individual lives in an unpredictable environment and does not have an abstract replica of reality, then . . .

The individual cannot plan.

If an individual cannot plan, then he/she cannot predict.

If an individual cannot predict, then he/she does not know cause and effect.

If an individual does not know cause and effect, then he/she cannot identify consequence.

If an individual cannot identify consequence, then he/she cannot control impulsivity.

If an individual cannot control impulsivity, then he/she has an inclination toward criminal behavior.

Feuerstein identified the missing links that occur in the mind when mediation has not occurred. He proved that the mind could be remediated. He called it modifiability. In other words, it can be developed in adults. What are these missing links?

MISSING LINKS

(Feuerstein, 1980; Sharron, 1994):

1. *"Mediated focusing"*—Ability to focus attention and see objects in detail. Opposite of blurred and sweeping perceptions.

2. *"Mediated scheduling"*—Based on routine. Ability to schedule and plan ahead. Ability to represent the future abstractly and therefore set goals.

3. *"Mediation of positive anticipation"*—Ability to control the present for a happy representation of the future.

4. *"Mediation of inhibition and control"*—Ability to defer gratification, think before acting, control impulsiveness.

5. *"Mediated representation of the future"*—Ability to construe imaginatively a future scenario based on facts.

6. *"Mediation of verbal stimulation"*—Use of precise language for defining and categorizing the environment.

7. *"Mediated precision"*—Ability to precisely define situations, things, people, etc., and use that precise thinking for problem-solving.

Missing links/mediations result in cognitive issues.

What Are These Cognitive Issues?

Blurred and sweeping perceptions and the lack of a systematic method of exploration mean that these workers and clients have no consistent or predictable way of getting information. They see only about 50% of what is on a page. If you watch these individuals in a new setting, they will rapidly go from object to object, touching everything. Yet when you ask them what they have seen, they cannot tell you. This area is related to the use of the casual-register story structure, which is episodic and random in the details or information presented. They simply do not have cognitive methodology for doing tasks or a systematic way to finish tasks.

Impaired verbal tools means they do not have the vocabulary to deal with the cognitive tasks. Vocabulary words are the building blocks of the internal learning structure. Vocabulary is also the tool to better define a problem, seek more accurate solutions, etc. Many persons from poverty who rely solely on casual register do not use or have many prepositions or adverbs in their speech.

Impaired spatial orientation is simply the inability to orient objects, people, etc., in space. Directions, location, object size, object shape, etc., are not available to them. They have neither the vocabulary nor the concepts for spatial orientation.

Impaired temporal orientation is the inability to organize and measure in time. One of Feuerstein's observations was that these individuals assign time to incidents on the basis of the emotional intensity of the experience, not the measured time that is part of educated thinking. I find among workers and clients from poverty that time is neither measured nor heeded. Being somewhere on time is seldom valued. And time itself is not seen as a thing to be used or valued.

Impaired observation of constancies is the inability of the brain to hold an object inside the head and keep the memory of the object constant. In other words, when there are impaired observations of constancies, objects change shape and size in the mind. If this is the case, then learning alphabet letters, retaining shapes, etc., are problematic. It is also the inability to know what stays the same and what changes. For example, east and west are always constant; left and right change based on the orientation of the moment.

Lack of precision and accuracy in data-gathering is another cognitive issue. It is related to several of the above issues. Problem-solving and other tasks are extremely problematic because individuals from poverty seldom have the strategies to gather precise and accurate data.

Another cognitive issue is the inability *to hold two objects or two sources inside the head while comparing and contrasting*. If a client or employee is unable to do this, he/she cannot assign information to categories inside his/her brain. If an individual cannot assign information to categories, then he/she cannot retrieve the information except in an associative, random way.

These issues explain many of the behaviors of clients and workers. How do we make interventions?

How Does One Mediate These Issues in the Workplace When the Adult Does Not Have the Necessary Strategies?

For employees to be able to negotiate the "terrain" of the workplace, some cognitive structures inside the head are needed. These abstract cognitive structures evidence themselves in the following kinds of activities: planning (and using abstract measures of time to do so), controlling impulsivity, sorting systematically through data using patterns, formulating questions (can invert the word order to make a question), and planning and labeling tasks (having a plan and vocabulary for the task).

What does that mean at work? Planning requires a mental model for time, space, and "part to whole."

▪ Time

First of all, the individual needs an abstract notion of time. Feuerstein found that individuals needing this type of mediation tend to keep time emotionally, not abstractly. In other words, time is kept on the basis of how it feels—not minutes, hours, etc. A mental model for time that includes a past, present, and future is necessary. In poverty, time is often only the present . . . namely, survival. Additionally, the ability to match the amount of abstract time a task will take is not developed. Often, therefore, the work does not get done because the judgment about the amount of time the task would take was highly inaccurate.

What can you do to help such persons develop better habits in response to time? Teach them to plan backwards. In other words, draw a simple grid for a task.

Monday	Tuesday	Wednesday	Thursday	Friday

If a task is due on Friday, go to the space marked Friday, and write in— Task is to be finished. Then say, "What do you have to do on Thursday, so that it will be done on Friday?" Break down the task into parts and then ask, "How much time will you need each day to get this done?"

For adults from poverty, the workday is often interrupted by personal demands. Relatives call, and they are in jail, their car broke down, etc. A clear understanding needs to be established that work time belongs to work. Just as they don't come in to work on their personal time, they also don't take care of personal matters on their work time.

▪ Space

To do math, read a map, put things together, and follow directions, an individual must have an orientation in space (i.e., north, south, east, west, left, right, up, down, etc.). The body operates in space. One way to keep track of space is through touch or concreteness. Another way is through the direction and abstract spatial references. Because math is about assigning order and value to the universe, we tend to do it via direction (i.e., we write small to large numbers from left to right or top to bottom).

For adults who don't have orientation in space, one way to teach it is to prepare a two-dimensional drawing/map and teach them to turn the map with their hands until they have the ability to turn it inside their head.

■ Part to Whole

The workplace requires individuals to have the notion of part to whole and whole to part. Again, one of the easiest ways to teach this is to list the parts of the task—or make a drawing of all the parts and identify each part.

WHERE TO BEGIN

In planning, the procedural steps are important. Where will you start? If you cannot plan well, you do not know where to begin.

Controlling Impulsivity

Controlling impulsivity exhibits itself when tasks are rushed through, projects are abandoned for another activity, budgets are not followed, etc. One of the best ways to address this with adults is to teach goal-setting. Goal-setting must be done in writing, or it has little power. It can be as simple as the workers or clients writing down their goals for that day. At the end of the day, they check to see if the goals were met.

Planning is the key to finishing tasks and controlling impulsivity. Even more importantly, brain research indicates that the primary filter for what gets noticed by the mind is what the goals are. So when there is no planning, there are no goals. Emotional need or association determines the activities that are done.

Planning and Labeling Tasks

Another aspect of planning is the completion of tasks. To complete tasks, labels (vocabulary) and procedures must be assigned. One of the biggest problems for individuals in poverty is the number of items or portions of the task that simply are not addressed because a systematic method is not used. Four systems can be used to systematically address a task: numbering, lettering, color-coding, and symbols/icons.

Sorting by Using Patterns

In recent brain research it is fairly clear that details are not remembered over time, but patterns are. Therefore, learning can be enhanced if the patterns are directly taught—particularly to individuals who have little or no prior knowledge of the patterns.

When patterns are known, sorting through information or tasks becomes much faster. In problem-solving, it becomes important to be able to sort through a great deal of information. Solutions can be generated or dismissed faster, based on the patterns involved.

A study done with individuals who worked in blue-collar technical fields (such as air conditioning, plumbing, etc.) found that information about patterns was passed on in story. For example: "This case is just like the problem we had at the Sutter house."

Mental Models of Vocations or Subjects

Furthermore, to be an excellent worker, one must know the structure of that area of work or discipline. Each vocation and subject has specific ways of coding and keeping its knowledge. If an individual knows those, it is much easier to access the pertinent information necessary for goal-setting, decision-making, etc.

WHAT IMPLICATIONS DOES THIS INFORMATION HAVE FOR THE SOCIAL SERVICE, HEALTH CARE, OR WORK SETTING?

Many organizations have limited contact with clients from poverty and therefore are not likely to employ any of the strategies outlined here. So why the emphasis?

We have included this chapter for the following reasons:

First, there is a myth that poor people are not intelligent. Jerome Bruner, the great psychologist, said that all intelligence is related to task and context.

So the information is here to counter the prejudice that often accompanies that myth. A lack of formal education should not be confused with a lack of intelligence.

Second, the situation can be changed for adults. One of the myths is that if you don't get the brain/mind development from birth to age 4, you can't get it. That simply is not true. What is true is that these individuals may never reach the level of potential they could have, had they had the early development.

So What Can You Do with Your Clients?

- We can encourage educators to provide these strategies to our clients and their children.

- We can encourage our clients to get help for their children and to learn parenting strategies, such as mediation, so they can help their sons and daughters too.

- We can provide staff development for front-line staff who have diagnostic responsibilities to identify issues around cognitive development.

- We can identify the mental models that our institutions use so that clients can better work with us and vice versa.

- We can focus more on their learning than our teaching.

- We can identify the mental models and patterns of the organizations with which clients must interact.

The fact that I'm neither dead nor still in prison is due not to any government program or fancy rehabilitation center but to some folks I met in prison—poets and playwrights, activists, theologians, and philosophers. . . . One of my favorite professors was Martha Connamacher, who taught chemistry and physics (at Western—a prison). . . . Even though Martha was white, she became a kind of surrogate mother for me, helping to free me from my dead-end quest for my real mother's approval. . . . Martha's influence is still with me today.

– Carl Upchurch, *Convicted in the Womb*

CHAPTER 11

Creating Relationships with People in Poverty

The key to achievement for students and workers from poverty is in creating relationships with them. Because poverty is about relationships as well as entertainment, the most significant motivator for these clients and employees is relationships.

To help someone, is it necessary to have "been there"?

There is a commonly held belief that alcoholics and addicts can only be helped by those who have "been there," that only veterans can help veterans, that only someone who has lived in poverty can truly understand and help another trying to work his/her way out. A movie such as *Good Will Hunting* supports the notion. The main character is a "Southie" in Boston who is sent to a number of psychiatrists (five in fact) before he finds one who can create a relationship with him. The therapist also grew up as a "Southie." In one scene illustrating their tight relationship, the two compare stories about their alcoholic fathers.

While it is certainly easier for those who share a common background to develop a relationship, it doesn't exactly follow that the only one who can help you is someone who has walked in your shoes. Those who work with people from the poverty culture but don't come from that culture themselves can, if they have the necessary skills, play a valuable role in the lives of others.

The question becomes, How does a formal institution create relationships? Two sources provide some answers to this question. These sources are (1) the recent research in the field of science and (2) the work Stephen Covey has done with personal effectiveness.

Margaret Wheatley, in her book *Leadership and the New Science* (1992), states quite clearly:

> *Scientists in many different disciplines are questioning whether we can adequately explain how the world works by using the machine imagery created in the 17th century, most notably by Sir Isaac Newton. In the machine model, one must understand parts. Things can be taken apart, dissected literally or representationally . . . and then put back together without any significant loss. . . . The Newtonian model of the world is characterized by materialism and reductionism—a focus on things rather than relationships. . . . The quantum view of reality strikes against most of our notions of reality. Even to scientists, it is admittedly bizarre. But it is a world where* relationship *is the key determiner of what is observed and of how particles manifest themselves. . . . Many scientists now work with the concept of fields—invisible forces that structure space or behavior.* (pp. 8–13)

Wheatley goes on to say that, in the new science of quantum physics, physical reality is not just tangible, it is also intangible. Fields are invisible, yet:

> *[They are the] substance of the universe. . . . In organizations, which is the more important influence on behavior—the system or the individual? The quantum world answered that question: It depends. . . . What is critical is the relationship created between the person and the setting. That relationship will always be different, will always evoke different potentialities.* It all depends on the players and the moment. (pp. 34–35)

Front-line staff and administrators of social service agencies and schools have always known that the relationships, often referred to as "politics," make a great deal of difference, sometimes all the difference in what could or could not happen in an agency or school. Yet social services and businesses all too often have concentrated on performance measurers. While the machine metaphor for business has led us to dissect our work into parts, the most important part of learning and change seems to be related to relationship—if we listen to the data and potent realities in the research emerging from the disciplines of biology and physics.

When students and workers who have been in poverty (and have successfully made it into middle class) are asked how they made the journey, the answer nine times out of 10 has to do with a relationship—a teacher, counselor, coach, or boss who made a suggestion or took an interest in them as an individual.

Stephen Covey (1989) uses the notion of an emotional bank account to convey the crucial aspects of relationships. He indicates that in all relationships one makes deposits to and withdrawals from the other individual in that relationship. In his view, the following are the deposits and withdrawals:

DEPOSITS	WITHDRAWALS
Seek first to understand	Seek first to be understood
Keeping promises	Breaking promises
Kindnesses, courtesies	Unkindnesses, discourtesies
Clarifying expectations	Violating expectations
Loyalty to the absent	Disloyalty, duplicity
Apologies	Pride, conceit, arrogance
Open to feedback	Rejecting feedback

Adapted from Stephen Covey, *The Seven Habits of Highly Effective People*

The first step to creating relationships between front-line staff members and clients or employees is to make the deposits that are the basis of relationships. Relationships always begin as one individual to another. The other relationships that have power to change are the relationships between the administrator and the clients and the relationships between the clients, students, or employees themselves.

What, then, is meant by relationship? A successful relationship occurs when emotional deposits are made to the client or employee, emotional withdrawals are avoided, and clients or employees are respected. Are there boundaries to the relationship? Absolutely—and that is what is meant by clarifying expectations. But to honor clients as human beings worthy of respect and care is to establish a relationship that will provide for enhanced learning and achievement.

What are the deposits and withdrawals with regard to clients from poverty? (See chart below.)

By understanding deposits that are valued by clients from poverty, the relationship is stronger.

DEPOSITS MADE TO INDIVIDUAL IN POVERTY	WITHDRAWALS MADE FROM INDIVIDUAL IN POVERTY
Appreciation for humor and entertainment provided by the individual	Put-downs or sarcasm about the humor or the individual
Acceptance of what the individual cannot say about a person or situation	Insistence and demands for full explanation about a person or situation
Respect for the demands and priorities of relationships	Insistence on the middle-class view of relationships
Using the adult voice	Using the parent voice
Assisting with goal-setting	Telling the individual his/her goals
Identifying options related to available resources	Making judgments on the value and availability of resources
Understanding the importance of personal freedom, speech, and individual personality	Assigning pejorative character traits to the individual

How does an organization create—and build—relationships? Through support systems, through caring about clients, by promoting achievement, by being role models, by insisting upon successful behaviors for the organization. *Support systems are simply networks of relationships.*

Will creating healthy relationships with clients or employees make all of them successful? No. But if we make a difference for 5% of our clients and employees the first year and 5% more each year thereafter, we will have progressed considerably from where we are right now.

In the final analysis, as one looks back on his/her career, it is the relationships one remembers.

WHAT IMPLICATIONS DOES THIS INFORMATION HAVE FOR THE SOCIAL SERVICE, HEALTH CARE, OR WORK SETTING?

- For adults from poverty, the primary motivation for their success will be their relationships.

- If your setting affords few opportunities for building relationships, find ways to establish natural connections that will enable this vital resource to take root and grow.

- Satisfaction studies show that customers and clients make up their mind about a store or agency in the first 15 minutes. Even more interesting, the opinion that is formed in the first 15 minutes is the opinion they hold from then on. Thus, it is extremely important that the staff person most skilled at creating relationships be the first contact with the customer or client.

The white teachers brought their white values into the school—values that negated my world entirely. The message was subtle, but it was clear to me: everyone I respected and loved was considered ignorant, irresponsible, and good-for-nothing.

– Carl Upchurch, *Convicted in the Womb*

CHAPTER 12

■ ■ ■ ■ ■ ■ ■ ■

Developing Personal Skills for Working with People in Poverty

CORE COMPETENCIES

In earlier chapters we described the characteristics of generational poverty. In this chapter we offer exercises designed to help readers evaluate personal skills for working with people from the poverty culture. The ability to work effectively with the employees, customers, or clients from the poverty culture is a core competency.

In the first table (starting on the next page) we recognize that we have relationships with clients based on the role we play in the agency. Receptionists set the tone of the relationship between the client and the agency. They need to be able to establish relationships quickly, put people at ease, and deal with difficult situations. At the other end of the spectrum are those who have long and involved relationships with clients as they assist them in building cognitive structures. They must have comprehensive skills.

Evaluate your skills. Make a check in the right column to indicate if you have the skill.

Personal Skills Applied by Position and Duties

POSITION AND DUTIES Personal Skills Required	HAVE THE SKILL?	
JUDGES, EMPLOYERS, POLICE: People in these positions motivate clients by use of orders and sanctions.		
Explain rules	☐ Yes	☐ No
Use adult voice	☐ Yes	☐ No
Avoid power struggles and manipulation	☐ Yes	☐ No
Use metaphor	☐ Yes	☐ No
Understand story structure and casual register	☐ Yes	☐ No
Assess resources	☐ Yes	☐ No
Teach middle-class rules	☐ Yes	☐ No
Use varied mentoring models and structures	☐ Yes	☐ No
Present concept of crisis as opportunity for change	☐ Yes	☐ No
Utilize community systems of care	☐ Yes	☐ No
RECEPTIONIST, SUPPORT STAFF: People in these settings greet public, gather data, orient clients, schedule appointments, collect fees. They have brief but perhaps frequent encounters. They set tone and climate for organization.		
Kindnesses, courtesies	☐ Yes	☐ No
Give clients time before "getting to the agenda"	☐ Yes	☐ No
Admit when wrong	☐ Yes	☐ No
Use adult voice	☐ Yes	☐ No
Appreciation and use of humor	☐ Yes	☐ No
Use informal mentoring techniques	☐ Yes	☐ No
Ability to detach and avoid power struggles	☐ Yes	☐ No
Teach middle-class rules	☐ Yes	☐ No
Knowledge of local resources	☐ Yes	☐ No

Personal Skills Applied by Position and Duties (continued)

POSITION AND DUTIES Personal Skills Required	HAVE THE SKILL?	
INTAKE WORKERS, DATA GATHERERS: People in these positions do screenings and make determinations about initial course of action. Their time with clients is limited.		
Understand story structure and casual register	❑ Yes	❑ No
Gather data from more than one person	❑ Yes	❑ No
Respect for client's loyalty to friends/family not present	❑ Yes	❑ No
Detach and avoid power struggles	❑ Yes	❑ No
Use adult voice	❑ Yes	❑ No
Evaluate assets and resources	❑ Yes	❑ No
Plan backwards	❑ Yes	❑ No
Teach procedural self-talk	❑ Yes	❑ No
Plan at beginning of each session	❑ Yes	❑ No
Avoid direct questions if possible	❑ Yes	❑ No
Who, what, when, where, how	❑ Yes	❑ No
Teach formal and consultative language	❑ Yes	❑ No
Teach middle-class rules	❑ Yes	❑ No
Use formal or informal mentoring for secondary issues	❑ Yes	❑ No
Mediate	❑ Yes	❑ No
THERAPISTS, COUNSELORS, CASE MANAGERS, INSTRUCTORS: People in these positions have long-term relationships with clients designed to assist clients in making changes. They gather data, develop plans, and monitor and process work with clients.		
These people must have all skills listed above—plus . . .		
Utilize team interventions	❑ Yes	❑ No
Provide mentors	❑ Yes	❑ No

continued on next page

Personal Skills Applied by Position and Duties (continued)

POSITION AND DUTIES Personal Skills Required	HAVE THE SKILL?
THERAPISTS, COUNSELORS, CASE MANAGERS, INSTRUCTORS (continued)	
Use metaphor stories	☐ Yes ☐ No
Assist client in developing support teams	☐ Yes ☐ No
Distinguish between enabling systems and positive support systems	☐ Yes ☐ No
Teach procedural self-talk	☐ Yes ☐ No
Offer structure and choices	☐ Yes ☐ No
Teach coping strategies, and provide respite	☐ Yes ☐ No
Offer bridge out of poverty culture	☐ Yes ☐ No
Use formal mentoring regarding primary and secondary issues	☐ Yes ☐ No
The most skilled will understand cognitive development, dynamic testing, instrumental enrichment, and mediation	☐ Yes ☐ No

The following table is simply another way to review personal skills for working with people in the poverty culture. This table invites you to mark a "+" if you already possess the listed skills, a "0" if you have some of the skills but need to improve them, and a "−" if your skills need lots of work.

Do the front-line staff in the organization have these skills?

Skills and Strategies for Working with Families from Poverty

+   Can Do Now
0   Needs Some Work
−   Needs Lots of Work

INTERNAL PROCESSES Skills and Strategies	+	0	−
CREATING RELATIONSHIPS			
Seek first to understand			
Keep promises			
Use kindnesses, courtesies			
Clarify expectations			
Show loyalty to absent friends/family			
Be willing to apologize			
Stay open to feedback (taken from Stephen Covey's book *The Seven Habits of Highly Effective People*)			
Show appreciation for humor and entertainment provided by individual			
Accept what individual cannot say about a person or situation			
Respect demands and priorities of relationships			
Use adult voice			
Assist with goal-setting			
Identify options related to available resources			
Understand importance of personal freedom, speech, and individual personality			
Use formal or informal mentoring; follow Wickman and Sjodin's "16 Laws of Mentoring"			

continued on next page

Skills and Strategies for Working with Families from Poverty (continued)

+ **Can Do Now**
0 **Needs Some Work**
– **Needs Lots of Work**

INTERNAL PROCESSES Skills and Strategies	+	0	–
GATHERING DATA			
Use humor			
Add 10 minutes			
Get more than one storyteller			
Comment; don't ask direct questions			
Pick data you need out of story as it is told to you			
Who, what, when, where, how			
Be aware of what is omitted from story			
Eye movement, neuro-linguistic programming			
GOAL-SETTING/TREATMENT PLANNING			
Use mediation			
Plan backwards			
Give all procedural steps			
Teach procedural self-talk			
Require a plan for each project			
Plan at beginning of each session			
Teach hidden rules of middle class			
Teach formal and consultative registers			

Skills and Strategies for Working with Families from Poverty (continued)

+ Can Do Now
0 Needs Some Work
– Needs Lots of Work

INTERNAL PROCESSES Skills and Strategies	+	0	–
DISCIPLINE, SANCTIONS, CONSEQUENCES			
Provide choices and consequences			
Reframe power struggles			
Use metaphor stories			
ORGANIZATIONAL STRATEGIES			
Examine client's life cycle at your organization			
Change internal processes to serve poverty culture			
Collaborate with other agencies that serve poverty culture to remove barriers			
Provide mentors, role models, sponsors			
Schedule for relationship-building			
Incorporate intermediary or peer mentoring programs			
Teach survival skills (hidden rules) of your organization			
Show videos			
Use team interventions			
Support staff development of skills to work with poverty culture			

A CASE STUDY

An environmental specialist working one of the more dangerous jobs in rural Ohio has the task of enforcing septic-systems standards with people who have consistently voted down zoning. Government officials are not usually welcome on their property. The environmental specialist developed the following strategies and skills.

He drives a beat-up pickup truck and wears casual clothes. When greeting clients at their home he takes time to talk about local fishing holes and gossip about friends and relatives. Before long he tells them that there's been a complaint about their septic system. He has learned to defuse the early moments by letting his clients know that he is willing to work with them. He doesn't throw around bureaucratic codes but simply asks what their septic system is like. If the clients get defensive he remains detached; he expects them to be angry. He doesn't take their anger personally. While they accuse neighbors for turning them in and of having worse septic systems than theirs, he waits them out. He returns to the issue and mediates by talking about the fish found in the creek nearby. He explains how runoff from improper sewage management kills fish and how that will impact them directly. "There won't be any fishing left," he says. Next he discusses how the system can be corrected and, by giving them choices, shows his respect for them. "How much time do you need to get that done?" he may ask. His ability is rewarded by the trust that his clients put in him. Several men have gone fishing with him. He has acted as mentor to a few, teaching them time management and goal-setting strategies, as well as ways to reward themselves when they have met short-term goals.

This professional has many core competencies required to work with people from the poverty culture. He can build relationships, understand the use of the casual-register language, and avoid power struggles and manipulations. He can mediate, teach middle-class rules, and even be a mentor to his clients.

WHAT IMPLICATIONS DOES THIS INFORMATION HAVE FOR THE SOCIAL SERVICE, HEALTH CARE, OR WORK SETTING?

Some front-line workers come to their work with many core competencies in place. This can be due to their cultural and ethnic backgrounds, educational credentials, emotional and cognitive health, and their spiritual well-being. Front-line workers who don't have core competencies not only undermine the mission of the organization for which they work, but they may have a detrimental impact on the people they are meant to serve. Administrators and supervisors must . . .

1. identify core competencies.

2. inform the front-line staff of core competencies they must have.

3. measure and evaluate core competencies of front-line staff.

4. budget for professional development.

5. provide training opportunities.

Managers have to learn to ask every few years of every process, every product, every procedure, every policy: "If we did not do this already, would we go into it now knowing what we now know?" . . . Indeed, organizations increasingly will have to plan abandonment rather than try to prolong the life of a successful product, policy or practice. . . .

– Peter Drucker, *Managing in a Time of Great Change*

Americans are good at moving on into a changing, contingent, turbulent, adverse, and largely unpredictable universe. That's the universe we're used to, and we're good at meeting the challenge, (re)making, (re)discovering, (re)presenting—in a word, reengineering—everything, including ourselves.

– James Champy, *Reengineering Management*

For the organization to perform to a high standard, its members must believe that what it is doing is, in the last analysis, the one contribution to community and society on which all others depend.

– Peter Drucker, *Managing in a Time of Great Change*

The conflict lies in the fact that theory, in a field like medicine, education, or sciences, may dictate one course of behavior, and the bureaucratic structure, set up supposedly to carry out these ends, may dictate another. There are certain structural needs or pressures which may conflict with theory, yet they may come to dominate practice.

– Chandler Washburne, "Conflicts Between Educational Theory and Structure"

Improving Agency Policies and Internal Processes

LEARNING FROM BUSINESS

In the previous chapter we argued that the core competencies of front-line staff members are crucial to the accomplishment of the mission of the organization. In this chapter we argue the reverse: that the skills of the individual are not enough to achieve the mission, that the theory of business, policies, and procedures, if not properly conceived, can frustrate and even negate the work of the individual.

Current reform movements share the common assumption that public-sector agencies and non-profit organizations would do better work if they were run in a more businesslike manner. This belief and the demand for change are leading to the retooling of most organizations. There are, of course, countless writers on business and many strategies for change. We offer the ideas of two writers—Peter Drucker and James Champy—because their concepts lend themselves to a simple way to couple a concern for the client with administrative change.

Consider the following concepts and definitions.

THEORY OF BUSINESS

Drucker defines the "theory of business" as those assumptions upon which a business is built and run. He says the theory shapes its behavior, dictates its decisions, and defines what the organization considers a meaningful result or outcome. Take, for example, a bookstore that redefined its theory of business.

It changed from a bookstore that looked like all bookstores with narrow aisles and tables covered with bargains to a place where people could meet, drink coffee, and talk about books. The aisles were widened, and chairs and benches were placed so that customers could sit down and read or talk with others. A coffee shop was added to the store. Staff members were encouraged to write book reports, which were placed where customers could read them. The bookstore became a place to spend time instead of a simple bookstore. In its new form it thrived.

Government and social service organizations have as much reason to examine their theory of business as the private sector. The current atmosphere of reform demands it. Perhaps the change is greatest for welfare organizations. For more than 60 years the theory of business was guided by the protocols of Aid for Dependent Children (ADC). The theory was to give basic support to poor women so that they could stay home and raise their children. Under ADC, welfare agencies were in the business of disbursing checks; now they are in the business of helping people find work. Welfare agencies will now be paid for putting people to work, *not* for disbursing checks. Meaningful results are measured in how many people leave the welfare rolls and how many find jobs, *not* how many people draw checks. The core competencies required by the system have changed.

It's important that we ask the seemingly obvious question: What is your organization's theory of business? During a period of reform such as this there will be subtle and not-so-subtle changes in the way business must be conducted in order to survive. Having a clear understanding of your agency's theory of business—and checking it frequently against the realities of the day —is necessary. When an administrator of an agency, whose mission was to work with misdemeanant young people, was asked how his agency went about helping troubled teens, he couldn't answer the question because the program director wasn't available. All workers in the organization must know what the theory of business is, especially the administrator. If they don't, the organization is in trouble.

Client's life cycle: The answer to the question about the theory of business leads naturally to an examination of how outcomes are to be achieved. In other words, what happens to the customer or client as they enter and go through your program *from their point of view?*

Champy writes about organizations that don't understand the importance of the customer: "We asked questions that only had relevance to us, not our consumers." When customers can't get their needs met because the office isn't open, or when they have to wait for services, or when the computer monitor gets the attention instead of the customer, you know the organization is built around the needs of the staff and not the client. Such organizations are bureaucracies.

Champy suggests that a flow chart of the client's life cycle be created, indicating who is primarily responsible for each step in the cycle. While creating the flow chart, keep in mind that the search is for deficits in the system, not for deficits in our clients. Imagine yourself as the client as you are asked these kinds of questions: Why did you come to the agency? Whom did you meet first? How long did you wait? How were you treated? What was expected of you? What did you do? What was done by others? What did you learn? What changed? Did your reason for coming to the agency get addressed? Were you satisfied?

These are not questions to actually throw at your clients. It's intended here to be an exercise in empathy, an attempt to visualize—and walk in the shoes of the client.

INTERNAL PROCESSES

An examination of the client's life cycle leads to the identification of checkpoints for every significant client-related event. The key question is: Who is responsible for that event or internal process? If several people share responsibility for an internal process, you will discover that no one is responsible.

Champy recommends that each internal process be assigned a "process champion," someone who controls the step and who is accountable for the outcome. Champy says, "The process champion works for the customer, not the organizational heads." The process champion, the person closest to the client, should have the authority to solve problems and to use his/her discretion.

Example: At a substance-abuse treatment facility, client orientation was done by several people. The front-office staff provided some information to the clients and gave them a client handbook. The counselors were expected to provide the rest of the orientation during the first visit or shortly thereafter. In practice, however, it was discovered that most of the orientation was provided by *other clients*. A satisfaction survey conducted after the first counseling session revealed that the clients had little idea of what was expected of them—that they were not getting an adequate orientation. Who was really responsible for the orientation? Who was accountable for the outcome?

With these few definitions and concepts in mind, ask yourself the following questions about your organization. By doing so you should begin to form ideas of what needs to be done at your organization to improve services for people from the poverty culture.

WHAT DRIVES *YOUR* INDUSTRY?

Welfare organizations are being driven by welfare reform. Health care industries are driven by managed care. Schools are driven by proficiency testing. In these instances outside forces are forcing a change in the theory of business. In other organizations the motivation to examine the theory of business can come from inside. Perhaps the administrators want to take advantage of new technologies, or perhaps they want to position their agency differently to meet the competition. A jail administrator of a new facility, knowing that other jails were being built in surrounding counties, recognized that keeping his jail full would become difficult as those jails went into operation. He decided that he would offer substance-abuse treatment and life-skills training to inmates. His theory of business was that if he could show a drop in recidivism because of the programming he would attract referrals to his facility and thus survive in a competitive environment.

WHO IS THE BUSINESS REALLY FOR? WHO IS IT TRYING TO SERVE? WHAT PERCENTAGE OF THE CLIENTS ARE FROM THE POVERTY CULTURE?

Who is the business really for? The answer to this question, taken immediately following the question about what drives the industry, isn't as simple as it might appear. In some instances there is a conflict between what drives an industry and who it is really for. The managed care debate is a case in point. Most agree that managed care drives the behavioral health care industry, but many believe that it does so at the expense of the people who are to be served. Take another field: Are schools really for children, for learning for learning's sake? Or are schools to serve the community at large, turning out young people ready for the workplace?

The private sector, driven by the profit motive, can be successful only if it identifies who is really to be served, then gives these people its complete attention. So should it be with governmental and non-profit organizations. The client must come first.

Who is it trying to serve? This is another deceptively simple question. Consider what happens over time in any organization. As it grows, grants are won, contracts written, new programs added, new sites opened. Before long the focus has shifted. Who is being served now? The answers to these questions should be matched with the agency's theory of business. Are they consistent? Who is being served and who should be served?

In any business, planners must know their customers. For social service and governmental organizations, it is crucial that planners know what percentage of their clients are from the poverty culture. This question is different from asking how many clients are in poverty. Granted, an administrator needs to know how many clients are on Medicaid or how many students receive free lunches, but the poverty culture is a lot more than a point on a financial guideline.

To what degree are people from the poverty culture a subset of the customers? Obviously a high percentage of clients of welfare departments will be from the poverty culture, but not all, as some will be from situational poverty. Law enforcement and corrections also see a large number of people from the poverty culture. The higher the percentage of clients from the poverty culture, the more the planners will need to design the theory of business, client's life cycle, and internal processes to meet their needs.

DO YOU NEED TO DEVELOP A CONTEMPORARY THEORY OF BUSINESS FOR YOUR AGENCY THAT TAKES INTO ACCOUNT WHAT YOU KNOW ABOUT THE POVERTY CULTURE?

If, by answering the above questions, you have come to the conclusion that your theory of business, client's life cycle, and internal processes are all consistent with the characteristics of those you are trying to serve, you won't need to develop a contemporary theory of business.

But . . .

- If reform is moving faster than you are, or

- You suspect that the client's life cycle is designed more to serve the staff than the customer, or

- You can't identify who is accountable for the internal processes at your agency, or

- You are serving a lot of people from the poverty culture and your staff isn't trained to serve them adequately . . . you might need to develop a contemporary theory of business.

WHAT IS THE CLIENT'S LIFE CYCLE AT YOUR AGENCY? HOW DO YOU ACHIEVE THE DESIRED RESULTS?

Your agency's theory of business can be revealed in a concrete form by a flow chart that details each step of the client's experience at your agency. The flow chart should start with the first contact a client has with the organization and end with where he/she goes upon departure. The key is to think through the experience from the client's point of view. Clients can be surveyed and/or included on boards and committees to gain their input.

Research on client satisfaction indicates that a customer makes up his/her mind about an organization in the first 15 minutes after walking through the door. For that reason alone planners should know what that experience is. Survey questions that will get to the experience of clients from the poverty culture are largely about relational issues.

- I was treated with respect by the staff.

- The staff gave me the time and attention I needed.

- I was treated fairly.

- The staff is concerned that I do well and helps me if I need it.

- The staff notices when I am doing well.

- The staff is calm when he/she talks to me.

- When I do something wrong the staff explains what I did wrong.

- I can trust the staff.

Questions should be on a 5- or 7-point scale for scoring purposes, and clients should be given an opportunity to comment on each question. Surveys can be used at key points in the client's life cycle to test how the client's life cycle is being perceived.

WHAT ARE THE INTERNAL PROCESSES OR CLIENT-RELATED EVENTS AT YOUR AGENCY? WHAT CHANGES SHOULD BE MADE IN YOUR AGENCY'S INTERNAL PROCESSES TO ASSIST THE CLIENT AND TO MAKE A SINGLE PERSON ACCOUNTABLE FOR THE OUTCOME?

Managers and front-line staff will be able to identify some problem areas immediately because certain areas cause the most tension and trouble. Some internal processes can be changed quickly and easily; others take a lot of work.

Returning to the earlier example of the substance-abuse treatment agency that had the confusing orientation process, its problem was solved by creating an orientation video. The counselors were relieved of the responsibility of doing orientations, and a single staff member was made accountable for answering any questions the clients had after viewing the video. This solution not only served the clients well by giving them all a carefully worded message, but it saved time for the counselors.

The changes illustrated in the table on the following pages were made the day after a welfare agency staff training on the poverty culture. The staff agreed that calling clients over the intercom was not a good way to begin a relationship with clients. The next day the staff began meeting their clients in the waiting room before taking them back to their offices.

The table illustrates how a particular internal process can be adjusted to meet the needs of those from the poverty culture. The first column describes the steps of the current process, the second highlights the survival-culture issues that apply, and the third column describes the steps of the new process.

Analysis of Intake Process at Welfare Agency

INTERNAL PROCESS AND RESPONSIBLE PERSON	POVERTY-CULTURE ISSUES	ADJUSTED PROCESS AND RESPONSIBLE PERSON
1. Receptionist seated behind window hands client papers and asks about emergency issues.	Distrust of organizations. Identity tied up in cynical attitudes about bosses, "professionals," importance of relationships. Sensitive to judgmental attitudes. Kids beg their mother for money for candy machine.	Receptionist greets client. Explains process for day, shows orientation video to client, offers help with paperwork. Children play with toys in waiting room. Candy machine removed. RESPONSIBLE: RECEPTIONIST
2. Receptionist makes appointment for client to return if caseworker is not available immediately.	Time occurs only in present. Lack of organization. Thus client cannot guarantee that she will get up in time for appointment, be able to get car that is running, or find someone willing to drive her. She agrees; what else can she do? Missed appointments are a problem.	Schedule caseworkers so that one is always open to take walk-ins. When clients do come in, give them longer appointments to get more work done. Have clients meet with more members of team, job placement, child support, income maintenance, substance-abuse assessment. RESPONSIBLE: RECEPTIONIST

continued on next page

Analysis of Intake Process at Welfare Agency (continued)

INTERNAL PROCESS AND RESPONSIBLE PERSON	POVERTY-CULTURE ISSUES	ADJUSTED PROCESS AND RESPONSIBLE PERSON
3. On day of appointment client sits in waiting room until her name is called over intercom.	Distrust of organizations, negative orientation, belief in fate, polarized thinking.	Caseworker goes to waiting room and introduces self, escorts client to private office, deals with motivation and practical issues, sets up meetings with other members of team. RESPONSIBLE: CASEWORKER
4. Caseworker begins to gather data from individual, entering data onto forms or into computer: "Let's get down to business."	Casual register, disorganized story structure, time oriented to present, rescuer/martyr role, lives in the moment.	Personal skills of caseworker come into play during data-gathering sessions. For example, caseworker spends a few minutes building relationship before "getting down to business." Other members of family are encouraged to attend so that information can be gathered from more than one person. Client is interviewed by two caseworkers (from different departments—income eligibility and jobs) so that one can enter data into computer while other attends to client. RESPONSIBLE: CASEWORKER

WHAT IMPLICATIONS DOES THIS INFORMATION HAVE FOR ORGANIZATIONS THAT WORK WITH PEOPLE IN POVERTY?

- When an organization redesigns its theory and structures along these lines the clients will no longer encounter an organization designed for and run by the middle class, but instead they will experience a process designed to meet their needs. Such a systems change removes a barrier to people not in the dominant economic culture.

- One business improved its retention rate of new hires from welfare from 29% to 85% by applying its new understanding of people in poverty to its processes.

- The organization will offer clients the necessary tools for change.

- Relationships with clients/customers/employees will improve.

- Results from satisfaction surveys will improve.

- Outcomes will improve.

. . . [T]he greatest change in corporate structure, and in the way business is being conducted, may be the largely unreported growth of relationships that are not based on ownership but on partnership: joint ventures, minority investments cementing a joint-marketing agreement or an agreement to do joint research; and semi-formal alliances of all sorts.

– Peter Drucker, *Managing in a Time of Great Change*

Our mental model of the way the world works must shift from images of a clockwork, machinelike universe that is fixed and determined, to the model of a universe that is open, dynamic, interconnected, and full of living qualities. . . . Once we see this fundamentally open quality of the universe, it immediately opens us up to the potential for change; we see that the future is not fixed, and we shift from resignation to a sense of possibility. We are creating the future every moment.

– Joseph Jaworski, *Synchronicity: The Inner Path of Leadership*

CHAPTER 14

■ ■ ■ ■ ■ ■ ■

Improving Interagency Collaboration

Earlier we made the argument that the success of an agency working with the poverty culture rests on the skills of the individual front-line worker, and then we made the argument that the success of the agency rests on a well-designed theory of business, client's life cycle, and internal process. Now we make the argument that the success also rests upon the quality of the collaboration between the agency and other organizations in the community.

Consider the story of Carl Upchurch, author of *Convicted in the Womb* , who wrote, "When I was released from BCC [a 'farm' for young offenders], everything I went back to was negative, dirty, racist, and violent. Instinctively, I reverted to my old feelings and actions. You cannot corrupt a child's spirit, give him a respite from the corruption, then return him to the original environment and expect him to be more moral than others in those circumstances." To frame Upchurch's experience in the language we are using here you could say that he began learning a second set of rules for survival and was motivated to succeed in his new environment. Unfortunately, the social service system did not collaborate to the extent that it could provide Upchurch with something other than a return to his original environment. In his view, the system clearly let him down; he fell through a gap in the continuum of services.

To look at his experience from the BCC's point of view we would have to know how BCC described their theory of business. Did it include a client's life cycle beyond the exit door of their facility? What other resources were available in the community? Was there any collaboration between the various agencies working with youthful offenders?

This story makes the argument for building connections between and among agencies. Community planners must see the client's life cycle as the *client's,* not their own. Planning for the client at your organization alone may not be enough. It may be necessary to plan with other organizations to span the client's experience.

Our primary understanding of what collaboration is and how to collaborate successfully comes from the work of Paul Mattessich and Barbara Monsey. In 1992 they published their research summary, *Collaboration: What Makes It Work —A Review of the Research Literature Describing Factors Which Influence the Success of Collaboration* .

They describe collaboration as a mutually beneficial and well-defined relationship entered into by two or more organizations to achieve common goals. The relationship includes a commitment to: (1) a shared vision and mutual goals; (2) a jointly developed structure, shared responsibility, and agreed-upon methods of communication; (3) mutual authority and account-ability for success; and (4) sharing of resources and rewards.

Coordination, cooperation, and collaboration are terms that are often used interchangeably but, in reality, they are very different things. Many grant applications call for some evidence of support from the community or other organizations, giving rise to countless "letters of support." These letters were generally regarded as courtesies that administrators extended to each other. With the advent of block grants, these courtesy letters are no longer sufficient. Funders and state officials have come to value—even demand—true collabo-ration.

Social service agencies that work with people in the poverty culture must close the gaps in the client's life cycle through effective collaboration. The table on pages 176 and 177 defines coordination, cooperation, and collaboration.

Example of collaboration: In a small, rural community, 10 agencies formed a network to provide services to the inmates of a new jail. The Life Skills Training (LST) Provider Network offered its services to the admin-istrator of the jail through one contract with a single unit cost. The network developed a common mission, philosophy, credentialing process, management information system, and quality improvement activities. One agency served as the administrative and fiscal agent for the network for which it was reimbursed by the other members. The network offered the following classes at the jail: GED preparation, résumé writing and job-search activities, alcohol/drug risk factors, parenting classes, healthy relationships, communicable diseases, anger management, stress management, goal-setting, and others. The network also contracted with the local welfare department to provide services to welfare-to-work participants and marketed its services to local employers as an Employee Assistance Program provider. The network provided staff-development classes to its own members on security issues and the poverty culture.

By the preceding definitions, the LST Provider Network is an example of collaboration.

- *Vision and goals:* All levels of each organization are invested in network activity. The leaders sign contracts, attend meetings, and advocate for the network. Mission and vision statements were developed early in the life of the group and are revisited frequently. The network has taken on four new projects.

- *Structure, responsibilities, and communication:* All network activities are coordinated, and the roles are defined. Grant and proposal writing, for example, are shared responsibilities. The network designed a database and computerized report writer that is maintained by a designated member. All levels of each organization are involved in communicating with the network. This is done through monthly meetings and via direct communication between front-line and middle-management staff.

- *Authority and accountability:* All network members are equal partners in the organization. The leadership structure is simple. A chairperson runs the monthly meetings. The members charged with administration and maintenance of the database report at the regular meetings.

Coordination, Cooperation, and Collaboration:

ESSENTIAL ELEMENTS	COORDINATION
VISION AND GOALS	Basis for coordination is usually between individuals.
	Individual missions and goals are not taken into account.
	Interaction is on as-needed basis.
STRUCTURE, RESPONSIBILITIES, AND COMMUNICATION	Relationships are informal; each organization functions separately.
	No planning is required.
	Information is conveyed at occasional intervals.
AUTHORITY AND ACCOUNTABILITY	Authority rests with individual organizations.
	Leadership is unilateral, and control is central.
	All authority and accountability rest with individual organization, which acts independently.
RESOURCES AND REWARDS	Resources (staff time, dollars, and capabilities) are separate, serving individual organization's needs.
	Rewards are specific to each organization.

A Table Describing the Elements of Each *

COOPERATION	COLLABORATION
Individual relationships are supported by organizations they represent.	Commitment of organizations and their leaders is fully behind their representatives.
Missions and goals of individual organizations are reviewed for compatibility.	Common new mission statement and goals are created.
Interaction is usually around one specific project or task of definable length.	One or more projects are undertaken for longer-term results.
Organizations involved take on needed roles, but they function relatively independently of each other.	New organizational structures and/or clearly defined and interrelated roles that constitute formal division of labor are created.
Some project-specific planning is required.	More comprehensive planning is required that includes developing joint strategies and measuring success in terms of impact on needs of those served.
Communication roles are established and definitive channels are created for interaction.	Beyond communication roles and channels for inter-action, many "levels" of communication are created —as clear information is keystone of success.
Authority rests with individual organizations, but there is cooperation among participants.	Authority rests with collaborative structure; individual organizations accept authority of group to achieve purpose for which it was formed.
There is some sharing of leadership and control.	Leadership is dispersed, and control is shared and mutual.
There is some shared risk, but most of authority and accountability falls to individual organization.	Risk is shared equally by all organizations in the collaborative structure.
Resources are acknowledged and can be made available to others for specific project.	Resources are pooled or jointly secured for longer-term effort that is managed by collaborative structure.
Rewards are mutually acknowledged.	Organizers share in products; more is accomplished jointly than could have been individually.

* Adapted from work of Paul Mattessich, Ph.D., and Barbara Monsey, M.P.H., who had compiled data from work of Martin Blank, Sharon Kagan, and Karen Ray

■ *Resources and rewards:* The network charges a single fee for services and is rewarded equally. Collaborative grant writing has been undertaken to extend services to populations for whom services would otherwise not be available. The network also was instrumental in changing Ohio law on how commissary funds can be used in county jails, thereby opening the door for a new funding source for jail services.

From Champy and Drucker we learn that partnerships are central to success in the private sector. We are told that businesses formerly grew from "grass roots" or by acquisition; now they grow through alliances. Downsizing too has led to alliances in which relationships between business entities are not based on ownership but on partnerships.

They both encourage partnerships between government and non-profits. Drucker says, ". . . [T]he delivery of welfare programs should be contracted out to non-governmental, community organizations as much as possible." He points to four factors for success: (1) Take advantage of emerging technology trends, (2) reduce cost, (3) minimize bureaucracy by making decisions and centralizing activity at the lowest possible level in the organization, and (4) do partnering.

This paradigm shift has now arrived at the doorstep of governmental entities and the non-profit social sector. Not only is it time to develop partnerships between government and non-profits, but among non-profits themselves. The table on pages 180 through 187, "Nineteen Factors Influencing the Success of Collaboration," is provided to define the elements of successful collaboration.

One planning group charged with the task of developing a Welfare-to-Work Community Plan called together the obvious organizations, plus a number of entities that might have an interest in contracting for some of the business. Group members kept the "Nineteen Factors" in front of them to review from time to time as they built their plan. They made conscious decisions to include middle-level and front-line staff in the design phase of the plan.

The planning group began by examining the client's life cycle of welfare recipients who used the services of the various agencies. A flowchart was developed to track a client through each of the agencies. An effort was made to see the experience through the customer's eyes so that the bureaucratic needs of the organizations didn't supersede the needs of the client. At the points where a client left one entity and went to another, special care was given to design referral and reporting procedures so that the client's experience was smooth.

Some features of the community plan that arose out of this planning process were:

- The client didn't have to repeat intake information for every agency he/she utilized. The state offered waivers on standards for each department represented, allowing common releases, intake data, and planning documents to be shared.

- The client's total needs were considered.

- As much as possible, the work with clients was strength-based. Client assets, both internal and external, were identified and built upon.

- Clients had a key contact that assisted them from the beginning of the process to the end. This person acted as case manager, mentor, and coach.

- A common management-information system was developed, largely as a result of keeping an eye on the "Nineteen Factors Influencing the Success of Collaboration." Clients were tracked through the entire process, and reports were made to the collaborative structure. They were seen as clients of the collective, not of the individual entities. An unduplicated count of individual clients was maintained.

Nineteen Factors Influencing the Success of Collaboration

FACTOR	DESCRIPTION
ENVIRONMENT	
1. History of collaboration in community.	History of collaboration or cooperation exists that offers potential partners understanding of roles and expectations, enabling them to trust process.
2. Collaborative group seen as leader in community.	Collaborative group is seen as leader, at least related to goals and activities it intends to accomplish.
3. Political/social climate favorable.	Political leaders, opinion-makers, those who control resources, public support, no obvious opposition to mission of group.
MEMBERSHIP	
4. Mutual respect, understanding, and trust.	Members share understanding of each other and their respective organizations (i.e., how they operate, cultural norms, values, limitations, and expectations).
5. Appropriate cross-section of members.	Collaborative group includes representatives from each segment of community that will be affected by its activities.

IMPLICATIONS

a. Goals should correspond to level at which collaboration is developed.

b. If there is little history of collaboration, address "environmental" issues before starting work (example: advocacy for legislation or funding that promotes collaboration, requiring education of potential collaborators).

c. Collaborators will have to address inhospitable environment, such as history of competition.

---

a. Must be perceived as legitimate leader by community it intends to influence.

b. Include assessment of group's leadership image—and correct it if necessary.

c. Communitywide projects will require broad legitimacy; smaller-scale projects will require legitimacy of narrower group.

---

a. Group must "sell" collaborative structure to key leaders.

b. If right climate doesn't exist, partners should plan strategies to change public commitment.

c. Set goals realistically to meet political and social requirements.

d. Goals and process should be seen as cost-effective and not in conflict with or drain on current endeavors.

---

a. In early stage of their work, partners should lay aside purpose of collaboration and devote energy to getting acquainted with each other.

b. Partners must present their intentions and agendas honestly and openly to facilitate building of trust.

c. Building strong relationships takes time.

d. Conflicts may develop.

e. Existing connections between partners may help with communication, trust, and sharing.

---

a. Carefully review membership needs, who has explicit and tacit control over relevant issues; invite them to participate.

b. Monitor whether new groups or individuals should be brought in; develop formal integration/education plan.

c. Membership that is too broad will become unmanageable.

Adapted from work of Paul W. Mattessich, Ph.D., and Barbara R. Monsey, M.P.H., *Collaboration: What Makes It Work—A Review of the Research Literature Describing Factors Which Influence the Success of Collaboration* (Amherst H. Wilder Foundation)

Nineteen Factors Influencing the Success of Collaboration (continued)

FACTOR	DESCRIPTION
MEMBERSHIP (continued)	
6. Members see collaboration as being in their self-interest.	Partners feel that collaboration, with its resulting loss of autonomy and "turf," will have benefits for them that exceed costs.
7. Ability to compromise.	Partners are able to compromise, since all decisions cannot possibly be molded to conform perfectly to preferences of each member.
PROCESS/STRUCTURE	
8. Members share stake in both process and outcome.	Group members feel "ownership" both in how group works and results of its work.
9. Multiple layers of decision-making.	Every level (upper management, middle management, operations) within each organization that is part of collaborative structure needs to participate in decision-making.
10. Flexibility.	Group remains open to varied ways of organizing itself and accomplishing its work.
11. Development of clear roles and policy guidelines.	Group clearly understands roles, rights, responsibilities— and how to carry out those responsibilities.

IMPLICATIONS

a. Make it clear that organizations will gain from collaboration; build those expectations into goals so they remain visible throughout life of group.

b. Build in incentives for organizations to get and stay involved; monitor whether those incentives continue to motivate members.

---

a. Representatives must have latitude in working out agreements; rigid rules and expectations will render collaboration unworkable.

b. Take time and be patient.

c. Members must know when to seek compromise or common ground and when to work through major decision points.

---

a. Devote time and resources to developing "ownership."

b. Operating principles and procedures must promote feeling of ownership.

c. Continuously monitor ownership and make changes in process/structure as required.

d. Developing interagency work groups, participating in regular planning, and monitoring effort can solidify ownership and ongoing commitment.

---

a. Create mechanisms to involve all layers.

b. At outset of collaboration, systems should be developed to include necessary staff from each organization.

c. Leadership may be insufficient to sustain major collaboration.

---

a. Flexibility needed in structure and methods.

b. Need and expectation for flexibility should be communicated at outset.

c. Monitoring group to ensure that it remains flexible is important, since groups often solidify their norms over time, thereby limiting their thinking and behavior.

---

a. Members need to reach agreement on roles, rights, responsibilities—and communicate them to all relevant parties.

b. Partners may need to adjust policies and procedures to reduce conflicts and competing demands on staff who work on collaborative issues.

c. People will gravitate toward their own interests; this tendency should be considered when making assignments.

Nineteen Factors Influencing the Success of Collaboration (continued)

FACTOR	DESCRIPTION
PROCESS/STRUCTURE (continued)	
12. Adaptability.	Group has ability to sustain itself in midst of major changes, even if it needs to change some major goals, members, etc., in order to deal with changing conditions.
COMMUNICATION	
13. Communication.	Group members interact often, update one another, discuss issues openly, convey all necessary information to one another and to people outside group.
14. Establish informal and formal communication links.	Channels of communication exist on paper, so that information flow occurs; members also establish personal connections that will produce better informed, more cohesive group working on common project.
PURPOSE	
15. Concrete, attainable goals and objectives.	Goals and objectives of group appear clear to partners and can realistically be attained.
16. Shared vision.	Partners share same vision with clearly agreed-upon mission, objectives, and strategy.

IMPLICATIONS

a. Group should stay aware of trends, environment, and directions of community and members.

b. Review vision and goals of group regularly and revise if necessary.

c. As member goals and outcomes change, it is important that collaborative goals and outcomes keep pace by group continually incorporating changes as necessary.

a. Set up system of communications and identify responsibilities of each member.

b. Staff function for communication may be necessary.

c. Provide incentives within and between organizations to reward or highlight effective communication.

a. Stable representation from each organization is needed to develop strong personal connections.

b. Meetings, trainings, and interagency work groups promote understanding, cooperation, and transfer of information.

c. Social time might be helpful for members of group.

d. Review systems regularly to upgrade and expand communications.

a. Clear, attainable goals will heighten enthusiasm.

b. Groups must experience some success in achieving objectives in order to be sustained.

c. Formulate clear goals and periodically report on progress.

d. Develop short- and long-term goals.

a. Group must develop shared vision, either when it's first planned or soon after it begins to function.

b. Engage in vision-building efforts and develop language and actions out of shared vision.

c. Technical assistance (outside consultation) may be useful to help establish common help vision.

Nineteen Factors Influencing the Success of Collaboration (continued)

FACTOR	DESCRIPTION
PURPOSE (continued)	
17. Unique purpose.	Mission and goals or approach of collaborative structure differ, at least in part, from mission and goals or approach of member organizations.
RESOURCES	
18. Sufficient funds.	Group requires adequate, consistent financial base to support its operations.
19. Skilled convener.	Individual who convenes group has organizing skills, interpersonal skills, reputation for fairness, and perceived legitimacy in convener role.

IMPLICATIONS

a. Mission and goals of group create "sphere of activity" that overlaps significantly but not completely with "spheres" of each member organization.

b. Mission and goals of each member of collaborative structure need to be known by all involved.

c. Development of collaboration among competing organizations around goals of each member may lead to failure; less demanding attempts to coordinate or cooperate might fare better.

a. Obtaining financial means for existence must be priority in forming group.

b. Collaborative work may be expensive in start-up phase; money should be available at outset.

c. Group needs to consider resources of its members, as well as approach outside sources, if necessary.

a. Care must be taken to choose convener with necessary skills.

b. Leaders of collaborative groups must give serious attention and care to convener role.

c. Grooming of new leaders and planning for transitions in leadership should be well-thought-out to avoid costly power struggles and loss of forward momentum.

- Each entity redesigned its internal processes to ensure that clients didn't fall through the cracks. Reports were made to the larger organization.

- Common goals were shared and tracked.

- Prevention programs were designed to help those at risk of losing their jobs to retain them, enhance the wellness of employees in general, and to provide immediate support if necessary.

- Funding of programs was managed through contracts with the Department of Human Services and the Welfare-to-Work Training Partnership Act/Private Industry Council.

WHAT IMPLICATIONS DOES THIS INFORMATION HAVE FOR COMMUNITIES THAT WORK WITH PEOPLE IN POVERTY?

- Clients will not fall through the cracks in the service-delivery system.

- Clients will no longer be blamed for the faults of the system.

- Service systems will improve.

- Staff knowledge of other systems, as well as appreciation for other disciplines and core competencies, will increase.

- The potential to capture competitive grants will improve.

- Outcomes will improve.

Crank is to coffee what sexual homicide is to a goodnight kiss. It's the black sheep of the speed family. Also called crystal meth, zip, or monster, crank is the rocket fuel for sputtering workers. Although supposedly a recreational drug—a fun thing—crank's usually taken to facilitate work performance. It treats your bloodstream as an assembly line and pushes up the production quota. . . . Crank is a homemade biohazardous brain-scalder produced by white outlaw chemists acting in the entrepreneurial tradition of their moonshining ancestors. . . . They disseminated illicit vitality to millions of (biker gangs and long-haul truckers) who couldn't afford to be tired.

– Jim Goad, *The Redneck Manifesto*

■ ■ ■ ■ ■ ■ ■

Poverty Culture, Addiction, Treatment, and Recovery

POVERTY AND ADDICTION

Given the prevalence of addiction in our society, it can be argued that every American should become an expert on addiction. Few of us make it through middle school without encountering the effects of addiction; by the time we graduate from high school more than 6% of our classmates have developed serious drinking or other drug problems.

Fifteen to 20% of people in poverty are thought to have substance-abuse problems, so recent welfare-reform strategies call for collaboration between those who provide treatment and TANF (Temporary Assistance for Needy Families) organizations.

Certainly, professionals who work with people in poverty should make it a core competency to understand addiction. The disease deeply affects individuals, their families, friends, co-workers, neighbors, and our society in the most profound ways. It is so powerful that all efforts to eradicate it have failed, and societal problems associated with it continue to grow.

This chapter is not designed to provide that education. That will have to be earned by attending workshops, 12-step meetings, and reading. In this chapter we make recommendations about contracting for assessments, referrals, and treatment. We examine some of the aspects of addiction and poverty that make recovery and change so complicated. Finally, we look at the features of Alcoholics Anonymous (AA) that provide hope for change. Not only can people recover from addiction, they can use the process of recovery as a model for other changes.

ALCOHOL/DRUG ASSESSMENTS: PRACTICAL CONSIDERATIONS

The stories of people trapped in poverty by their addictions are countless. For them, efforts to change are ruined by crisis and chaos brought on by addictive lifestyles. When addiction and poverty culture combine to bring a person to the door of a welfare agency, an opportunity to identify and treat the person is created. To miss that opportunity is to participate in the entrapment of the addict just like a family member who "enables" the addict with just enough support to keep the addict alive while the disease worsens.

Federal and state planners are quite right in demanding that treatment facilities and welfare agencies work together to identify those with addictions and offer them treatment. Given the impact of addiction on families and given the delusional nature of the addictive mind, it would be wise for planners to give this phase of the client's life cycle and internal processes considerable attention. Who is to do the assessment? What training and skills are needed to do it accurately? Should the work of assessments be outsourced? If so, what should the contract cover?

Consider these features of addiction:

Addiction is a primary illness, not the symptom of some other disorder or problem. Just as stomach ulcers due to drinking won't truly be healed until the patient stops drinking, so it is that poverty is not likely to be overcome if the addiction is still active. As with any other primary disease, addiction has a distinct set of symptoms. The work of the person doing the assessment is complicated because: (1) The symptoms and the consequences of the alcohol and other drug use are disguised from the addicts themselves, (2) the addicts may consciously subvert the history-taking process because they don't want to stop using, and (3) they may not be motivated to do any more than play the game so that they can get their immediate needs met.

Addiction is progressive. This means that, left untreated, addiction will always get worse. It doesn't, however, get worse in a predictable pattern. The problems and symptoms might steadily and relentlessly worsen over time, or they might also progress in fits and starts as the addicted person struggles to control his/her use in an attempt to avoid the consequences that come with drug abuse. The person doing the assessment must be aware of the early-, middle-, and late-stage symptoms. The exact nature of an individual's addiction can initially be difficult to determine with precision. A thorough history is needed to expose the hidden addiction.

Addiction is chronic. Treatment isn't a surgical procedure that removes the problem once and for all. Addicts are prone to relapse; no matter how many years have transpired since a person stopped using, the disease will quickly be reactivated if he/she starts using again.

Addiction is a family illness. Everyone in the family is affected by the drinking and drug use, its consequences, and the efforts to survive. A complex enabling system usually grows up around the addict, which has the effect of keeping the addict from suffering the full impact of the consequences of his/her addiction. Someone in the family will take on the responsibilities of the addict, others will clean up after him/her, "solving" the addict's problems and making excuses. Others will make the family look good by becoming family heroes, and someone will become the jokester who dispels tension and keeps everyone laughing. Each person's role is designed to keep the family system (and thus the addiction) going.

Addiction is fatal. Left untreated, addiction leads to an early death. Physical complications, accidents, and violence take their toll.

Addiction is treatable. Outcome studies indicate that treatment works; for those people who have jobs, work performance improves following treatment.

ADEQUATE ASSESSMENTS

There are two ways to ensure that adequate assessments are done. First, the welfare agency could train staff and purchase the necessary screening instruments to do a thorough screening for clients. A screening should not be mistaken for an assessment; it is only a search for red flags and doesn't gather enough data to make a diagnosis. Red flags may include some of the more obvious symptoms of the disease, such as blackouts, withdrawal, and physical deterioration. Screenings also include a review of such consequences of alcohol and other drug use as accidents, arrests, emergency-room visits, and the like. Those who are red-flagged would be sent to a treatment provider for a complete assessment.

The disadvantage of doing in-house screenings is that some of the early- and middle-stage cases may be missed. A welfare-to-work participant with an undiagnosed addiction may get well into the three-year time limit before his/her primary problem is identified. In essence, the individual is being set up for failure.

The second method is to arrange for a treatment provider to do the screening and/or assessment. A contract with a provider should include the following elements . . .

1. *Agency qualifications*: Treatment programs are certified by state departments and/or private credentialing entities. Private, for-profit entities may join the mix of community-based, private, non-profit, and public providers (that have traditionally served the poor) to bid for welfare-reform business. As the competition heats up, the cost of treatment will likely drop. When choosing a provider, one should remember that price isn't everything. Access is important. Where do the clients have to go for an assessment? Are there evening and weekend hours? Is there a waiting list? How quickly will they be seen? The quality of treatment and mix of community support services should also be examined. Some providers have little experience working with coerced clients or people from the poverty culture. These skills too should be required. The provider of assessment services can be asked to conduct and report on satisfaction surveys of welfare-to-work participants to ascertain their opinions of the services.

2. *Staff qualifications*: Each state has its own method for credentialing professionals who work in addictions. Check with your state department for this information. Be certain to include in the contract the credentials of the staff who will be responsible for direct care. Certified chemical-dependency counselors (names vary by state)

are sufficiently qualified to work with addictions, yet the current managed care thrust is to require higher degrees and credentials. This has the effect of limiting access to services and raising costs, as there are fewer professionals who can deliver the service.

3. *Assessment elements*: An adequate assessment will include no fewer than two written instruments and an interview covering all life domains. Consequences of alcohol and other drug use should be thoroughly explored, as should the symptoms of the disease. The best assessments include an interview with at least one other family member. Some providers are doing group and one-day assessments. The details of these, along with the process used by the provider, need to be compared with those of other potential contractors. One-session assessments should be viewed with an extremely critical eye.

4. *Drug-testing*: Clients entering the workforce will need to be prepared for pre-employment drug-testing, so requiring drug-testing of program participants may make some sense. On the other hand, overreliance on drug-testing as an assessment tool can lead to missed diagnoses. Most, but not all, drugs will be on the panel, which means that some drug users will not be identified. Also, alcohol is difficult to test for. It is a legal drug, and it also detoxes out of the body in a very short time. Reliance on drug-testing tends to draw the energy and focus away from doing a meaningful assessment. Employers, agencies, and schools that drug-test tend to use it as a benchmark: "Ninety-five percent of our population is drug-free." The facts may be different. Any organization contemplating drug-testing should also know that boundaries must be established to avoid unethical practices. Drug-testing should be used only to determine illicit drug use and not to determine or discover pregnancy, the use of prescribed drugs for mental-health purposes, or health-related problems of a potential employee.

REFERRALS TO TREATMENT AND CONTRACTING FOR TREATMENT SERVICES

When considering a contract with substance abuse treatment providers you will want to cover the following elements:

1. *Treatment modality:* What is the treatment approach or philosophy of the organization? Is it a 12-step, behavioral, or cognitive model? Is it a combination of modalities? Does it feature "brief" therapy? In order to contain treatment costs, managed care organizations have put pressure on treatment programs to shorten the number of sessions that a client receives or the length of stay—this despite the fact that research shows that the longer clients are involved in treatment the better they do. Most treatment programs in the United States are based on the 12-step model of Alcoholics Anonymous and introduce their clients to 12-step programs during treatment.

2. *Access:* How long will it take your clients to be served? Where will they have to go? Are evening hours available? Obviously, the easier and quicker the access the better. Ask for initial appointment and waiting-list reports.

3. *Levels of care:* A contract should describe the levels of care provided by the agency. These may include outpatient treatment, intensive outpatient programming (IOP), ambulatory detox, medically monitored detox, inpatient, and residential halfway house. The more levels of care that are available to your clients the better. Treatment technology has improved considerably in the last decade, so that many clients can be served by community-based outpatient treatment programs.

4. *Credentials:* Any contract should describe the credentials of the

staff who will be providing treatment. Once again, you can check with your state department about the standards in your state.

5. *Outcomes:* You need to know exactly what a treatment program measures, which results are considered important. Some organizations have "report cards" that present outcomes about their treatment program. You should know that there are stages of recovery, just as there are stages in the progression of the disease. These are described in the developmental model of recovery (DMR) as observable behaviors that can be itemized. They include abstinence from alcohol and other drug use but also describe the lifestyle changes that are required of someone who is developing a sober way of life. Some states have standardized outcome measures. Check with the department responsible for substance-abuse treatment in your state.

6. *Feedback:* A contract should cover frequency and content of reports on the client's progress. Confidentiality releases, according to federal laws, need to be specific and time-limited. Clients have the right to withdraw them at any time. Clients should know ahead of time what will happen if they pull their releases. Ask for summary reports on your clients on a regular basis, so that at a glance your staff can check their progress.

7. *Support services:* A contract should detail the support services available to clients. Transportation, child care, case management, wraparound, and family and children services enhance outcomes considerably. The more support services an agency has the better.

8. *Grievances:* What mechanisms are in place for the client to file a grievance? Reports on grievances filed by clients referred by your organization should be made available to you.

RECOVERY FROM ADDICTION AND CLIMBING OUT OF POVERTY

For addicts and alcoholics from generational poverty, recovery is not an automatic ride out of poverty. Consider Paul's story.

Paul had two part-time jobs. He was the driver for a substance-abuse treatment facility and the night manager of a homeless shelter. Neither of the jobs paid well or offered health insurance. Paul had an apartment with his girlfriend, but because of their frequent fights, he would often live with his ex-wife.

At the time that Paul read *A Framework for Understanding Poverty* he had 11 years sobriety and was active in AA. His program of recovery had brought about significant changes in his lifestyle. Fighting, stealing, and other criminal behavior were things of the past. Paul was now honest, direct, dependable, humorous, humble, and willing to ask for help and accept feedback. There were, however, many things that Paul did not have. His expectation that long-term sobriety would bring about "the good things of life" wasn't coming true. He didn't have a good job, a house, stable relationships with women, financial security, or (for that matter) much hope of ever having those things.

As he said after reading the book, "Of all the things in the book I could relate to, the thing that made the most sense to me was the bit about being fated. I figured that this was just the way my life was meant to be." Paul was raised in generational poverty, and many of the hidden rules of that culture continued to sabotage his attempts to climb out of poverty, even after his recovery. He continued to distrust organizations and hold them and the people in them to high standards of conduct. When the organizations and people failed to meet those standards, he quit in disgust. The life changes he had made and his obvious intelligence would earn him good job opportunities that would later be sabotaged by his inability to use the formal register to write or to negotiate with supervisors and co-workers. The mating dance and his identify as a fighter/lover caused problems at work and at home, contributing to his chaotic lifestyle.

COMPLICATING ISSUES

Someone who has coexisting problems of poverty and addiction is obviously going to have a very hard time making long-lasting lifestyle changes. Addiction may complicate attempts to escape poverty, and poverty may complicate attempts to get clean and sober. What exactly is it that makes it so difficult? The following is an attempt to present key aspects of the poverty culture and corresponding features of addiction in parallel columns. By reading the two, one can begin to see how interwoven the conditions are, how the two problems feed each other.

Addiction and Poverty

Survival-Culture Characteristics	Features of Addiction
Self-image, episodic memory, fatalistic attitude, and lack of motivation make it difficult to see the need to change.	Addicts cannot see the problem they have with drugs because they have learned to rationalize and explain away the consequences of alcohol/drug use. Addicts cannot see the problem because of memory issues associated with their alcohol/drug use. Blackouts rob them of vital information about their behavior by simply not storing in their memory the things they did while under the influence. The repression of painful memories also robs them of information they need to see their addiction. The addict's self-image is not based on reality.
Discipline: Punishment is about penance and forgiveness, not about change. Ownership of people: People are possessions. There is a great deal of fear and comment about leaving the culture and "getting above your raisings." Importance of relationships: One only has people upon which to rely, and those relationships are important to survival.	Most addicts have an enabling system of people who will cover for them, clean up after them, lecture them, assist them, care for them, and forgive them. Their enabling system absorbs the pain and consequences of the alcohol/drug use, thus robbing them of the chance to learn from the pain or correct their own mistakes. Addicts use their enabling system to survive and to retain their primary relationship with their drug of choice. They often manipulate the people in their enabling system to keep it intact. "I'll leave you (kill myself, kill you, run away) if you..."

Addiction and Poverty (continued)

Survival-Culture Characteristics	Features of Addiction
Identity is tied to lover/fighter roles for men and rescuer/martyr role for women. The rules are rigid: A man is expected to work hard, be a lover and fighter; a good woman takes care of and rescues her man and children.	In families where there is addiction, survival roles are established to help the family deal with frequent crises that arise from the alcohol/drug use. The spouse generally becomes the chief enabler, taking on additional responsibilities and relieving the addict/alcoholic of his/her responsibilities. The eldest child will often act as the family hero to make the family look good and bring balance and stability back to the situation. Other children will take on the roles of scapegoat, the lost child, and the clown. Each role assists the family in hanging together as a unit and weathering the storms.
The importance of entertainment, humor, and personality: When one can only survive, then any respite from the survival struggle is important. Entertainment brings respite. Individual personality is what one brings to the setting because money is not brought. The ability to entertain, tell stories, and be funny are valued.	In the early stages of the disease, preoccupation with alcohol/drug use increases, and a pattern of use is established. During this phase the spouse and family may enjoy the socializing that goes with the alcohol/drug use. A tolerance is developed, demanding larger dosages and activities, and some relationships are given up in order to make time for alcohol/drug use. The addict gravitates toward people who use as he/she does. Later, as the disease progresses, the family falls under rigid rules: Keep the family secrets, don't talk, don't trust, don't feel; even family members can't be relied upon. For the alcoholic/addict, the drugs become the only solution. For the family members, their survival roles become their only solution. Humor and entertainment are key survival techniques for a family in deep trouble with addiction.

Addiction and Poverty (continued)

Survival-Culture Characteristics	Features of Addiction
Lives in the moment—does not consider future ramifications: Being proactive, setting goals, planning ahead are not a part of generational poverty. Most of what occurs is reactive and in the moment.	Addicts and their families lead reactive lives. They are constantly having to react to crisis, unpredictable behavior, and problems brought on by alcohol/drug use. Efforts to control the drug use by the addict, along with efforts by the family to control the addict, fail repeatedly. The family members cannot plan ahead with any certainty.
Casual-register language and episodic story pattern may result in an episodic, random memory pattern and thus make learning difficult. A failure to provide children with adequate mediation will likely result in cognitive deficiencies.	Alcohol/drug use can cause memory problems other than blackouts and repression. When a person stops using and has detoxed, he/she often experiences short-term memory problems as part of post-acute withdrawal (PAW). During the six to twelve months of PAW, the individual also may experience emotional swings, cognitive interruptions, and sleep disturbances.
	Women who drink during their pregnancies expose their children to Fetal Alcohol Syndrome (FAS) and Fetal Alcohol Effects (FAE). FAS often causes mental and physical retardation. Symptoms of FAE may include problems with impulsivity. Drug-affected babies and their mothers have great difficulty bonding because the babies cannot handle the stimulation required to bond.
	Alcoholics/addicts may not provide sufficient mediation for their children. They spend time planning to use, using, and recovering from using. They are often away from home and/or emotionally absent.

People in the poverty culture and in homes where there is addiction have complex and compounding problems. The poverty culture can be seen as an ideal environment for the development and entrenchment of addiction. First, it provides a norm of heavy drinking and drug use. Here is how Jim Goad describes it: "Working-class amusement is always too much. It operates from an Overdose Aesthetic. It's nominally leisure, but it often seems more like an endurance test. You don't make love, you f--- your brains out. You don't laugh, you piss yourself laughing. You don't listen to music, you pump up the volume until your ears bleed. You don't drink, you drink yourself blind. You don't want to get high. You want to get F----- UP. BLASTED. OBLITERATED. You don't punch someone, you beat the shit out of him, kick the snot out of him, and thrash him until he pisses blood."

In this environment individuals could be long into their disease before it would look any different than the drinking and drug using that is happening around them (e.g., "My drinking isn't near as bad as John's"). It would disguise the disease from the victim, as well as from the others in their family. The consequences of drinking that would make a middle-class alcoholic sit up and take notice, such as an arrest and a night in jail, are not unusual occurrences for people in the poverty culture.

It has been said that ours is an addictive society. Our culture facilitates those who abuse alcohol and other drugs. Wealthy addicts and alcoholics are enabled by their wealth and status. For a long time money can solve problems caused by alcohol and drug abuse. Connections in high places can protect middle-class folks from consequences. They live in the suburbs, isolated from their extended families and neighbors by distance and backyard fences. Their secrets can more easily be kept. As long as no one knows what's really going on, the disease can progress. Alcoholics in any culture—regardless of its norms and attitudes of its members toward addiction—will find that an enabling system will grow up around them. Such is the nature and power of the disease.

The poverty culture also is an enabling culture. It will automatically follow that friends, relatives, and lovers will try to help the alcoholic and, in their ignorance of the disease, will eventually be drawn into covering up, protecting, and cleaning up after the alcoholic. In the case of the alcoholic or addict in the poverty culture, he/she finds a ready-made enabling system. The women are already taught to rescue their men, to be martyrs. The matriarchal structure ensures that there is a fall-back position for any man whose wife lays down the law about his drinking and kicks him out. He can always count on his mother to take him in. Doing penance with the important women in his life and waiting out their anger will earn their forgiveness and, in this culture, no one will expect real changes to be made. The women can be angry for a while, but they can't afford to burn bridges with anyone, for they might need that person again someday to fix a car or give them money. People are possessions. Hope, love, relationships, and a fuzzy view of the future will keep the cycle of drinking-related problems and broken promises going for a long time.

PROFESSIONAL ENABLING

Workers in the fields that serve the poverty culture who don't understand the dynamics of addiction often become enablers themselves, because they can be and will be confused. Not having asked the questions about alcohol and other drug use, they go on a search for understanding. They grasp for theories or accept the explanations of the addict or the family members: "He drinks because he's depressed. His dad died last winter and he hasn't been the same. She was abused as a child, and now she has an abusive husband." Alcoholics and addicts who by definition want to protect their primary relationship— their drugs—will take advantage of the ignorant and confused and manipulate them so that they can continue using.

Those who choose to work with people from the poverty culture must commit themselves to learning about addiction so that they can avoid the confusion that drives the disease. They are working with two very powerful dynamics: a culture to which their client *belongs* and a disease that *owns* the client. The coexisting dynamics don't respond to isolated and confused individuals, and they won't respond to isolated agencies with confused programs and processes.

TREATMENT AND CHANGE

It's ironic and paradoxical that in addiction, with all of its complexities and despair, lies the hope for change for addicts and alcoholics from the poverty culture. Addiction is one door through which people may pass on their way to new ways of life. Having an addiction is how you start moving toward a new lifestyle of recovery. Even though Paul didn't move out of poverty despite being in recovery, there is now hope that he will. Having learned about poverty culture, he can name the problem: "I'm stuck in poverty, and I'm stuck in a culture. Am I ready to give up many of my relationships for achievement? Do I have the tools I need to make the move? Do I need a mentor?" If he is motivated, he can apply the strategies he learned from his recovery from addiction to work his way out of poverty. Let's examine how the process of recovery holds within it the tools, skills, and relationships required to move out of poverty.

A Comparison of What It Takes to Get Out of Poverty with the Process of Recovery from Addiction

To Get Out of Poverty	What Happens in Recovery from Addiction
People in the survival culture need motivation to move from poverty to middle class. Self-image can be a barrier and may need to be changed.	In order to recover, alcoholics and addicts must experience the consequences of their alcohol and drug use (i.e., "I was sick and tired of being sick and tired"). The delusional self-image must be replaced with a vision of what is real. The work of the 12 steps restores the person to sanity.
To move from poverty to middle class, an individual must give up many relationships for achievement.	To move from the drug culture to a lifestyle of recovery one must be in "dry places with dry people." Recovery can mean making 180-degree changes. Giving up alcohol/drugs and the using crowd starts a grieving process that must be acknowledged and dealt with.

A Comparison of What It Takes to Get Out of Poverty with the Process of Recovery from Addiction (continued)

To Get Out of Poverty	What Happens in Recovery from Addiction
People in the poverty culture must learn the hidden rules of the middle class.	The rituals of AA are learned by going to a lot of meetings. Newcomers are encouraged to go to "90 meetings in 90 days." The meetings have a structure and ritual that are simple and welcoming. AA is based on the 12 steps and 12 traditions. These form the basis of recovery and the fellowship of AA.
It helps to have someone teach you the ropes.	In AA members are encouraged to ask someone who works "a good program" to be their sponsor. This person should know and be working the 12 steps of recovery himself/herself. The sponsor is more than a friend, he/she is a guide.
Mediation is needed to explain the stimuli, meaning, and strategies of past issues and present conditions.	AA mediates the drinkers' past experiences by exposing them to a series of speakers who share their leads or stories. They describe their own drinking, "what it was like," and thus point to the stimuli. This is reframed in terms of the disease— "I am an alcoholic"—thus providing the meaning. Next the speaker tells "what I did," thereby providing strategies. Finally the speaker tells "what it's like now," which offers hope. This is mediation at its best.

continued on next page

A Comparison of What It Takes to Get Out of Poverty
with the Process of Recovery from Addiction (continued)

To Get Out of Poverty	What Happens in Recovery from Addiction
People in poverty need to learn how to use formal and consultative language registers, along with the casual register. New story structures need to be learned, as the episodic storytelling structure is ineffective for storing memory or communicating clearly.	AA leads or speakers often use the casual register to tell their stories. The three-part format (what it was like, what I did, and what it's like now) teaches a simple story structure with a beginning, a middle, and an end. It helps in remembering. Over the course of the meetings the listener will hear some stories by speakers who also model formal and consultative registers.
People in the poverty culture value relationships, entertainment, and humor.	AA members often gather for coffee after the meetings. Humor plays a large part in the fellowship and in storytelling. Relationships, entertainment, and humor continue to be valued, but honesty, humility, and becoming accountable are values that are also very important. New values are taught.
People in poverty need to be afforded the respect of making choices about their lives—whether or not they want to build or cross bridges to the middle class.	AA is a choice. Meetings are opened with a statement acknowledging that the AA program doesn't work for everyone. Members are encouraged to "take what you want and leave the rest."
People from the poverty culture must overcome their general distrust of organizations.	The 12 Traditions of AA describe an organization with no entrenched leadership. Chairmanship and other roles rotate among the members. AA is not affiliated with any other organization, including treatment centers. There are no dues.

A Comparison of What It Takes to Get Out of Poverty
with the Process of Recovery from Addiction (continued)

To Get Out of Poverty	What Happens in Recovery from Addiction
Some people from the poverty culture will need to develop cognitive structures.	The AA fellowship, its slogans, and the sponsors provide mediation. Short-term memory problems are mediated through the use of short, memorable phrases, such as: *HALT (Don't get too Hungry, Angry, Lonely, or Tired); Easy Does It; Live and Let Live; One Day at a Time; Think, Think, Think; Let Go and Let God.* Sponsors and others in the fellowship interrupt impulsive behavior by encouraging the newcomers not to make important decisions for a year and to ask for the help of others to "reason things out."
Memory problems and self-image make change difficult for most people from the poverty culture. The use of metaphor assists people in learning about themselves, then choosing new behaviors.	AA is one of the few remaining oral traditions. The many leads that are heard over the course of the first year are metaphors for the life of individual alcoholics. They can identify with the feelings (if not the precise particulars) of "how it used to be," they can get new ideas for managing their lives from "what we did," and they can begin to visualize the telling of their own story when they hear "what it's like now." The story structure begins to build memory and store it where it can be found. A new self-image can be built: "I'm an alcoholic, a recovering alcoholic."
Gender roles may need to be changed. The fighter/lover role for men and martyr/rescuer role for women tend to keep the pattern of crisis revolving.	People new to the program are encouraged to avoid serious romantic relationships for at least a year. Spouses, significant others, and family members are encouraged to attend Al-Anon meetings.

Those familiar with AA know its remarkable depth. As a vehicle for change, it has elements of many therapeutic approaches: cognitive therapy, behavioral therapy, rational emotive therapy, and others.

Interestingly, much of the transforming power of AA comes from story-telling. Ernest Kurtz, who has studied and written about AA, says in *The Spirituality of Imperfection:* "The stories that sustain a spirituality of imperfection are wisdom-stories. They follow a temporal format, describing, 'what we used to be like, what happened, and what we are like now.' Such stories, however, can also do more: the sequential format makes it possible for other people's stories to become part of 'my' story. Sometimes, for example, hearing another's story can occasion profound change. Telling the story of that change then follows the format of telling a story within my story: 'Once upon a time, I did not understand this very well; but then I heard this story, and now I understand it very differently.' "

Storytelling, we have learned, is suited to the poverty culture for its entertainment value and because of how it builds relationships, helps with developing cognitive structures, and the storing of memory. But what about spirituality? Does spirituality play a role in the way one leaves the poverty culture? If so, how? And, even if it does, should the organizations that work at welfare reform do anything about it?

Kurtz again: "The language of recovery that is storytelling involves not dogma or commandment, not things to be done or truths to be believed, not theory, conjecture, argument, analysis, or explanation, but a way of conversation shared by those who accept and identify with their own imperfection. Following the tradition of Western spirituality, AA aims to convey experience rather than to 'teach' concepts. . . . [T]he 'language of recovery' works, not because those telling their stories describe Release, Gratitude, and so on, but because, in the very telling of their stories, they actually experience those realities."

AA generates change without a heavy organizational structure or any agenda other than that people who want to stop drinking go to the meetings and work the 12 steps. Ernie Kurtz's words bring up perhaps the greatest difference between welfare reform as it's being conceived and recovery from addiction. Those involved in substance-abuse treatment know that change from addiction to recovery is, at least in part, a spiritual journey. Of course, no one is suggesting that moving from the poverty culture to middle class is a spiritual journey, or that the attainment of any economic class should be a spiritual goal. So it isn't sensible for organizations involved in welfare reform to take on the role of spiritual guide, but the people in them can acknowledge that spirituality can and probably does play an important role in any major change.

The parallels between what is needed by people who wish to bridge out of poverty and those who wish to recover from addiction are striking. What AA offers alcoholics seems to be a possible model for people working out of poverty. It offers a way to change self-image, learn new rules, change relationships, and move toward a new lifestyle. It uses memory aids, metaphor, story, mentors, mediation, and cognitive restructuring. Does it offer a model for recovering addicts to use to move out of poverty? Perhaps. Is it a model for people in poverty (who are not addicts) to use to move out of poverty? No more so than it's a model for a healthy lifestyle for anyone to adopt as a way of life. That, of course, is saying a lot.

WHAT IMPLICATIONS DOES THIS INFORMATION HAVE FOR THOSE WHO PROVIDE SUBSTANCE ABUSE TREATMENT?

Treatment programs, no matter how closely their philosophy and treatment approach approximate AA, are more like other agencies and social service organizations than they are like AA. After all, they have boards, administrators, tables of organization, policies, mission statements, budgets, goals, outcome measures, programs, projects, and employees. For that reason the administrators and staff of those agencies might want to examine their core competencies, personal skills, internal processes, and collaborative arrangements just like any other organization. Until the client's life cycle is examined closely through every step of his/her treatment, how is an agency to be sure that those from the poverty culture are being well-served?

Epilogue

This book would not be complete without including the stories of individuals who have endeavored to build and then cross their own bridges of economic class. Included here are paraphrases of interviews conducted for this project. The summaries are written in first person so that the stories may reflect the timbre and tone of each person interviewed. Summaries are divided into three sections which tell of the way things were in poverty, the process of bridging, and finally, the current situation at the time of the interviews. These stories are similar to the scenarios in Chapter One, with the exception that the Epilogue stories demonstrate how resources and circumstances worked together to create positive change in the lives of real people!

The Epilogue is presented with a minimum of embellishment in order to clearly illustrate the complexities and variations that exist within the framework discussed in the previous chapters. It is left to the reader to determine how this framework of hidden rules, internal and external resources, and life experiences were woven together to make a difference in the lives of four women.

The authors very much appreciate the contributions of these women to this book.

LORI

Background: The Way It Was

In my childhood, my teachers described me as "spirited," a trait I believe has served me well. When I was 9 years old, I had that intense realization that "comes over" some children who are raised in families like mine. I felt as if my family was "foreign" to what and who I was. I thought, "This is crazy. I'm not going to live my life like this." I vowed I would do whatever I could to improve my life. There was a vague sense something was amiss, that the family dynamics were wrong at some level. More than anything, I desired a life in which I had some control over my circumstances.

Most of my adult relatives had not attended high school. My family lived in the projects in a large Eastern city. I was the fourth of five children, having two brothers and two sisters. My Dad worked in a steel mill and was an alcoholic. He lost that job and all his other jobs due to his drinking. My mother never worked outside the home once she was married. The entire family experienced repeated crises, which put us further in "the hole." On both sides of the family, very few of the women worked. We were all on welfare.

Even when I was little, I sensed that a life on welfare was not a life that included personal power. Someone else has control of your life. My father had established a pattern of leaving for long intervals. When I was 5 years old, he left for good, and we never heard from him again. Six years later, he was found dead and destitute in a ditch (literally) 1,000 miles away. Since he had no identification, it had taken the authorities 30 days to identify him. Ironically, this marked my family's "progress" by moving us from welfare to Social Security. Incredibly, this was a "step up." My mother purchased a washer and dryer. This was true luxury!

I honestly was embarrassed by my family. My mom took on the "martyr" role, looking after everyone else, never taking care of her own physical or emotional needs. I was ashamed of my mother and often introduced her to my friends as my grandmother. Once I talked Mom into getting a perm and being more concerned about how she dressed. However, these changes in her appearance were short-lived. Mom just did not value those types of things. Even at a young age, I was determined to not model this.

School was precious to me. When I was 14 years old, we moved to the Midwest where my sister Jean had settled after her marriage. My other sister, Linda, had dropped out of school at age 15 and had a baby at the age of 17.

Linda later decided to go back to school and ended up in my high school class, even though she was in her late 20s at this point. "Great!" I thought. "How dare you steal my time?" I asked that we be placed in separate classes. My school time belonged only to me.

My fifth-grade art teacher had allowed me to be "a class helper," setting the stage for what occurred with the next art teacher. He would let me spend time in the art room, doing various jobs. It made me feel useful and special, increasing my self-image. I remember that he mailed me a postcard from Alaska and brought me a polished rock from his vacation. He treated me with respect.

When he moved on to another job, I met Mrs. Carter, who was highly nurturing. She let me spend time in the art room as her helper, but she would sometimes take me home to her townhouse if we were out running errands after school. This was the first time I ever saw a middle-class home. I met her husband and little 3-year-old girl, who was simply charming. Mrs. Carter told me how she had become an art teacher by attending the University of Maryland. I was stunned by the beautiful original artwork in her home, with how the furniture matched, with little extras such as candles and ceramic pieces. I decided to be an art teacher.

When Mrs. Carter dropped me off at my house in the projects, she never expressed displeasure or shock at my home and family. Even my mother liked Mrs. Carter. I remember thinking, "She accepts me for me." Mrs. Carter planted "incredible seeds" for me, opening the window to a life that I had not previously known. She was a truly genuine person. Mrs. Carter assisted me with goal-setting. She was a fine teacher who helped develop my art talent. She told me, "You must have an education to get out of where you are. You too can have a nice house and a caring husband." I began to want to go to college in order to become "just like Mrs. Carter." Can you imagine that I had not previously heard anyone talk about college, especially in such detail? So, art became my "First Love." I had a plan. During a sixth-grade field trip to the University of Maryland, I told the other children, "This is where I'm going."

I actively sought out new friends in my high school. I had a sense of who would be beneficial to develop as a friend. Three good friends helped me learn about their lives. I had a girlfriend who even had a horse! I was invited to dinner at their home, and I was surprised at the number of forks and spoons at each place setting! All three friends lived in beautiful homes. How to dress, fashion, make-up, and proper social skills were all part of what I learned from them. One young woman lived in a single-parent home with her father. Her friend's father was like no male in my family! It was amazing how well he parented and cooked! One of the girls was African-American. Our families were somewhat concerned about this relationship. In fact, I was thankful to learn about different lifestyles and cultures. I was extremely eager to remove myself from my own culture. Academically, I enjoyed great success. My classwork came easily to me. It is probably my achievement in school that gained me positive attention from my classmates and teachers.

I imagine that I was considered a "model Christian teen" by my church. We moved to the Midwest, and my family became involved in a conservative Apostolic church. The rules of the church were that women were never to cut their hair, were to be conservative in dress, and that the youth were not to spend too much time away from the other church members. Even though the church was strict, the structure of the church helped me avoid parties and behaviors that could have jeopardized my progress. The spiritual nature of the church was generally supportive in helping me believe that there was hope. However, as I look back on the church group now, I identify that the group oppressed individual growth, even while providing safeguards.

The only other church experience my family had was attending Vacation Bible Schools (VBS) each summer. Basically, my family sought out these events because they were "freebies" offered by the church. They were fun and provided food; basically VBS was considered a "resource" to my family. The churches often helped out at holidays with food baskets and clothing.

Bridges

When we moved to the Midwest at age 14, I explored some art schools, but realized art education was not what I really wanted. Commercial art was more attractive to me, but through college visits I discovered that these schools treated students as a commodity, a number. I sensed that this was a competitive field that would "take the fun" out of art as I knew it. Honestly, I craved warmth.

I started getting desperate about my college plans the summer after high school graduation. I visited a community college, which was close to home, and I thought the campus was gorgeous! Looking back, I see this as a rather humorous way to choose an institution of higher learning.

I was uncertain about which field to enter. I wanted to make good money, be with warm people, and do something enjoyable. One of my required courses was Applied Psychology, which I thought was fascinating. During the quarter, I made friends with a woman who was majoring in Mental Health/Mental Retardation. That somehow sounded good to me. So I "fell into" that field. It happened to be the right choice.

During my second year, my family and the members of the church began to express negative attitudes toward getting an Associate's Degree. "Who do you think you are?" "What makes you think you will get a job?" "You're not the same." "You're pulling away from us." The members of the church denounced college as "humanist." I wanted to be physically and emotionally separated from home. I knew I needed to be away from this negative energy toward my accomplishments. I'm still unsure how that insight came about. Now that I look back, I see that I basically severed all old relationships and sought out new ones. This was an unsettling experience, to say the least. Now I realize this was the hardest thing I ever did!

During my college years, encouragement came from several areas: classmates, supervisors at the school and at field experience sites, and from a friend who was a physician. He encouraged me to go on to get a Bachelor's Degree and not "settle" for just the Associate's Degree. He told me, "You're too smart. Don't you dare stop now." I took his advice.

Current Situation: The Way It Is

I did continue to attend college throughout my adult life. I now hold a Master's Degree in Social Work and am working on my doctorate. I met my husband in one of my classes at the community college. He was from a lower-middle-class home and was taught a mixture of values from middle class and generational poverty. He was amused at my "checklist" for a potential husband. He must . . .

- be emotionally stable.
- pay all his bills on time.
- own his own home.
- have career and education goals similar to mine.
- possess proactive coping mechanisms.
- have savings in the bank.
- display positive values and ethics in both himself and his family.

He passed! We have been married for many years now. To this day, I have no remorse or guilt for breaking away from the relationships that bound me to poverty. I believe I have always been good at recognizing what was healthy for me—and that my "spirit" helped me not to stick around what was unhealthy any longer than necessary.

■ ■ ■ ■ ■ ■

AUTHORS' NOTE: Today, Lori directs a program for people who are seeking higher education in the field of human services. Many of these students are seeking achievement in order to move out of poverty toward middle class. Lori has been described as a support and a role model by students interviewed. She says that 20 years ago she would have considered her present career and lifestyle "inconceivable."

RANDI

Background: The Way It Was

You want to know about my childhood? Can't you tell my dad abused me? I didn't get this ugly all by myself! But once upon a time, we had a good life. Both my mom and dad worked until I was about 9 years old.

Now, I gotta cipher (figure this out). They had a baby when I was about 9 years old. That baby lived 15 months, then she died. When that happened, my dad started drinking real bad. See, his mother (my grandmother) had died the year before that. Well, after Grandma died, Grandpa and my dad would go across the street to the bar and drink. I'd wake up in the night hearing my mom and dad fighting. Before Grandma died, they didn't go to the bar. We went square-dancing. Sure, there was a little drinking, but nothing like later. My little baby sister, she died of pneumonia—she had a weak heart. Dad blamed Mom for not taking good care of her, for not being a good mom. Mom blamed Dad because of his drinking. Things were different than before. We never went hungry, though. But sometimes all we had to eat was "butter beans and skillet bread." My kids call it "silly bread." Even now, sometimes my kids beg me for it!

Before the baby died, there were toys for us kids. But afterwards, Dad couldn't hold a job. Mom worked at a local department store, Dad worked at factories and service stations. Most of the jobs were short-term, even before the baby died. We were doing all right before. After the baby died, Mom quit altogether. She had worked afternoons before that. She figured that Dad took to drink in the evenings and didn't trust him to take care of us. So she stayed home with us.

Dad got in trouble stealing at his job and had to go to jail for a time. This is when I was about 11. It was his second offense, so he had to go to the penitentiary for 13 months. That's when the real trouble started. Why did he steal? He thought if he wasn't there, the state would take care of us. I think it's pride. My parents didn't think much at all.

Before he went to jail, they had another baby girl. But life didn't get any better. This baby, she was supposed to help Mom get over the other baby.

We moved a lot, about seven times. I don't really think I saw anything wrong with our family. Everyone else had the same kind of parents. Everybody's dad drank. My mom was so enabling. But some of the dads in the neighborhood worked. Mine didn't. I figured everyone was getting hit at home, it's just that I didn't see it happen.

I didn't really start thinking about how bad things were until I had my own baby.

My dad drank every other night. He'd smack me around. And when I was around 15 years old (I was the oldest) I had to protect my sisters and brothers (they were 11, 3, and 2). Occasionally he would get to them before I figured out what he was up to. Mom started working nights from 3-11. In all honesty, I think she wanted things to be better for us. But I was angry. Really angry. How could she leave us alone with him?

He'd go on binges for days. Drinking was a big thing in Dad's family. He'd drink with his brother for days. Then they'd fight. They were crazy. Even now, I get stressed out when I hear loud voices.

After I got married, I'd take my sister and brothers to my house if I even saw one beer on his kitchen table. We grew up having a phone. Sometimes the kids would call me to come get them. And I'd go get them.

I got pregnant when I was 17. Dad wouldn't speak to me except when he cussed at me and hit me. Back then, the cops would just not get involved. They'd set foot on the front porch, and he'd tell them to back off. He sure wasn't afraid of them. Everyone just thought there was nothing to be done. "He's your dad." I was so determined to get my baby out of there. The strange thing is, he would never ever dream of hitting my Timmy. See, the grandkids are my dad's life. But I knew, I just knew, that he could hurt Timmy without laying a hand on him.

I dropped out of school when I was 16; I just didn't want to go. Why bother? I'm going to be stuck on the wrong side of the tracks forever! The bummer is I had three more kids before I woke up! When I was 16 and had Timmy, my Mom didn't want me to take the baby and move out. Mom and Dad even called the cops on me because I was leaving with the baby. Dad was really mad I was taking Timmy from him. But when I was 18 in February, I moved out and me and Timmy went on welfare.

My first husband, he drank a lot and went out on me. He had no ambition; he'd work for a couple months and quit. And I was home with two babies. Well, all that didn't work out.

Bridges

When I met my present husband, that's when my life changed. Took a new direction. We've been together 19 years now. He cared. We both came out of bad marriages. We moved out of town to a smaller town nearby. It was quiet. People didn't bother us. He made $13 an hour when I met him.

All of a sudden, there were groceries, the bills were paid, no worries. We've had another son and daughter together. I want them to have nice toys, shoes, and some stuff they don't need. He was the first man to ever buy me a diamond ring! He's four years older than me. He was raised in poverty too. They had nothing growing up. He never graduated from high school.

I had to go to work when my husband's company went out of business. We had a bit of a hard time then. He had trouble keeping his new jobs. See, all he knew was the concrete business. For four years we received assistance. I knew how to, that's for damn sure! But things eventually worked out. One thing we did together was to get our GEDs. I told him, "We're going nowhere fast here. We have to do something." Really, he went because I did. We went to classes once a week for a few months. I really can't remember how we got into the classes, or who told us about them.

College was always a dream for me. But stuff happened to get in the way of that dream. I just knew I wanted to work for Children's Services. The local college branch had a four-year program, but I had kids!

See, when they were little, I didn't feel comfortable leaving my husband with the kids. It took him forever to get me over some things. Like, I'd ask him if I could use the car. I'd ask him! It drove him nuts! I was afraid of everything. Afraid to make supper without asking him what he wanted. I'd make a meal for the kids, but I'd wait until he got home to make his supper. Maybe he didn't want what we had. I was afraid of making him mad. Silly little things like that. If there was one can of pop left in the refrigerator, I'd leave it there. It could be the hottest day of the year, and I'd leave it there no matter how bad I wanted it.

I wasn't fully aware that all men weren't like my dad. I tried to keep the kids quiet. My husband would say, "They're boys, they're supposed to make noise." He was 2 years old when his mom and dad got a divorce. His dad had some mental illness. Come to think of it, I don't know why he grew up to think so straight! Or maybe it's just that I thought so crooked! If something's wrong, he doesn't take off. We work things out together. We don't fight. We try to figure it out.

Then one day I saw the sign at the community college. My friend Pam had been trying to get me to go there for a long time, ever since I got my GED. At first, I wanted to be a labor and delivery nurse. Well, they had a nursing program at that college, but I wanted to cut that "crap" and just learn about labor and delivery. Well, it didn't work like that. So I thought, "Forget it." Then I saw the sign at the college, "New: Human Services Degree." I thought, "Now I can get a job with Children's Services." So Pam helped me sign up.

After I got into college, I was totally amazed at how much there is in the world! Our instructor was so neat. In our very first day of our first course, she asked us to do a paper evaluating ourselves. You know, how you value yourself. She gave it back to us when we graduated. She kept them all that time. We were the first class to get the Human Services degrees. There were a lot of major differences when I read that paper again. It's like someone finally pulled the cotton out of my head!

You want to know the people in my life who have been the best influence on me? Well, Larry, my present husband, he's been the best. And then Pam, always on my butt to take a class at that college of hers! You know, I did admire her for going to college. Well, maybe not at first. I'd say, forget that, let's go shoot the loop! Not Pam. You know, I didn't even go to her first graduation!

You know, when I think back on what happened to the guys who were my age and lived in the neighborhood, none of them have their own home. Some of them still live with their parents! It really helps to get out of the neighborhood. You have to get away from it to look at it and see what it is. My friends and I used to borrow money from each other, but not anymore. I don't like to feel like I owe them anything.

One other person who was good to me was my Uncle Don. He loved me and he took me everywhere. He'd come and get me and take me places with his family. My Aunt Molly loved me too. She'd come and get me to spend the night. She never said why. Maybe she wanted to get me out of there.

I never had a teacher who made a positive difference in my life until I was in college. There was this teacher, the one who asked us to evaluate ourselves. That woman made me think for myself, helped to open my eyes. And then, this other teacher . . . I never met a man like him; he's fair. I've never seen him put a male above a female. He'll change his mind during a class discussion! He's a great father. He's changed his share of diapers and everything.

Current Situation: The Way It Is

Now I work at a children's home. I make $8.50 an hour. I had it rough when I was a kid. These kids have it rougher. Some of them want help. Some of them will never change. I've been working at the children's home almost two years. My husband had a heart attack, the fool! I can't get him to quit smoking and eat more veggies! We own a campsite nearby in a nice trailer resort. We spend our summers there. I like camping and reading Stephen King and V.C. Andrews.

I always did like to read. I liked to play on the softball team too! I played 14 years! No, I've never been to the symphony! That comes with the third column on that hidden-rules sheet, doesn't it? I love to crochet. I've crocheted three blankets in three months.

I've never been to an art museum. But I loved Bob Ross.

■ ■ ■ ■ ■ ■

AUTHORS' NOTE: Randi is not ugly in any way, despite her joking about her looks. She is a caring and humorous woman who is taking steps to ensure that her children's lives will be better than the life she has experienced. Randi is the woman referred to in Chapter Seven who did not allow her mother into the limousine to the graduation ceremony. (By the way, Bob Ross is an artist who has appeared on PBS.)

PAM
Background: The Way It Was

> **"IF YOU CAN'T HELP YOURSELF, YOU DON'T NEED TO ASK FOR HELP"**

I can't believe that I'm trusting you enough to tell you all this. But I figure, if Lori thinks you're OK, then it must be all right.

I've always lived in this town. For years, I thought our neighborhood was this town. I am the second of five children. My dad died of cancer when I was 7 years old. They had separated the year before his death. My mother was a diabetic requiring insulin injections. There was no alcoholism or drug abuse that I remember. But, it's kind of hard to admit, but Dad mentally, verbally, and physically abused my mother—and sometime us kids. It's especially hard because my dad was a minister and I was a "Daddy's Girl." I think he basically lost control when he was told he had cancer. Once when my mother was in labor, he refused to take her to the hospital. Dad wouldn't budge. Someone called the ambulance, but the baby was delivered in a corner of the bedroom. I hated him for that. But I needed him. Even though I was only 7, I was the one who took on the father's role in our house after he died. I just naturally took charge. Funny, even today, I think of myself as "Daddy's Girl."

My mother was "there" for us. By that I mean that she provided food, clothing, and a roof over our head. But she wasn't "there for us" in other ways. After Dad died, she always had to have an adult there. At one point, three other families were living with us! She would take away from us to give to friends. That made me so angry! Can you believe that only twice did my mother tell me that she was proud of me? Those times were my high school graduation and when I got my first degree from the technical college. Twice. Mom's first boyfriend was physically abusive to everyone in the family. But she stayed with him for financial reasons. When I was 14, my mother married another man who drank but was not abusive.

In the neighborhood, the neighbors looked out for each other. If anyone needed food or shoes, the others pitched in. Almost the whole neighborhood was on welfare. Some had factory jobs. Once someone called Children's Services on my family because we didn't have an indoor bathroom. The neighbors helped us build the bathroom, digging the footer, laying the tiles. The rule was, however, that domestic violence/abuse was family business. The police were not called, and no one offered any assistance during domestic incidents. I remember a neighbor repeatedly cracking his wife's head against a building during the night. No one assisted the woman. Once my mother gave this woman a considerable amount of money for an airline ticket so that she could leave her abusive husband.

The woman kept the money and never left. I asked my mother if she was angry at this, or felt the woman used her. I knew our own family needed that money really badly. But Mom was not angry—she was just "helping the woman out."

In elementary school, I was shy and did what was needed to be moderately successful. There were several early-childhood teachers who were especially kind. One of my sister's teachers sent clothing home for the family. That teacher would help any child. My first-grade teacher chose me to be a helper. Other than that, no particular interest was shown in me or my abilities.

In high school, my grades began to decline. I was losing interest and did whatever it took in order to get a "C." The other kids didn't like me. It was really painful. I considered myself to be unattractive and overweight, and I didn't have nice clothes. I never even tried to meet new friends. In the ninth grade, my family moved to another state with Mom's boyfriend, to be near his family. But we moved back here after about six months. I don't remember any high school teachers offering me any extra help. I had no plans to go to college. At one point, the only person I knew who went to college was my neighbor's son.

My dad's parents lived in the same town but were somehow estranged from my family. I remember thinking, "I want to prove to my dad's side of the family that I'm not bad like the rest."

I did work occasionally for my stepgrandpa. He was a hard-working man, but he made his own liquor in the garage. He gave me money to watch the door! I'm not sure if I was watching out for the law or just for Grandma!

Bridges

I think the most significant role model I had was a widow who lived next door. We called her Grandma Sheila, though now I suppose she was only about 50 years old. Grandma Sheila's son had graduated from college, and she believed in getting an education. On report card days, all the neighborhood children would make a stop at Grandma Sheila's house on the way home. In third grade I got an "F" in math. Grandma Sheila loudly declared that I needed to bring this grade up! "You can do it," she said.

And then there was an African-American family in the neighborhood who kind of took me under their wing. The girls in that family were taught to value education. One of them, who became a teacher, had that drive to become something. I really admired that, but I had no real hope of going to college. Still, looking back, they had a really positive influence on me.

Later, when I found out it was possible, I did go to college. I enrolled in a two-year community college using federal assistance. Can you believe that I walked to and from school for two years and never asked anyone for a ride? No one offered one. It was at least two miles one way. And my diabetic mother expected me to come home midday every day to give her an insulin shot. She couldn't understand how that was not possible for me. Nothing should come before my mother. Sometimes I did go home to help her.

Current Situation: The Way It Is

I am 40 years old. I've worked in a clerical position at the community college for 20 years now. I began working here when I started attending classes. I feel really proud that because of working here, I was able to get an additional Associate's Degree. And this degree is not federally funded! Employees get free tuition. This has really done a lot to improve how I view myself. The community college, it's security. I think I've stayed at my present job for such a long period of time because the college is a safe place for me.

I have Associate's Degrees in both Business Management and Paralegal Studies (1997). I someday hope to get a job as a paralegal in a nearby city. I keep sending out those résumés! I am single and live with one of my brothers. One thing I do is encourage all my nieces and nephews, my brothers and my friends, to work hard at school—and to go back to school/college in their adult years.

I think financially I am now middle class. However, in "society" I will always be "poverty." If I had children, they would be more middle class than I am. But hey, I now own three stereos! I always wanted a stereo when I was young. I'm not married, but to me "a man" is synonymous with alcohol, abuse, and control. I'm safer alone. In high school I fell in love with a red Z-28 sports car. I still hope to someday buy one of these cars. Truth is, I think I'm still looking for outside approval. I want to be motivated inside instead!

I would not give up my childhood, though. I've learned not to be critical of others. I admit that I'm sometimes slow to accept new acquaintances because I'm not sure whether they are being critical of me. Some of those middle-class "hidden rules" seem shallow, especially the one that says "things are more important than people."

■ ■ ■ ■ ■

AUTHORS' NOTE: Pam was responsible for influencing Randi to attend classes at the same college, which resulted in the completion of Randi's goal to get a degree and work in the field of social services.

SALLY

Background: The Way It Was

I grew up in Council Housing in Suffolk County, England. Council Houses are government, subsidized, semi-detached homes for those in poverty and middle class who need affordable housing. The housing estate where I lived was considered to be "rough" or "trashy," a higher crime area.

I am an only child. My mother had a debilitating form of mental illness and could not cook, clean, or take care of me. Up until I was 6 months of age, my parents lived with my grandparents. My dad was a blue-collar worker, until he finally quit work to take care of me (age 2) and my mother. We lived on government assistance due to her illness. When I was 8 years old, my father started to teach me to cook and clean for the family. In return, I received a small allowance.

Unfortunately, my father became alcoholic and spent at least four nights a week drinking at a local pub. I was left with my mother, although Dad did attempt to do some cooking and cleaning while I was at school. Basically, I was left to raise myself. I watched a lot of TV to break the monotony. A social services worker would visit the family regularly to check on me. Everyone just seemed to assume that I was doing all right. I always had enough to eat, even though it was not always the "greatest food."

Not all the children at school were on welfare. I was teased and picked on because of my clothing. I had to get myself ready for school, and once (age 7), I went to school wearing seven sweaters. The headmaster had to call my mother to see what was happening. Actually, I did have quite a few friends, mostly children of the Irish "drinking buddies" who associated with my father. The Irish community stuck together. I remember no one teacher in particular who stands out as exceptionally supportive. I have the impression that there was some general concern from the school about my home situation. I was extremely shy, however, and did not open up to the teachers about my home. I admit that I was somewhat lazy in school. There were too many other distractions.

I was considered to be of average intelligence. I did not excel at any particular art form or academic discipline. I was not a particularly attractive child. I was generally left to raise myself and take care of my mother. I had no great goals or dreams. I was not a particularly spiritual child or teen. I could see how my middle-class relatives lived, their beliefs, their dreams. But I did not consciously aspire to these in my early life.

I knew if I wanted to have something of my own, I would have to work. By the time I was 14, I was going to school, babysitting, and working at a fast-food restaurant on Saturdays. Really, I believe my father's work ethic was good. Once he began working, he managed to keep his job. Even when we were on assistance, he would do spading and tilling for extra money. I still remember the pride he showed when he felt he had completed a job well done. Eventually, the disability checks were denied, and he was forced to find work.

Bridges

My mother had been raised in middle class, my grandfather being a major in the army. My aunt and grandmother were concerned about my welfare. However, they lived some distance from us. The extended family met about four times a year, mostly during the summer holidays. I looked forward to these visits because my grandmother would pay attention to me and outfit me with new shoes. My dad never bought me clothing or shoes. My aunt gave me my cousins' hand-me-downs. I was grateful for the clothing. My aunt was upper middle class, really, and would take me on family vacations. We traveled to South England, Wales, Cornwall. In fact, even today at 29 years of age, I still recall a restaurant from one of these vacations. It was the nicest and most formal restaurant to which I've ever been.

Aunt corrected my accent and grammar and tried to give instructions on the basics of good hygiene and fashion. She stressed good posture and taught me how to walk straight and tall. I welcomed the help, but I was frustrated at her somewhat condescending tone. My relatives should have realized the reason that I talked, dressed, and acted the way I did was that no one had ever instructed me otherwise! Aunt would make comments about the house and cleaning. This bothered me to no end. After all, there was only I to be responsible for the cleaning. I was doing the best under the circumstances. Aunt kept asking me what I wanted to do with my life. She stressed that I had options. Of course, all my cousins would be going to college. Actually, I was planning to go to technical college when I graduated, but I eventually dropped that idea to work in a factory. I really needed to get out of my father's home, and financial resources were needed in order to do this.

I had a friend who lived with her mother, who was divorced. This was relatively uncommon in our community. They often invited me over to spend the night. They were Jehovah's Witness, and I learned about morality issues from my friend's mother. They treated me as family. We are friends even today. I also "fell into" a family for which I babysat. I began babysitting to make extra money when I was 12. This family also took me on vacations.

I was also drawn to a Baptist youth group through some friends. This group provided fun activities for the Council Estate youth. We would gather together and go to the church activities for something to do. Sometimes we received instruction on the Bible. When I was 14 a neighbor who was a Church of England minister took an interest in my spiritual life. He convinced me to be baptized and confirmed. I went through a three-month confirmation course and was confirmed. I now recognize that I did this to please Aunt, who was also Church of England. My father was an Irish Catholic, but he left my spiritual choices up to me. The Church of England instruction offered me new patterns of viewing the world, which I probably have used to build my later life.

When I graduated (at the age of 16—common in England), I went to work in a factory. I met Jack when I was 18, the legal age in England. I worked for a brief amount of time before we married. Even though Jack was not from a middle-class family, we shared goals to attain a better life. We dated about three months before we were married and expecting a child. Jack offered me a love and respect I had not yet experienced. Together, we slowly struggled toward forming our own family.

For a time Jack was supported by his job in the armed forces. When he was finished with his term, we moved to the U.S., and Jack worked for a fertilizer company while we lived with his parents. Jack lost his job and was unable to find another. We went on ADC and welfare. He went to technical college to get a degree as a medical lab technician but never found a job in that field. His degree did enable him to get a job at a local hardware store chain and then finally as a supervisor in state facility. More than once we moved back home with our parents before finally breaking out on our own.

When the opportunity arose for me to attend technical college, I decided to go into the field of human services. I seem to have a strength and persistence, and I enjoyed school and the people I met there. I was a good student. I guess I'm quite practical in my decision-making.

Current Situation: The Way It Is

Jack is still employed at the state facility. He has excellent benefits and a good salary. We have two sons and I am working for a government preschool facility. I truly enjoy my job. I am a professional woman working in a profession that I love. I love children. I am teaching my sons the importance of learning and doing well in school. We live in our own home now, even though it is a sort of "fixer-upper." I guess I found the right job, the right man, and have persistently struggled to slowly move toward middle-class lifestyles. I don't think I'm middle class yet, but my children are. Today I am determined that my children will have the resources I lacked. I am now in the position to give them what they need.

■ ■ ■ ■ ■ ■

AUTHORS' NOTE: Sally is a polite, rather polished, attractive young woman who seems to have learned how to get what she needs for herself and her family. She is the woman referred to in Chapter Seven who is actively involved in her children's education, including frequent visits to the public library.

Each woman had in some way encouraged and supported at least one other interviewee. It is our hope that the reader also will show encouragement, support, and understanding—and use the strategies discussed—to lend a hand in helping someone who desires to cross the bridge out of poverty.

Research Notes

■ ■ ■ ■ ■ ■ ■ ■ ■ ■ ■ ■

AUTHORS' NOTE: The following Research Notes have been selected to correlate with the content of this book. The quotations and sourcing are intended to supplement, not replace, the Bibliography. The intent also is to buttress the primary premises of this book with the perspectives of many other keen observers in the field. It is the authors' hope that this book and these notes will spark further study of—and caring involvement in—the culture of survival in North America.

Introduction

"The poverty rate in 2004 (12.7 percent) was 9.7 percentage points lower than in 1959, the first year for which poverty estimates are available. From the most recent low in 2000, both the number and rate have risen for four consecutive years, from 31.6 million and 11.3 percent in 2000 to 37.0 million and 12.7 percent in 2004, respectively."

DeNavas-Walt, Carmen, Proctor, Bernadette D., & Lee, Cheryl Hill. (2005). *Income, Poverty, and Health Insurance Coverage in the United States: 2004.* Washington, DC: U.S. Bureau of the Census, Current Population Reports, P60–229, U.S. Government Printing Office. p. 9.

"Median household income was $44,389 in 2004, unchanged from 2003 in real terms. Median household income was also unchanged in real terms between 2002 and 2003."

Ibid. p. 9.

"The historical record is marked by a 12-year period from 1987 to 1998 when the uninsured rate (12.9 percent in 1987) either increased or was unchanged from one year to the next. After peaking at 16.3 percent in 1998, the rate fell for two years in a row to 14.2 percent in 2000, and the rate increased for three years before stabilizing at 15.7 percent in 2004."

Ibid. p. 16.

"The percentage of people covered by employment-based health insurance decreased to 59.8 percent in 2004, from 60.4 percent in 2003.

Ibid. p. 16.

"The percentage and number of people covered by government health insurance programs increased between 2003 and 2004, from 26.6 percent and 76.8 million to 27.2 percent and 79.1 million."

"The lack of health care is symptomatic of a larger challenge of childhood in America. Poor children largely come from low-wage working families. Seventy-one percent of poor children are members of families who work but do not make a living wage. These families are predominantly headed by two parents of working age."

Glasmeier, Amy K. (2006). *An Atlas of Poverty in America: One Nation, Pulling Apart, 1960–2003.* New York, NY: Routledge Taylor & Francis Group. p. 7.

"Over the last two decades, the United States has seen a substantial increase in the number of persons and families who are working but poor. The working poor are individuals who spend at least 27 weeks in the labor force, but whose incomes fall below the official poverty level. These are not individuals who choose voluntarily to work part-time or only part of a year. Instead, these are persons who would work full-time, 40-hour jobs if that type of employment was available. Of the more than 35 million persons classified as living in poverty in the U.S., most are children, disabled, or elderly, but about seven million of them, men and women, fathers and mothers, young women and men, are working at jobs that do not pay a wage they can live on over the course of a year."

Ibid. p. 26.

"Intergenerational immobility is also observed in rich countries: new evidence from the United States (where the myth of equal opportunity is strong) finds high levels of persistence of socioeconomic status across generations: recent estimates suggest that it would take five generations for a family that earned half the national average income to reach the average."

World Bank. (2005). *World Development Report 2006: Equity and Development.* New York, NY: Oxford University Press. p. 6.

"We argue that an equity lens enhances the poverty reduction agenda. The poor generally have less voice, less income, and less access to services than most other people. When societies become more equitable in ways that lead to greater opportunities for all, the poor stand to benefit from a 'double dividend.' First, expanded opportunities benefit the poor directly, through greater participation in the development process. Second, the development process itself may become more successful and resilient as greater equity leads to better institutions, more effective conflict management, and a better use of all potential resources in society, including those of the poor."

Ibid. p. 9.

Chapter Two: The Role of Language and Story

"In the welfare families, the utterances addressed to the children were both fewer in quantity and somewhat less rich in nouns, modifiers, verbs, past-tense verbs, and clauses. Although the welfare parents were just as likely to respond to their children and ask them questions, they displayed fewer floorholding utterances—after initiating or responding, these parents continued talking to their children less than half as often as did the working-class parents. The result was that the welfare children received in each hour of their lives less than half the language experience of working-class children."

Hart, Betty, and Risley, Todd R. *Meaningful Differences in the Everyday Experience of Young American Children.* Baltimore, MD: Paul H. Brookes Publishing Co., 1995. p. 125.

"There was a striking difference, too, in affirmative feedback. The professional parents gave their children affirmative feedback every other minute, more than 30 times per hour, twice as often as the working-class parents gave their children affirmative feedback and more than 5 times as often as parents in welfare families gave their children affirmative feedback. The children in welfare families heard a prohibition twice as often as they heard affirmative feedback."

Ibid. p. 126.

Chapter Three: Hidden Rules Among Classes

Mayer says America has " 'vacillated between trying to improve the material well-being of poor children and . . . the moral character of their parents' " for 200 years.

Samuelson, Robert J. "The Culture of Poverty." *Newsweek.* May 5, 1997. Volume 129. Number 18. p. 49.

The test of "welfare reform" is fewer teen pregnancies, more marriages that are stable and children living in "better homes," not a reduction in welfare cases.

Ibid.

"Mayer writes: 'The parental characteristics that employers value and are willing to pay for, such as skills, diligence, honesty, good health, and reliability, also improve children's life changes, independent of their effect on parents' incomes. Children of parents with these attributes do well even if their parents do not have much income.' "

Ibid.

A character in a story/scenario knows the "rules of middle-class life."

Sennett, Richard, and Cobb, Jonathan. *The Hidden Injuries of Class*. London/Boston: Faber and Faber, 1993. First published in U.S.A. in 1972 by Alfred A. Knopf, New York, NY. p. 21.

Children at the Watson School did not feel that the time in the classroom was " 'real time.' " Instead "they would come alive" when they were able to go to work and be "on their own." Adults on the job view their time at work the same way. In an example, one individual felt that " 'the job's just cash to live; the things that matter every day to me are at home . . . the family, people . . . the neighborhood.' "

Ibid. p. 93.

Theories of why poor children fail more often than rich children: (1) "Parents who are present-oriented, fatalistic, and unambitious raise children who are the same. Both generations tend to be jobless and poor." (2) Material deprivation and parental stress of poverty cause failure because children can't compete if their basic needs are not met.

Mayer, Susan E. *What Money Can't Buy*. Cambridge, MA: Harvard University Press, 1997. p. 16.

The definitions of class by each group: People at the bottom define class by your amount of money; people in middle class value education and your line of work almost as much as money; at the top, people emphasize "taste, values, ideas, style, and behavior"— regardless of money, education, or occupation.

Fussel, Paul. *Class*. New York, NY: Ballantine Books, 1983. p. 3.

Middle class is characterized by " 'Correctness' and doing the right thing."

Ibid. p. 34.

A sign of middle class: desire to belong and to do so by a "mechanical act," such as purchasing something.

Ibid. p. 35.

Middle class: believes in the "likelihood of self-improvement."

Ibid. p. 37.

Upper middle class: The emphasis of cookbooks, and books about food and food presentation addressed to them, was about " 'elegance.' " At their dinner parties, the guests are an audience.

Ibid. p. 111.

The farther down socially one moves, the more likely that the TV set will be on.

Ibid. p. 100.

A sign of the upper classes is silence; proles are identified by noise and vociferation.

Low-income families differ from higher-income families in more ways than just economics (i.e., they're not as likely to have the two biological parents living in the household, to have adults with college degrees or high-status jobs present); "they are more likely to live in poor neighborhoods, receive income from welfare, contain adults with mental or physical problems, and so on."

Ibid. p. 196.

Brooks-Gunn, Jeanne, Duncan, Greg J., and Maritato, Nancy. Poor Families, Poor Outcomes: The Well-being of Children and Youth. Duncan, Greg J., and Brooks-Gunn, Jeanne, Editors. *Consequences of Growing Up Poor*. New York, NY: Russell Sage Foundation, 1997. p. 14.

"In communities with limited resources like Humboldt Park and East L.A., sophisticated survival structures evolved, including gangs, out of the bone and sinew tossed up by this environment."

Rodriguez, Luis J. *Always Running*. New York, NY: Simon & Schuster, 1993. p. 8.

The author says that in the first Christmas his family had (the presents were from a church group), "I broke the plastic submarine, toy gun and metal car I received. I don't know why. I suppose in my mind it didn't seem right to have things in working order, unspent."

Ibid. pp. 22–23.

When the family moved from South Central L.A. to Reseda after their dad obtained a substitute teaching job, he writes, "Even my brother enjoyed success in this new environment. He became the best fighter in the school . . ."

Ibid. pp. 30–31.

Rodriguez says his dad "went nuts in Reseda," buying things such as new furniture, a new TV, a new car. He went into debt to do so, but "his attitude was 'who cares.' We were Americans now." But then his dad lost his job, and these things were repossessed.

Ibid. p. 31.

"It seemed Mama was just there to pick up the pieces when my father's house of cards fell."

Ibid.

During the time in Reseda, his mother was "uncomfortable." . . . "The other mothers around here were good-looking, fit and well-built. My pudgy mom looked dark, Indian and foreign, no matter what money could buy."

Ibid.

"The economic traits which are most characteristic of the culture of poverty include the constant struggle for survival, unemployment and underemployment, low wages, a miscellany of unskilled occupations, child labor, the absence of savings, a chronic shortage of cash, the absence of food reserves in the home, the pattern of frequent buying of small quantities of food many times a day as the need arises, the pawning of personal goods, borrowing from local money lenders at usurious rates of interest, spontaneous informal credit devices (*tandas*) organized by neighbors, and the use of second-hand clothing and furniture."

Lewis, Oscar. The Culture of Poverty. Penchef, Esther, Editor. *Four Horsemen: Pollution, Poverty, Famine, Violence.* San Francisco, CA: Canfield Press, 1971. pp. 137–138.

". . . [T]he city jail is one of the basic institutions of the other America."

Harrington, Michael. The Invisible Land. Penchef, Esther, Editor. *Four Horsemen: Pollution, Poverty, Famine, Violence.* San Francisco, CA: Canfield Press, 1971. p. 153.

In a conversation the author describes "work hard, get ahead" as a "middle class promise."

Capponi, Pat. *Dispatches from the Poverty Line.* Toronto, Ontario, Canada: Penguin Books, 1997. p. 41.

The author says she "didn't spend a lot of time worrying about nutrition, just volume enough to quell hunger pains."

Ibid. p. 53.

"The poor are usually as confined by their poverty as if they lived in a maximum security prison. There is not much exposure to other ways of life, unless their neighborhood starts to undergo gentrification."

Ibid. pp. 82–85.

Lisa, an interviewee, says: " 'I never felt like I was middle class. I didn't live in a renovated house, we didn't have cable or colour television, junk food, ketchup in bottles, new cars, yearly family vacations.' My mother says: 'Of course you were raised in a middle-class family. You went to camp, you took gymnastics and ballet, you read books for entertainment, both your parents were educated and working.' "

Ibid. pp. 173–174.

"This is how the Midtown researchers described the 'low social economic status individual': they are 'rigid, suspicious and have a fatalistic outlook on life.

Harrington, Michael. *The Other America.* New York, NY: Simon & Schuster, 1962. p. 133.

They do not plan ahead, a characteristic associated with their fatalism. They are prone to depression, have feelings of futility, lack of belongingness, friendliness, and a lack of trust in others.'"

Of the poor, the author says that, "they do not postpone satisfactions that they do not save. When pleasure is available, they tend to take it immediately."

Ibid. p. 134.

"Like the Asian peasant, the impoverished American tends to see life as a fate, an endless cycle from which there is no deliverance."

Ibid. p. 161.

"No matter what else they may be, the people of these higher circles are involved in a set of overlapping 'crowds' and intricately connected 'cliques.'"

Mills, C. Wright. *The Power Elite*. New York, NY: Oxford University Press, 1956. p. 11.

The upper social class "belong to clubs and organizations to which others like themselves are admitted, and they take quite seriously their appearances in these associations."

Ibid. p. 57.

"They have attended the same or similar private and exclusive schools, preferably one of the Episcopal boarding schools of New England. Their men have been to Harvard, Yale, Princeton, or if local pride could not be overcome, to a locally esteemed college to which their families have contributed."

Ibid. p. 58.

"As a selection and training place of the upper classes, both old and new, the private school is a unifying influence, a force for the nationalization of the upper classes."

Ibid. p. 64.

"The major economic fact about the very rich is the fact of the accumulation of advantages: those who have great wealth are in a dozen strategic positions to make it yield further wealth."

Ibid. p. 115.

In describing the rich: ". . . [T]heir toys are bigger; they have more of them; they have more of them all at once."

Ibid. p. 164.

". . . [U]nlike the more affluent classes, the poor cannot mask their occasional inability or unwillingness to practice mainstream behavior, which is why the more affluent imagine the poor have bad values."

Gans, Herbert J. *The War Against the Poor: The Underclass and Antipoverty Policy*. New York, NY: Basic Books, 1995. p. 83.

"What may turn out to be one of the important challenges for education is helping poor people seek employment in the office-centered world of 'service' jobs. Manufacturing work takes place in the working-class culture of the shop floor, but offices are run by the rules and social relations practices of middle-class and professional cultures. Many poor people who obtain jobs in offices learn these cultures on their own, but some may need a kind of schooling, not in punctuality and dress code, but in the subtler cultural practices that are needed for success in the office world, and which the middle class learns almost automatically."

Ibid. p. 116.

"One of the reasons the rich get richer, the poor get poorer, and the middle class struggles in debt is because the subject of money is taught at home, not in school. Most of us learn about money from our parents. So what can poor parents tell their child about money? They simply say, 'Stay in school and study hard.' The child may graduate with excellent grades but with a poor person's financial planning and mind-set. It was learned while the child was young."

Kiyosaki, Robert T., and Lechter, Sharon L. *Rich Dad, Poor Dad*. Paradise Valley, AZ: TechPress, 1998. p. 12.

Chapter Four: Characteristics of Generational Poverty

"Moreover, Lewis himself initially felt that some of the culture of poverty's traits were positive, thus implying that they deserve being copied by better-off Americans. These included what Rigdon described as 'family loyalty, generosity and sharing, spontaneity, gaiety, courage and the ability to love.'"

Gans, Herbert J. *The War Against the Poor: The Underclass and Antipoverty Policy*. New York, NY: Basic Books, 1995. p. 93.

"Americans are willing to entertain a more descriptive and less judgmental view of the poor, of how they live and why some behave in ways that deviate from those of the mainstream. To describe or to explain is not to justify, but to point out that the world of the poor differs in many respects from that of the better-off, that the poor act on the basis of understandable reasons just like everyone else, and that knowing these is, at least in the long run, helpful to the reduction of poverty."

Ibid. p. 119.

The extended family "makes the dependence of family members on each other into a code of honor." This works by age usually, "the older people having a right to set the standard for the younger."

Sennett, Richard, and Cobb, Jonathan. *The Hidden Injuries of Class.* London/Boston: Faber and Faber, 1993. First published in U.S.A. in 1972 by Alfred A. Knopf, New York, NY. p. 106.

Low-income parents compared to rich parents:
- Are not as likely to be married.
- Typically have less education.
- Typically have poorer health.

Mayer, Susan E. *What Money Can't Buy.* Cambridge, MA: Harvard University Press, 1997. p. 8.

The role-model version of the good-parent theory contends that "because of their position at the bottom of the social hierarchy, low-income parents develop values, norms, and behaviors that are 'dysfunctional' for success in the dominant culture."

Ibid. p. 50.

Men and women from low-income background are less likely to marry when they have a child than those from higher income. When they marry, "they are more likely to separate and divorce."

Ibid. pp. 65–66.

"Absent any state support, some women and children will be more likely to remain in abusive and destructive relationships with men. Others will turn to 'social prostitution,' serial relationships with men willing to pay their bills."

Ibid. pp. 151–152.

Having income well above the poverty line does appear to reduce teen out-of-wedlock births. A family characteristic frequently associated with poverty—the number of years spent living with a single parent—is also a significant determinant of teenage fertility choices, particularly if a child spends the teenage years from twelve to fifteen living in poverty."

Haveman, Robert, Wolfe, Barbara, and Wilson, Kathryn. Childhood Poverty and Adolescent Schooling and Fertility Outcomes: Reduced-form and Structural Estimates. Duncan, Greg J., and Brooks-Gunn, Jeanne, Editors. *Consequences of Growing Up Poor.* New York, NY: Russell Sage Foundation, 1997. p. 443.

"Criminality in this country is a class issue. Many of those warehoused in overcrowded prisons can be properly called 'criminals of want,' those who've been deprived of the basic necessities of life and

Rodriguez, Luis J. *Always Running.* New York, NY: Simon & Schuster, 1993. p. 10.

therefore forced into so-called criminal acts to survive. . . . They are members of a social stratum which includes welfare mothers, housing project residents, immigrant families, the homeless and unemployed."

He says his mother "held up the family when almost everything else came apart."

Ibid. p. 23.

"We changed houses often because of evictions."

Ibid. p. 30.

The family then moved in with Seni, the author's half-sister, and her family. A grandmother also lived there, making a total of 11 in the apartment. "The adults occupied the only two bedrooms. The children slept on makeshift bedding in the living room." The author and his brother "sought refuge in the street."

Ibid. p. 32.

"We didn't call ourselves gangs. We called ourselves clubs or *clicas*. . . . It was something to belong to— something that was ours. We weren't in [B]oy [S]couts, in sports teams or camping groups. Thee Impersonations (club name) is how we wove something out of threads of nothing."

Ibid. p. 41.

"But 'family' is a farce among the propertyless and disenfranchised. Too many families are wrenched apart, as even children are forced to supplement meager incomes. Family can only really exist among those who can afford one."

Ibid. p. 250.

"Even when income is used to define poverty, one finds relatively high ownership of televisions and automobiles among the poor."

Seligman, Ben B. The Numbers of Poor. Penchef, Esther, Editor. *Four Horsemen: Pollution, Poverty, Famine, Violence*. San Francisco, CA: Canfield Press, 1971. p. 95.

"Poverty does different things to different people. Walk into the home of a poor family. A stench may offend the nostrils; filth may offend the eyes. Or the home may look immaculate."

Dicks, Lee E. The Poor Who Live Among Us. Penchef, Esther, Editor. *Four Horsemen: Pollution, Poverty, Famine, Violence*. San Francisco, CA: Canfield Press, 1971. p. 118.

Boyd and his wife believe education provides the best chance for his son. He said, " '. . . [T]hey won't

Ibid. p. 123.

get any place at all without high school education, and most likely college to boot.'"

"Some of the social and psychological characteristics include living in crowded quarters, a lack of privacy, gregariousness, a high incidence of alcoholism, frequent resort to violence in the settlement of quarrels, frequent use of physical violence in the training of children, wife beating, early initiation into sex, free unions or consensual marriages, a relatively high incidence of the abandonment of mothers and children, a trend toward mother-centered families and a much greater knowledge of maternal relatives, the predominance of the nuclear family, a strong predisposition to authoritarianism, and a great emphasis upon family solidarity—an ideal only rarely achieved. Other traits include a strong present time orientation with relatively little ability to defer gratification and plan for the future, a sense of resignation and fatalism based upon the realities of their difficult life situation, a belief in male superiority which reaches its crystallization in *machismo* or the cult of masculinity, a corresponding martyr complex among women, and finally, a high tolerance for psychological pathology of all sorts."

Lewis, Oscar. The Culture of Poverty. Penchef, Esther, Editor. *Four Horsemen: Pollution, Poverty, Famine, Violence*. San Francisco, CA: Canfield Press, 1971. p. 138.

"First rule of the streets: don't display weakness, sentimentality."

Capponi, Pat. *Dispatches from the Poverty Line*. Toronto, Ontario, Canada: Penguin Books, 1997. p. 150.

The author asks an interviewer how she feels about hooking. The response is: " 'You just turn off part of your mind. You gotta think, well, a guy goes out, he buys work boots, and he puts them to work to make money. I put my body to work. It's the same thing, really.'"

Ibid. p. 153.

"Poverty in the United States is a culture, an institution, a way of life."

Harrington, Michael. *The Other America*. New York, NY: Simon & Schuster, 1962, p. 16.

"But within a slum, violence and disturbance are often norms, everyday facts of life. From the inside of the other America, joining a 'bopping' gang may well not seem like deviant behavior. It could be a necessity for

Ibid. p. 127.

dealing with a hostile world. (Once, in a slum school in St. Louis, a teacher stopped a fight between two little girls. 'Nice girls don't fight,' she told them. 'Yeah,' one of them replied, 'you should have seen my old lady at the tavern last night.'")

Some of the evidence to support the changes in family life includes: "Large numbers of adult males are only loosely attached to the families and households that contain their offspring. Many among these see their children sporadically, if at all, and contribute little or nothing to the financial support of their children."

Zill, Nicholaus. "The Changing Realities of Family Life." *Aspen Institute Quarterly*, Winter 1993. Volume 5. Number 1. p. 37.

When walking with five children (two are 7 years old, two are 9 years old, and the other is described as a tiny child), Kozol says: "None of the children can tell me the approximate time that school begins. One says five o'clock. One says six. Another says that school begins at noon." The children then tell him of the rape and murder of one of their sisters.

Kozol, Jonathan. *Savage Inequalities*. New York, NY: Harper Perennial, 1991. pp. 12–13.

A 12-year-old boy named Jeremiah tells Kozol that " 'white people started moving away from black and Spanish people in New York' " in 1960. Kozol asks him where the white people went. Another boy says he thinks they moved to the country. Jeremiah then says, " 'It isn't where people live. It's *how* they live.' " Kozol asks him to repeat what he said. " 'It's *how* they live,' he says again. 'There are different economies in different places.' " Kozol asks Jeremiah to explain what he means, and Jeremiah refers to Riverdale, "a mostly white and middle-class community in the northwest section of the Bronx." " 'Life in Riverdale is opened up,' he says. 'Where we live, it's locked down.' " Kozol asks him, " 'In what way?' " He responds, " 'We can't go out and play.' "

Kozol, Jonathan. *Amazing Grace*. New York, NY: Crown Publishers, 1995. p. 32.

A 15-year-old student, Isabel, says she thinks Jeremiah's description of feeling " 'locked down' " is "too strong." " 'It's not like being in a jail,' she says. 'It's more like being "hidden." It's as if you have been put in a garage where, if they don't have room for something but aren't sure if they should throw it out, they put it where they don't need to think of it again.' "

Ibid. pp. 38–39.

Chapter Six: Support Systems

"Other fruitful strategies might be more indirect programmatic ones, such as helping mothers read more to their children (as well as read more themselves) and teaching mothers about intellectually stimulating learning activities that they can do at home with their children" (Brooks-Gunn, Denner, and Klebanov, 1995; Snow, 1986).

Smith, Judith R., Brooks-Gunn, Jeanne, and Klebanov, Pamela K. Consequences of Living in Poverty for Young Children's Cognitive and Verbal Ability and Early School Achievement. Duncan, Greg J., and Brooks-Gunn, Jeanne, Editors. *Consequences of Growing Up Poor.* New York, NY: Russell Sage Foundation, 1997. p. 167.

"Parents' economic resources can influence self-esteem in several ways. Parents' income brings both parents and children social status and respect that can translate into individual self-esteem. Income can also enhance children's self-esteem by providing them with the goods and services that satisfy individual aspirations."

Axinn, William, Duncan, Greg J., and Thornton, Arland. The Effects of Parents' Income, Wealth, and Attitudes on Children's Completed Schooling and Self-esteem. Duncan, Greg J., and Brooks-Gunn, Jeanne, Editors. *Consequences of Growing Up Poor.* New York, NY: Russell Sage Foundation, 1997. p. 521.

In models by Rand D. Conger, Kathy J. Conger, and Glen Elder, "[L]ow income produces economic pressures that can lead to conflict between parents over financial matters, which in turn affects the harshness of the mother's parenting and the adolescent's self-confidence and achievement."

Duncan, Greg J., and Brooks-Gunn, Jeanne. Income Effects Across the Life Span: Integration and Interpretation. Duncan, Greg J., and Brooks-Gunn, Jeanne, Editors. *Consequences of Growing Up Poor.* New York, NY: Russell Sage Foundation, 1997. p. 602.

The author makes several points that he says "conservatives may find troublesome." One of these includes: "*Federal programs have made a difference in children's lives.* As noted earlier, the character of child poverty in this country has been changed for the better by

Zill, Nicholaus. "The Changing Realities of Family Life." *Aspen Institute Quarterly,* Winter 1993. Volume 5. Number 1. pp. 47–48.

programs such as food stamps, WIC, Medicaid, Chapter 1 and equal opportunity efforts."

Reasons Wage-Supplement Workers Lost Their Jobs

Fired

Failed to show up	24%
Absenteeism	23%
Unable to perform work	12%
Shift closed	9%
Conflict with others	8%
Failed drug test	1%

Quit

Transportation problems	7%
Medical/health problems	5%
Day-care problems	4%
Found new wage-supplement job	2%

Deavers, Kenneth L., and Hattiangadi, Anita U. "Welfare to Work: Building a Better Path to Private Employment Opportunities." *Journal of Labor Research*, Spring 1998. Volume 19. Number 2. Source: Local Investment Commission in Forsey Davis Workforce Pilot Program, *Wall Street Journal*, September 2, 1997.

Chapter Seven: Mentoring and Bridging

"Observe calmly the natural unfolding of events. Rapid growth and advancement are unnatural. Hold to the inner vision of gradual flowering of potential. Avoid haste. Do not jump ahead blindly. Enjoy the moment of waiting to be!"

Huang, Chungliang Al, and Lynch, Jerry. *Mentoring: The TAO of Giving and Receiving Wisdom*. San Francisco, CA: HarperSanFrancisco, 1995. p. 76.

"Attentive listening to others is important regardless of their stations and positions. Wise people consider the deep meaning and true values of all suggestions. Learning and teaching are exchanged joyfully through deep listening and mutual appreciation."

Ibid. p. 64.

"The elevator to success and wealth is out of order; you have to use the stairs. A step at a time" (John Hughes).

Wickman, Floyd, and Sjodin, Terri. *Mentoring: The Most Obvious Yet Overlooked Key to Achieving More in Life Than You Dreamed Possible: A Success Guide for Mentors and Protégés*. Chicago, IL: Irwin Professional Publishing, 1997. p. 172.

"Mentoring is several steps beyond advice. In its simplest terms, it's someone sharing their knowledge and wisdom . . . knowledge about the 'how-tos'" (Sam Cupp).

Ibid. p. 102.

"Many of the seeds that we plant may not become visible to us for years, if ever."

Bluestein, Jane. *Mentors, Masters, and Mrs. MacGregor: Stories of Teachers Making a Difference.* Deerfield Beach, FL: Health Communications, 1995. p. xviii.

Chapter Eight: Discipline, Choices, and Consequences

"The distinction between divergent and harmful behavior is crucial from a policy perspective, because in a diverse or multicultural society punishing divergent behavior cannot be tolerated. Indeed, the distinction may be useful for showing people that the limited facilities and resources available for punishment and therapy should be spent only on truly harmful behavior."

Gans, Herbert J. *The War Against the Poor: The Underclass and Antipoverty Policy.* New York, NY: Basic Books, 1995. p. 122.

". . . [O]ur affinity for myth and metaphor comes hardwired into our brainstems. For most of our natural history, explains psychologist Richard Nisbett, 'vivid information' has been the only way to learn. 'I'd put it in evolutionary terms,' he explains. 'We're accustomed to the use of narrative information. That's the way we learned things in our previous, preliterate cultures. It's a relatively recent thing to learn about the world by statistics and by logical argument.' "

Shenk, David. *Data Smog: Surviving the Information Glut.* New York, NY: HarperCollins Publishers, 1997. p. 158.

Chapter Nine: Resources and Resiliency: Internal Assets

"A few central questions . . . What are the mechanisms that spur ongoing resilient capacities? Are there identifiable themes in people's lives that tell us how some people surmount . . . so effectively? I assume that resilience is not a collection of treats, but a *process* that builds on itself over time."

O'Connell Higgins, Gina. *Resilient Adults: Overcoming a Cruel Past.* San Francisco, CA: Jossey-Bass, 1994. p. 4.

"Because alcohol is an enabler of both sexual and physical abuse as well as neglect, it is crucial to note that roughly 10 percent of adults in the United States grew up in alcoholic homes. Many children also grow up in abject poverty, and . . . receive no financial support from their non-custodial parent (usually the father) five years after the divorce. Low income

Ibid. pp. 8–9.

status can be considered intrinsically abusive, as it exposes children and adolescents to many other associated stressors, such as poor nutrition, community violence, and substandard housing and health care."

"By defining resilience broadly for the moment and calling it the ability to function psychologically at a level far greater than expected given a person's earlier developmental experiences, there are many studies that suggest that resilience occurs often in groups at high risk for the development of psychopathology. The figure frequently cited is approximately 10 percent of the population under scrutiny (although because definitions of resilience differ across studies, it is difficult to know what this figure represents). Emmy Werner and Ruth Smith's thirty-year study of 700 insular, low-mobility, ethnically diverse subjects in Kauai, Hawaii, yielded a 10 percent resilient sub-group, although most of these subjects often had effective parenting amidst the strain of impoverishment."

Ibid. pp. 17–18.

"That ability is the badge of individual worth, that calculations of ability create an image of a few individuals standing out from the mass, that to be an individual by virtue of ability is to have the right to transcend one's social origins—these are the basic suppositions of a society that produces feelings of powerlessness and inadequacy in the lives of people. . . ."

Sennett, Richard, and Cobb, Jonathan. *The Hidden Injuries of Class*. New York, NY: W.W. Norton & Company, 1972. p. 62.

"There are hints in the literature that suggest variables which may be operative in stressful life situations. One is the modification of stressors brought about by temperament, such as activity level, reflectiveness in meeting new situations, cognitive skills, and positive responsiveness to others. Another core of variables is to be found in families in poverty that are marked by warmth, cohesion, and the presence of some caring adult (such as a grandparent) in the absence of responsive parents. . . . A third variable is the presence of a source of external support as exemplified by a strong maternal substitute or a kindly concerned teacher, or the presence of an institutional structure, such as a caring agency or a church that fosters ties to a larger community" (Garmezy, 1985, 1987).

Garmezy, Norman. "Resiliency and Vulnerability to Adverse Developmental Outcomes Associated With Poverty." *American Behavioral Scientist*. March/April 1991. Volume 34. Number 4. ©1991, Sage Productions. p. 421.

"This definition says that resilience is competence despite chronic and severe adversity. It is important to remember that it is chronic and severe adversity such as lifetime poverty or cancer; although everyone faces hard times, not everyone faces such chronic and severe adversity. . . . What it means to be resilient varies depending on one's developmental level. Considering these limitations, about one-third of the population is high risk and one-third of that high-risk population is resilient, leaving 10 percent of the general population resilient" (Emmy Werner, 1994).

Gordon Rouse, Kimberly. "Resilience from Poverty and Stress." *Human Development Bulletin.* Columbus, OH: Ohio State University Extension, Spring 1998. Volume 4. Number 1. p. 1.

"The question then is: What are the personal qualities and social conditions that make it possible for some people to flourish when they have grown up in 'bad' families?

Rubin, Lillian. *The Transcendent Child.* New York, NY: HarperCollins Publishers, 1996. pp. 4–7.

"One major theme that emerges from these life histories is clear: *Some families have to be left behind.* And the transcendent child is one who, for a variety of reasons, is able to do that relatively early in life. . . . These were children . . . who were in the family but not of it and who, therefore, became the observers of family life. . . .

"I was seven years old when, bewildered by [my mother's] rage and hurt by her rejections, I began consciously to remove myself psychologically from the family scene. It was then I first said to myself clearly, *I won't be like her.* . . .

"So when, at eight, a friend who had watched me walk down the street said as I approached, 'You walk just like your mother,' I spent the next year training myself to walk differently."

"Since 1955, Werner and Smith have followed the lives of 698 children born on the island of Kauai in Hawaii. . . . All were reared in poverty; almost one-third also had experienced stress either before or at birth, were raised by parents with little education, or lived in families torn apart by fighting, divorce, alcoholism, or mental illness.

Wolin, Steven, and Wolin, Sybil. *The Resilient Self: How Survivors of Troubled Families Rise Above Adversity.* New York, NY: Random House, 1993. pp. 18–19.

"Nevertheless, many of these children developed into fine human beings as measured by the familiar triple standard of mental health: working well, playing well, and loving well. . . .

"Here are Werner and Smith's conclusions . . . : 'Our findings appear to provide a more hopeful perspective than can be had from reading extensive literature on "problem" children. . . . Risk factors and stressful environments do not inevitably lead to poor adaptation. It seems clear that . . . there is a shifting balance between stressful events that heighten vulnerability and protective factors that enhance resilience.' "

Chapter Ten: Improving the Work Performance: Teaching What Is Needed to Do the Job

"Feuerstein changes Piaget's formula for the 'free' and 'transparent' interactions between children and the world, denoted by the formula Stimuli-Organism-Response (S-O-R) by inserting the role of a mediator —a parent, grandparent, sibling or caretaker—who shapes the way the child perceives the world."

Sharron, Howard, and Coulter, Martha. *Changing Children's Minds: Feuerstein's Revolution in the Teaching of Intelligence.* Third Edition. Birmingham, England: Imaginative Minds, 1996. pp. 36–38.

"The formula now becomes S-H-O-R, the H standing for human intervention."

"Contrary to what conventional theories tell us, the way in which parents and other mediators construct their children's world is not through bombarding them with stimuli but by selecting, ordering, emphasizing and explaining some stimuli at the expense of others."

"Although 'deprivation' is often associated with poverty, what Feuerstein understands by cultural deprivation has its origin in many different social circumstances. It is associated, along with poor education achievement, with the lower socioeconomic classes. But while material constraints may be a very significant factor in ensuring that the parents do not have the time and energy to mediate a wide range of cultural needs to their children, they do not necessarily lead to cultural deprivation. Things are more complex: history, politics and economics as well as cultural traditions all take a role."

Ibid. p. 76.

Chapter Twelve: Developing Personal Skills for Working with People in Poverty

"So far the discussion of core competencies has been largely anecdotal. But a number of highly specialized mid-sized companies . . . are developing the methodology to measure and manage core competencies. The first step is to keep careful track of one's own and one's competitors' performances, *looking especially for unexpected successes and for unexpected poor performance in areas where one should have done well*" (emphasis added).

Drucker, Peter F. *Managing in a Time of Great Change.* New York, NY: Truman Talley Books/Dutton, 1995. p. 133.

"The individual knowledge worker will also have to learn something that today practically no one has learned: how to switch from one kind of team to another; how to integrate himself or herself into teams; what to expect of a team; and in turn, what to contribute to a team."

Ibid. p. 241.

"A good traveler has no fixed plans and is not intent upon arriving. A good artist lets his intuition lead him where it wants. A good scientist has freed himself of concepts and keeps his mind open to what is.

Mitchell, Stephen. *Tao Te Ching.* New York, NY: HarperCollins Publishers, 1988. p. 27.

"Thus the Master is available to all people and doesn't reject anyone. He is ready to use all situations and doesn't waste anything. This is called embodying the light.

"What is a good man but a bad man's teacher? What is a bad man but a good man's job? If you don't understand this, you will get lost, however intelligent you are. It is the great secret."

"The problems for which the poor are blamed have often been economic; they have been held partly responsible for the decline of the American economy. For example, to accuse the poor of being lazy and unwilling to adhere to the work ethic and its dress and time codes is easier than to confront the inability of the economy to create enough jobs, especially for unskilled people."

Gans, Herbert J. *The War Against the Poor: The Underclass and Antipoverty Policy.* New York, NY: Basic Books, 1995. p. 85.

Chapter Thirteen: Improving Agency Policies and Internal Processes

"... [T]he underclass label poses a danger for poor people in that the agencies with which they must deal can hurt clients who are so labeled. For one thing, agencies for the poor sometimes build labels into their operating procedures and apply them to all of their clients. As a result, either evidence about actual clients is not collected, or the label is assumed to fit regardless of evidence to the contrary. Agencies responsible for public safety typically resort to this procedure as a crime prevention or deterrence measure, especially when those labeled have little legal or political power."

Gans, Herbert J. *The War Against the Poor: The Underclass and Antipoverty Policy.* New York, NY: Basic Books, 1995. p. 66.

"Admittedly, labeling of clients is only a small part of staff-client misunderstandings and client mistreatment. The ... lack of funds and staff, the stresses of operating in stigmatized agencies and with stigmatized clients, normal bureaucratic rules that always put the demands of the agency and its staff ahead of the needs of the clients, as well as differences of class and race between staff and clients, wreak their own cumulative havoc."

Ibid. p. 68.

"The other major source of the reproduction of stigma and the stigmatized is the routine activities of the organizations that exist to service welfare recipients, the homeless, and other stigmatized poor. These activities continue to take place partly because the organizations involved lack the funds or power to provide the resources that would help their clients to leave welfare or rejoin the housed population, or for that matter, to escape poverty altogether. One major reason they lack these funds and this power is because the clients are stigmatized, and thus not viewed as deserving of much help."

Ibid. p. 100.

"The first step of a comprehensive crime policy has to remove people who are guilty of violent street and other major crimes from everyday life, but it must treat them in such a way that some or many can eventually be returned to that life and are not likely to become recidivists. The preventive part of the program must aim once more to try to transform prisons and work camps into rehabilitative institu-

Ibid. pp. 104–105.

tions or camps for all but the most chronic, violent, or otherwise disturbed lawbreakers. When a political and organizational opening for innovation and experimentation becomes available, such prisons and camps should be 'workplace prisons' that would also offer schooling and job training oriented to the world outside."

"Many social sector organizations will become partners with government—as is the case in a great many 'privatizations,' where for instance a city pays for street cleaning and an outside contractor then does the work. . . . These social sector organizations, while partners with government, also clearly compete with government. The relationship between the two has yet to be worked out—and there is practically no precedent for it."

Drucker, Peter F. *Managing in a Time of Great Change.* New York, NY: Truman Talley Books/Dutton, 1995. pp. 257–258.

Chapter Fifteen: Poverty Culture, Addiction, Treatment, and Recovery

"Researchers at the National Institute on Alcohol Abuse and Alcoholism (NIAAA), based on data from the 1992 National Longitudinal Alcohol Epidemiologic Survey, estimated that 17.9 percent of welfare recipients are dependent on alcohol or drugs, compared to 8.9 percent of non-recipients.

Making Welfare Reform Work: Tools for Confronting Alcohol and Drug Problems Among Welfare Recipients. New York, NY: Legal Action Center, September 1997. p. 5.

"The National Center for Addiction and Substance Abuse at Columbia University, based on 1991 National Household Survey on Drug Abuse data, reported that 20 percent of welfare recipients abuse or are addicted to drugs and alcohol."

"Sampling of welfare participants in a Montgomery County, Maryland, welfare program in 1990 found that between 16.1 and 20.8 percent were addicted to drugs or alcohol."

"Alcoholism is a fatal disease, 100 percent fatal. Nobody survives alcoholism that remains unchecked. . . . It is a myth that alcoholics have some spontaneous insight and then seek treatment. Victims of this disease do not submit to treatment out of spontaneous insight—typically, in our experience they come to their recognition scenes

Johnson, Vernon E. *I'll Quit Tomorrow.* New York, NY: Harper & Row Publishers, 1973. p. 1.

through a buildup of crises that crash through their almost impenetrable defense systems. They are forced to seek help; and when they don't, they perish miserably.

"This disease involves the whole man: physically, mentally, psychologically, and spiritually. The most significant characteristics of the disease are that it is primary, progressive, chronic, and fatal. But it can be arrested. The progress of alcoholism can be stopped, and the patient can be recovered. Not cured, but recovered."

"We have lost our sense of inner life; we have become so alienated from ourselves by work in the industrial era that abuse of alcohol or drugs or some other addiction is often the nearest thing we have to an inner life. Addiction is a larger industry in America today than automobile production. The effort to combat addiction is also a rapidly expanding industry."

Fox, Matthew. *The Reinvention of Work: A New Vision of Livelihood for Our Time.* New York, NY: Harper-Collins Publishers, 1994. pp. 21–22.

"Psychologists speak of this process as 're-framing,' but within the context of a spirituality of imperfection, the term *re-mapping* far more accurately conveys the idea of journey as well as the sense of discovering a new 'map' through storytelling. When newcomers to Alcoholics Anonymous become immersed in story-telling and storylistening, they begin to see the form and outline of a new map, which details where they are, and how they got there, and—most importantly —the way to get where they want to go.

"The active alcoholic does have a 'way of life,' a map— but it is the *wrong* map. . . . As an A.A. member once observed: 'The drinking alcoholic is trying to find his way around on Earth with this beautifully detailed map of Venus.' "

Kurtz, Ernest, and Ketcham, Katherine. *The Spirituality of Imperfection: Storytelling and the Journey to Wholeness.* New York, NY: Bantam Books, 1992. pp. 114–115.

". . . [A]ddictions are similar to other chronic disorders such as arthritis, hypertension, asthma, and diabetes. Addicting drugs produce changes in the brain path-ways that endure long after the person stops taking them. Further, the associated medical, social, and occupational difficulties that usually develop during the course of addiction do not disappear when the patient is detoxified. [These] protracted brain

O'Brien, Charles P., McLellan, A. Thomas. "Myths about the Treat-ment of Addiction." *Lancet,* January 1996. Volume 347. Number 896. p. 237.

changes and the associated personal and social difficulties put the former addict at great risk of relapse.
Treatments for addiction, therefore, should be
regarded as being long term, and a 'cure' is unlikely
from a single course of treatment."

". . . [S]tudies of abstinence rates at 1 year after completion of treatment indicate that only 30–50% of
patients have been able to remain completely absti-
nent throughout the period, although an additional
15–30% of patients have not resumed compulsive use." | Ibid. p. 238.

"Studies of treatment response have uniformly shown
that patients who comply with the recommended
regimen of education, counseling, and medication
that characterizes most contemporary forms of treatment, have typically favorable outcomes during
treatment and long-lasting post-treatment benefits.
Thus, it is discouraging for many practitioners that
many drug-dependent patients do not comply with
[the] recommended course of treatment and subse-
quently resume substance use. Factors such as low
socioeconomic status, comorbid psychiatric conditions, and lack of family or social supports for continuing abstinence are among the most important
variables associated with lack of treatment compli-
ance, and ultimately to relapse after treatment. | Ibid. p. 239.

"The diseases of hypertension, diabetes, and asthma
are also chronic disorders that require continuing care
for most, if not all, of a patient's life. . . . As with the
treatment of addiction, treatments for these chronic
medical disorders heavily depend on behavioral
change and medication compliance to achieve their
potential effectiveness. In a review of over 70 outcome
studies of treatments for these disorders patient compliance with the recommended medical regimen was
regarded as the most significant determinant of treatment outcome. Less than 50% of patients with insulin-
dependent diabetes fully comply with their medication
schedule, and less than 30% of patients with hypertension or asthma comply with their medication regi-
mens. . . . It is interesting in this context that clinical
researchers have identified low socioeconomic status,
comorbid psychiatric conditions, and lack of family
support as the major contributors to poor patient
compliance in these disorders."

Additive Model:

The aha! Process Approach to Building Sustainable Communities

by Philip E. DeVol

T he mission of aha! Process, Inc. is to positively impact the education and lives of individuals in poverty around the world. This mission is informed by the reality of life in poverty, research on the causes of poverty, and Dr. Ruby K. Payne's research and insights into economic diversity. The issues that aha! Process addresses are economic stability; the development of resources for individuals, families, and communities; and community sustainability. aha! Process provides an additive model that recognizes people in poverty, middle class, and wealth as problem solvers. The focus is on solutions, shared responsibilities, new insights, and interdependence. This work is about connectedness and relationships; it is about "us."

USING THE KNOWLEDGE OF PEOPLE IN POVERTY TO BUILD AN ACCURATE MENTAL MODEL OF POVERTY

Going directly to people in generational poverty, the people working the low-wage jobs, and listening to them talk about their concrete experiences is to learn from the experts, the people with the knowledge. The circle of life for a family at the bottom of the economic ladder is intense and stressful. Cars and public transportation are unreliable and insufficient, low-wage jobs come and go, housing is crowded and very costly, time and energy go into caring for the sick and trying to get health care, and many of the interactions with the dominant culture are demeaning and frustrating. For people in poverty, the arithmetic of life doesn't work. Housing costs are so high and wages so low that people have to double up, usually with family members, but often with people they may not know very well. All the elements in this mental model of poverty are interlocking: When the car won't start it sets off a chain reaction of missed appointments, being late to work, losing jobs, and searching for the next place to live. Vulnerability for people in poverty is concrete. When the price of gas goes to $2.20 a gallon it can mean having to work half a day to fill the tank. When one's attention is focused on the unfolding crisis of the day, people in poverty fall into what Paulo Freire calls the tyranny of the moment. Adds Peter Swartz: "The need to act overwhelms any willingness people have to learn." In this way poverty robs people of their future stories and the commitment to education. It requires them to use reactive skills, not true choice making, to survive. And finally, it robs them of power; the power to solve problems in such a way as to change the environment—or to make future stories come true.

By continuing to listen, one learns that people survive these circumstances by developing relationships of mutual reliance and facing down problems with courage and humor. It is family, friends, and acquaintances who give you a place to stay, food to eat, a ride to work, and help with your children. It's not Triple A that you call when your car breaks down; it's Uncle Ray. People in poverty are the masters at making relationships quickly. Above all, they are problem solvers; they solve immediate, concrete problems all day long.

Unfortunately, the current operating mental model of our society appears to be that people in poverty are needy, deficient, diseased, and not to be trusted. Again, this can be learned by simply listening: listening to policymakers, commentators, and taxpayers who don't want their tax dollars to go to someone who isn't trying, isn't motivated, is lazy, and so on. Another way to discover the underlying mental model is to observe its programs in action and work backwards. Three- to five-year lifetime limits for assistance, 90 days of services, work first . . . These policies point to frustration felt by those whose mental model of the poor is that they are needy, deficient, and diseased.

This inaccurate mental model is fed by media reports that favor soap operas to conceptual stories and individual stories to trends and the broader influences. The public hears about a fictitious "welfare queen" but not comprehensive studies. What is needed is a thorough understanding of the research on poverty.

STUDYING POVERTY RESEARCH TO FURTHER INFORM THE WORK OF AHA! PROCESS

David Shipler, author of *The Working Poor*, says that in the United States we are confused about the causes of poverty and, as a result, are confused about what to do about poverty (Shipler, 2004). In the interest of a quick analysis of the research on poverty, we have organized the studies into the following four clusters:

- Behaviors of the individual
- Human and social capital in the community
- Exploitation
- Political/economic structures

For the last four decades discourse on poverty has been dominated by proponents of two areas of research: those who hold that the *true* cause of poverty is the behaviors of individuals and those who hold that the *true* cause of poverty is political/economic structures. The first argues that if people in poverty would simply be punctual, sober, and motivated, poverty would be reduced if not eliminated. For them, the answer is individual initiative. Voter opinion tends to mirror the research. Forty percent of voters say that poverty is largely due to the lack of effort on the part of the individual (Bostrom, 2005). At the other end of the continuum, the argument is that globalization, as it is currently practiced, results in the loss of manufacturing jobs, forcing communities to attract business by offering the labor of their people at the lowest wages, thus creating a situation where a person can work full time and still be in poverty. In a virtual dead heat with the countering theory, 39 percent of voters think that poverty is largely due to circumstances beyond the individual's control. Unfortunately, both two sides tend to make either/or assertions as if to say, *It's either this or that—as if "this" is true and "that" is not.*

Either/or assertions have not served us well; it must be recognized that causes of poverty are a both/and reality. Poverty is caused by both the behaviors of the individual and political/economic structures—and everything in between. Definitions for the four clusters of research and sample topics are provided in the table on the next page.

Typically, communities put a great deal of effort into the first area of research: the behaviors of the individuals. "Work first" was one of the key themes of the welfare reform act of 1996. TANF (Temporary Assistance to Needy Families) organizations focused on getting people to work. The idea was that getting a job, any job, and learning to work were more important than going to job-training classes or receiving treatment. Community agencies offered treatment for substance abuse and mental-health problems, money-management classes, and programs to address literacy, teen pregnancies, language experience, and more. The mission of these agencies is not to work directly on poverty issues but to deal with co-existing problems. All of these agencies encourage their clients to change behaviors, recording and managing the changes through the use of plans and contracts, and often sanction clients who fail to adhere to treatment plans.

Community efforts to enhance human and social capital include the strategies found in Head Start, WIA programs, One-Stop centers, Earned Income Tax Credit, and other anti-poverty programs. In this area too, accountability and sanctions are used to measure and motivate community organizations. Schools that don't meet certain benchmarks are taken over by state departments; TANF organizations that don't meet certain benchmarks don't receive incentive funds. This isn't to make a blanket criticism of any of the programs that serve low-wage workers. In fact, many programs have great value to those who have used them. Rather, it's the almost exclusive focus on these two areas of research that is the problem.

Communities rarely develop strategies to restrict, replace, or sanction those who exploit people in poverty. Even those organizations charged with fighting poverty sometimes neglect this cause of poverty. In part, this comes

CAUSES OF POVERTY

1. Behaviors of the Individual

Definition: Research on the choices, behaviors, characteristics, and habits of people in poverty.

Sample topics:

Dependence on welfare	Racism and discrimination
Morality	Commitment to achievement
Crime	Spending habits
Single parenthood	Addiction, mental illness, domestic violence
Breakup of families	Planning skills
Intergenerational character traits	Orientation to the future
Work ethic	Language experience

2. Human and Social Capital in the Community

Definition: Research on the resources available to individuals, communities, and businesses.

Sample topics:

Intellectual capital	Childcare for working families
Social capital	Decline in neighborhoods
Availability of jobs	Decline in social morality
Availability of well-paying jobs	Urbanization
Racism and discrimination	Suburbanization of manufacturing
Availability and quality of education	Middle-class flight
Adequate skill sets	City and regional planning

3. Exploitation

Definition: Research on how people in poverty are exploited because they are in poverty.

Sample topics:

Drug trade	Gambling
Racism and discrimination	Temp work
Cash-advance lenders	Sweatshops
Sub-prime lenders	Sex trade
Lease-purchase outlets	Internet scams

4. Political/Economic Structures

Definition: Research on the economic, political, and social policies at the international, national, state, and local levels.

Sample topics:

Globalization	Taxation patterns
Corporate influence on legislators	Salary ratio of CEO to line worker
Declining middle class	Immigration patterns
De-industrialization	Economic disparity
Job loss	Racism and discrimination
Decline of unions	

from departmentalizing community services. People who work in organizations charged with serving those in poverty don't think of exploiters as their responsibility. That falls to law enforcement and policymakers.

Departmentalizing is even more pronounced when it comes to the causes of poverty that arise from political and economic structures. Community economic development is left to the market system, developers, businesses, corporations, the Chamber of Commerce, and elected officials. People who typically work with those in poverty don't see a role for themselves in the debate on economic development issues any more than those who are engaged in business ventures make a direct connection between their work and the well-being of people in poverty. And yet, in concrete terms, there is direct connection between quality of life and the actions of government and business. For the person in poverty it comes down to this: A person can get vocational training in a particular skill, get a job, and still be in poverty.

This all-too-common reality is the reason why communities must develop strategies across all four areas of research, not just the first two. To continue to focus exclusively on the first two areas of research is to invite more of the same—in short, more poverty. There is good research in all four areas; communities must develop strategies in all four areas if they are going to build resources and sustainability.

Alice O'Connor, author of *Poverty Knowledge*, says our society has typically looked at poverty through the prism of race and gender. She suggests that another analytic category is needed, that of economic class (O'Connor, 2001). In her seminal 1996 work *A Framework for Understanding Poverty*, Ruby Payne offered that prism. Since then aha! Process has published many books and produced many videos and workbooks that are used to address poverty across all four areas of research.

THE NEED FOR CHANGE: NAMING PROBLEMS AND FINDING SOLUTIONS

Any community or organization that sets out to address poverty, education, health care, justice, or community sustainability must acknowledge that it seeks change: change in the individual's behavior, change in community approaches, and/or change in political/economic structures. Put another way, there is no agency that receives money—be it federal, state, or private—to keep behaviors and conditions exactly as they are. We seek change because we perceive something to be wrong.

Naming the problem is the first step toward a solution, and the most important step, for if the problem is not named accurately the course of action based on that faulty assumption will only lead further and further from a solution. So naming problems accurately—making the correct diagnosis—is crucial because it is on those definitions that the theories of change and program activities are based.

But naming the problem isn't as simple as it seems. If a problem exists, is it due to something that is lacking, a shortage, a disadvantage, a handicap? It is here that planners, providers, and problem solvers tend to slide into what often is referred to as the deficit model. This model seems to derive from what William Miller calls the righting reflex. He says, "Human beings seem to have a built-in desire to set things right" (Miller, 2002). We see something that is wrong; we want to fix it. This tendency is all well and good as long as it's confined to one's own problems, but as soon as our fix-it intentions are focused on others, this approach quickly loses its charm and questions arise. Who is it that names the problem? Who is it a problem for? What evidence is provided? How broad or deep is the investigation? People from minority cultures and dominated groups are the first to ask these questions, for it is often their ways of raising children, their language uses, and their problem-solving strategies that are being labeled as having deficits by the mainstream culture. Nobody likes deficit labeling. So it is that the righting reflex leads to deficit models that few of us like—and even fewer defend, for good reasons.

There is no known father or mother of the deficit model. Nobody claims it, but the title or slur gets hung around the neck of those who use it, or appear to use it. Some people hold that James Coleman, who has been called the "father of busing," proposed a deficit model. A review of the body of his work would refute that label. His research on education, one of the largest research projects ever undertaken, discussed economic class and achievement in its complexities. It was legislators, businesspeople, school administrators, and others who were under pressure to "Fix it!" who simplified Coleman's work when they turned it into policy. There are two things to be learned from this. First, the deficit model is simplistic; it oversimplifies the research and applies the righting reflex. Second, there is research—and then there are those who use the research.

It's important to take a closer look at how problems get named and what the distinction is between naming problems and deficit labeling. The deficit model names the problem and blames the individual; the individual must change, whereas society can be left unaltered. It is, however, possible to name problems and not blame the individual. For example, Dr. James P. Comer, not by any stretch a proponent of the deficit model, does identify the family environment as crucial to a child's academic success. He points to hard science—brain research—that confirms the interactive process between the mediation (interpretation of reality) that children receive from caregivers before they come to school with the continuous mediation when children enter school. Quoting Comer: "Without [mediation] children can lose the 'sense'—the intelligence potential—they were born with. Children who have had positive developmental experiences before starting school acquire a set of beliefs, attitudes, and values—as well as social, verbal, and problem-solving skills, connections, and power—that they can use to succeed in school. They are the ones best able to elicit a positive response from people at school and bond with them." Read another way, this could appear as labeling low-income families with deficits. Of course, it isn't that because Comer acknowledges the problems that exist across the system; it's never as simple as the fault of a single person or group. The body of Comer's work reveals the true nature of his model (Comer, 2001).

Despite the fact that the deficit model seems to have no father or mother and is the work of policymakers more than researchers (and gets confused with the naming of problems), the deficit model is still for real. Its features are that it fixes the problems on the individual and therefore focuses on fixing the individual. Environmental conditions are translated into the characteristics of the individual and gradually turn into negative stereotypes. The talents, gifts, and skills of an individual get lost. In the deficit model the "glass is seen as half empty." The message becomes "you can't," and the impulse to care for and protect arises. Thus we have "special needs," "special programs," "special rooms," and "special personnel," all of which can lead to and foster dependency.

The lack of staff training can result in the deficit model appearing in the attitudes of the professionals, in individual bias, and inaccurate assumptions. Notes Comer: "Many successful people are inclined to attribute their situations to their own ability and effort—making them, in their minds, more deserving than less successful people. They ignore the support they received from families, networks of friends and kin, schools, and powerful others. They see no need for improved support of youth development" (Comer, 2001). Without training, staff members are likely to see deficits where there are none. A child who comes to school after getting up early to pump water from an outside well and whose mother hand-washes clothes once a week may be seen as dirty, less presentable, more lacking in physical resources than children who can shower in their own bathroom before coming to school and whose mother uses a washer and dryer. The first child has the resources and skills but isn't readily able to demonstrate those capabilities.

The lack of understanding on the part of the staff can lead to labeling that is hard to shake. If the school or agency doesn't provide some way for individuals to demonstrate their skills and resources, the glass will always appear to be half empty.

Problems are identified with student performance, drug use, teen pregnancy, inadequate skill sets, job retention, criminal behavior, poverty, and so on, all of which gives rise to fix-it programs. One Teacher Leaders Network online discussion participant offered this analogy about deficit-model programs: "We call it the 'chicken inspector' mindset. You see, the chicken inspector has been trained to look for something that isn't right, so that's his focus and that's what he finds—the things that are wrong. The more things he finds wrong, the better he feels he is doing his job."

The deficit model finds its way into the design of programs. Legislators and professionals set policy and create departments and programs. Each department is expected to fix the piece of the pie that falls under its purview. These reactions to the latest problem set up a random approach to problem solving and result in remedial programs focused on the behaviors of the individual while losing sight of the whole system made up of families, neighborhoods, communities, and sociopolitical/economic structures.

This isn't to suggest that policymakers and program designers set out to apply the deficit model. It's more likely that they select some other approach but for any number of reasons fail to adhere to their espoused theory (what is said) and slide into a "theory of use" (what is done) that resembles the deficit model (Senge, 1994). Perhaps the most common reason for this slip is that it's easier to describe, plan for, monitor, and sanction the behaviors of individuals than it is to hold organizations, communities, and systems accountable in the same way (Washburne, 1958). The fact is that the deficit model is resilient, and we slide back into it easily.

Opposite the deficit model are many models that offer what the deficit model does not. They go by many names: positive model, developmental assets, competency, value-based, and strength-based . . . to name a few. Other models have been assigned names by their developers: Health Realization, Resiliency in Action, Comer Model, and Motivational Interviewing to name but four. Each of these models has its distinct theory and practices, but the one thing they have in common is that they see "the glass as half full."

Positive models too are not without their critics. For example, child-protection workers point out that reframing the behaviors and characteristics of victims of abuse into strengths is naïve. No matter how resilient the child, the fact remains that the child has very little control over his/her environment and the behaviors of adults. Educators note that children in poverty have been exposed to more in their few years than many adults. In some ways they seem to have adult capabilities; they take care of themselves and feel confident they can handle big decisions. But the educators caution against accepting this claim. According to a recent piece by Craig Sautter, "We as adults need to remember that they are not adults. They still have a lot of growing and developing to do and still need the guidance of adults who can be there to help them through their growing-up period" (Sautter, 2005).

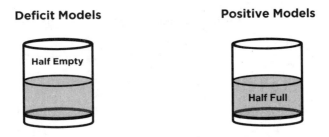

The additive model, a term used by Ruby Payne to describe the work of her company, aha! Process, combines the value of accurate problem identification with a positive, strength-based, communitywide approach to change. Applying the glass half empty/half full model to the three economic classes and the work of aha! Process would look like this:

For the Person in Poverty

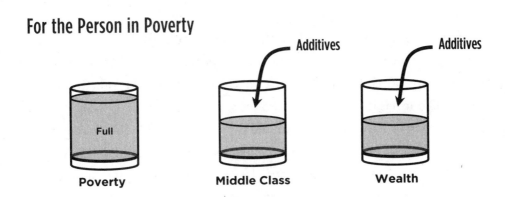

To survive in poverty, individuals must have reactive, sensory, and non-verbal skills. This means they have the ability to read situations, establish relationships, and solve immediate and concrete problems quickly. In that environment, individuals have a full glass; they have the assets and strengths to survive.

When individuals in poverty encounter the middle-class world of work, school, and other institutions, they do not have all the assets necessary to survive in that environment because what is needed there are proactive, abstract, and verbal skills. The additive model offers insight into how hidden rules of economic class work, along with a framework for building resources, a way to fill up the glass.

When the person in middle class encounters wealth, the same is true—but to a greater extent.

For the Person in Middle Class

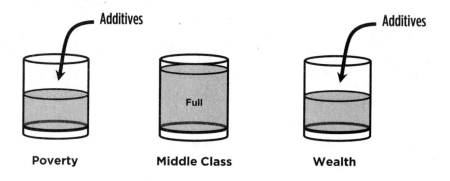

Individuals raised in a middle-class environment learn the hidden rules, mindsets, and means of survival the same way persons in poverty or wealth do: through osmosis. To learn the survival rules of one's environment, virtually all one has to do is breathe. So the glass is full so long as individuals remain in their environment. But should those persons suddenly find themselves in poverty—or even in a poverty neighborhood—would they have the assets needed to survive there? The glass would be half empty. But there is a more common scenario that brings people in middle class and people in poverty together; that is in the institutions run by middle-class people. In this scenario both groups come with a glass half full because they may not understand the rules or value the assets of the other person or the other class. Here is where the additive model can help. It names the problem and offers insight and awareness; it opens the way to build relationships and eventually to better outcomes for both.

As middle-class individuals interact with people in wealth they may not know any more about the rules of survival in wealth than the person in poverty knows about the rules of middle class (and how the values of the additive model apply).

The additive model has something to offer people in wealth as well.

For the Person in Wealth

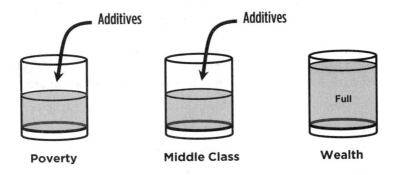

Where the worlds of wealth, middle class, and poverty intersect, the additive model can assist. Due to their connections, influence, and power, people in wealth often are in the position to design the policies and directions of the institutions that the middle class run and that the people in poverty use. If wealthy individuals' poverty and middle-class glass is only half full and all they know is their own rules of survival, then it can result in policies that are ineffective and counterproductive.

To better understand the additive model, we must consider aha! Process definitions and core concepts.

RESOURCES

Resources: The following resources are quality-of-life indicators that are described in almost all aha! Process publications.

- Financial
- Emotional
- Mental
- Spiritual
- Physical
- Support systems
- Relationships/role models
- Knowledge of hidden rules

Poverty: the extent to which an individual or community does without these resources.

Prosperity/sustainability: the extent to which an individual or community has these resources.

By these definitions it is easy to see that an individual may have low financial resources and at the same time have other resources that are very high. Of course, the opposite is true too: One can have high financial resources and be impoverished in other ways.

This approach emphasizes that every individual's story is different and takes into account the culture in which one lives. And yet, as a general rule, the additive model holds that to have high resources is better than to not have high resources. It's preferable to have financial stability than to be unable to pay for basic needs. It's preferable to have many positive relationships than to live in isolation. It's preferable to be able to identify feelings, choose behaviors, and get along with others than to be emotionally destructive.

The additive model holds that:

- Resources are to be developed by communities, families, and individuals. In fact, it is the appropriate role, or "job" if you will, of individuals, families, and communities to grow resources for oneself, one's family, and the community.

- The optimal way to build resources is to build on one's strengths. Focusing on low resources, weaknesses, and what is absent not only is no fun, it simply isn't effective.

- We must develop resource-building strategies across all four areas of poverty research. The deficit model is at work when a community focuses its anti-poverty strategies on the behaviors of the individual.

Ruby Payne's research on the hidden rules of economic class is another key component of the aha! Process approach. It is this analytic category that provides a new lens through which to examine poverty and prosperity issues. Again, some definitions will help clarify the additive model.

HIDDEN RULES OF ECONOMIC CLASS

Hidden rules: the unspoken cues and habits of a group. All groups have hidden rules; you know you belong when you don't have to explain anything you say or do. These rules are held by racial, ethnic, religious, regional, and cultural groups . . . to name a few. An individual's cultural fabric is made up of many threads, one of which is economic class. Where the threads are woven together the different cultures act on behaviors of the individual and group. Of these rules, economic class is a surprisingly strong thread, one that is often overlooked—or at least minimized.

The additive model holds that:

■   The hidden rules arise from the environment in which a person lives, that they help persons survive in the class in which they were raised. This means that the rules of class are not to be criticized, but that we simply add options, new rules, a wider range of responses, an ability to negotiate more environments. While these are framed as choices and not identity, any individuals who begin to work on achievements—such as economic stability, education, or getting sober—are changing their identity. How they make the transition is a choice: Will they stay connected with people from their past, or will they move into new circles? This is an individual and often painful choice/process. Being aware of the choice can smooth the process, whatever the decision.

■   It is beneficial for middle-class people to learn the hidden rules of poverty—and not just so they're able to help people in poverty make changes, but because the hidden rules of poverty have value in their own right. Perhaps first among these is the value of relationships and the time given to them. The ability people in poverty have to establish quick but intimate relationships is an asset. In the additive model, change takes place, not just in the individual but in the theories of change and program designs of organizations. Middle-class organizations often have based their work on middle-class mindsets without an adequate mental model of poverty or knowledge of the hidden rules of the people they serve.

It is by adding to the hidden rules that one is raised with that people develop a range of responses that will give them control over their situations and open doors to new opportunities.

LANGUAGE ISSUES

The aha! Process approach calls for an extensive discussion of language issues, including definitions of the registers of language, discourse patterns, story structures, language experience in the first three years of life, cognitive issues, and strategies to deal with all of these. As a body of work, aha! Process's many books, workbooks, videos, classroom strategies, program design strategies together make up a remarkable representation of the additive model. It is here that the model calls for an accurate naming of problems where the word deficit is used.

The additive model holds that:

- People build relationships by using the registers of language and discourse patterns skillfully.

- The strengths and uses of each register are encouraged where they can be most skillfully applied.

- Classroom interventions and agency strategies must be based on a clear understanding of the issues and a clear definition of the problems.

- The interventions themselves are built on the assets of the individual and the necessary changes fall as much on the professionals as on the individuals in poverty.

- Learning structures in the brain can be enhanced, but only by knowing the exact nature of the thinking that is occurring. In school settings the intervention cannot be random or general. The strategies offered by aha! Process are grade- and subject-specific.

- A rich language experience benefits children and prepares them for the world of work and school.

- Teachers value the language experience that children bring with them to school and prepare students to be able to skillfully navigate a wide range of language situations.

- In social service settings with adults, the additive model calls for the staff to become bilingual (able to translate from formal register to casual register).

- Change messages—be they about cardiovascular disease, breast feeding, birth weight, or the prevention of drug use—often taught in the formal register are now taught through a self-discovery process and by using mental models. Communication is meaningful and not just what Robert Sapolsky calls middle-class noise (Sapolsky, 1998).

FAMILY STRUCTURE

Matriarchal structure: All families have capabilities and strengths, and all families are faced with demands. In the course of life all families must face suffering and hard times, but some families seem to have more than their share of suffering to contend with. Under ordinary demands and stressors, families will become stronger as a result of their struggles. But there are some things that can overrun and overwhelm a family's capabilities; those include chronic addiction, mental illness, physical illness, and poverty (Henderson, 1996). People in poverty sometimes contend with more than poverty alone, and poverty itself is so stressful that there is a direct correlation between poverty and stress-related illnesses (Sapolsky, 1998). In high-demand conditions, families take on a structure that fits the survival needs of the family. In that context, the matriarchal structure and associated patterns of behavior are assets, but if viewed in light of a deficit model are often seen as negative or even as lacking in morals. A matriarchal family is not synonymous with a dysfunctional family. As in all economic classes, dysfunctional things may happen, but living in poverty does not equate with dysfunctional behaviors. The additive model provides an understanding and appreciation of matriarchal families and offers new information and ways of increasing resources.

The additive model holds that:

- Family structures evolve to meet the survival needs of the family and that they are strengths.

- As with aha! Process knowledge, awareness gives people optional ways to stabilize the chaotic circle of life, to envision new patterns and stories, to practice choice, and to build new resources.

SHARING AHA! PROCESS KNOWLEDGE WITH ADULTS IN POVERTY

Co-investigation: Sharing aha! Process knowledge with people in poverty is done through a group investigation of the causes of poverty, examining the impact of poverty on the individual, and exploring new information. Individuals in the group assess their own resources and make plans to build their own future story. Here's one way of articulating the challenges faced by people in poverty:

Poverty traps people in the tyranny of the moment, making it very difficult to attend to abstract information or plan for the future (Freire, 1999; Sharron, 1996; Galeano, 1998)—*the very things needed to build resources and financial assets. There are many causes of poverty, some having to do with the choices of the poor, but at least as many stemming from community conditions and political/economic structures* (O'Connor, 2001; Brouwer, 1998; Gans, 1995).

The additive model holds that:

- People in poverty need an accurate perception of how poverty impacts them and an understanding of economic realities as a starting point both for reasoning and for developing plans for transition (Freire, 1999; Galeano, 1998).

- Using mental models for learning and reasoning, people can move from the concrete to the abstract (Freedman, 1996; Harrison, 2000; Sharron, 1996; Mattaini 1993; Jaworski, 1996; Senge, 1994).

- People can be trusted to make good use of accurate information, presented in a meaningful way by facilitators who provide a relationship of mutual respect and act as co-investigators (Freire, 1999; Sapolsky, 1998; McKnight, 1995; Pransky, 1998; Farson, 1997).

- Using Ruby Payne's definition of the resources necessary for a full life, as well as her insights into the hidden rules of economic class, people can evaluate themselves and their situation, choose behaviors, and make plans to build resources (Miller, 2002).

- The community must provide services, support, and meaningful opportunities during transition and over the long term (Putnam, 2002; Kretzmann, 1993).

- In partnership with people from middle class and wealth, individuals in poverty can solve community and systemic problems that contribute to poverty (Phillips, 2002; Kretzmann, 1993).

AHA! PROCESS KNOWLEDGE AND COMMUNITY SUSTAINABILITY

Community sustainability: This is an issue that all communities, states, and nations must now face. The world has seen several revolutionary changes: the change from hunter/gatherer societies to agriculture, the industrial revolution, the information age, and now the era in which we must determine how to use our resources and live in our environment—and yet retain vital resources for our children and grandchildren.

The mission of aha! Process—to directly impact the education and lives of individuals in poverty around the world—leads to a role in this revolution. Communities are awakening to the reality that they do not offer a sustainable way of life to their children and are looking for direction. Equity and critical mass impact the changes that are taking place. If a community allows any group to be disenfranchised for any reason (religion, race, class), the entire community becomes economically poorer (Sowell, 1998). When poverty reaches the point of critical mass in a community and efforts to reverse the problem don't succeed, the people with the most resources tend to move out of the community, leaving behind enclaves of poverty. At this point the community is no longer sustainable.

Responding to the impending crisis with the mindset that created it and with the strategies that have been used to address poverty to date is to invite more of the same results: more poverty and more communities at risk.

aha! Process defines community as any group that has something in common and the potential for acting together (Taylor-Ide 2002). The rich social capital that peaked in the post–World War II era—and that has been on the decline since—must be restored (Putnam, 2000). The barn-raising metaphor for communities where citizens contribute to the building of the barn with their particular skills, gifts, and talents must replace the vending-machine metaphor, which is currently in use. The vending-machine metaphor reduces community members to consumers or shoppers who put 75 cents into the machine expecting 75 cents of goods and services in return. With that mindset, it's no surprise that we find people kicking, shaking, and cursing the vending machine.

The additive model holds that:

- It's better to be a barn raiser than a consumer.

- All three classes must be at the table.

- Communities must have a shared understanding and a common vocabulary to build critical mass that is willing and motivated to make the necessary changes.

- Strategies must cover all the causes of poverty—from the behaviors of individuals to political/economic structures.

- Communities must build intellectual capital.

- Long-term plans of 20 to 25 years are needed.

- Quality-of-life indicators must be monitored and reported regularly in the same way that economic indicators are monitored and reported.

CONCLUSION

aha! Process offers a unique understanding of economic diversity that can give individuals, families, and communities new ways of solving problems. It is the hope of aha! Process that 100 years from now poverty will no longer be viewed as economically inevitable. Two hundred years ago slavery was thought to be an economic necessity. It was not. One hundred fifty years ago it was believed that women were not capable of voting. That also was not true. We fervently hope that by 2100 individuals and society at large will no longer believe that poverty is inevitable. It is only by applying an additive model that we will understand and address both poverty and the underlying factors that have perpetuated it.

WORKS CITED

Andreas, Steve, & Faulkner, Charles. (Eds.) (1994). *NLP: The New Technology of Achievement*. New York, NY: Quill.

Bostrom, Meg. (2005). Together for Success: Communicating Low-Wage Work as Economy, Not Poverty. Ford Foundation Project. Douglas Gould & Co.

Brouwer, Steve. (1998). *Sharing the Pie: A Citizen's Guide to Wealth and Power in America*. New York, NY: Henry Holt & Company.

Comer, James P. (2001). Schools That Develop Children. *The American Prospect*. Volume 12. Number 7. April 23.

DeVol, Philip E. (2004). *Getting Ahead in a Just-Gettin'-by World: Building Your Resources for a Better Life.* Highlands, TX: aha! Process.

Farson, Richard. (1997). *Management of the Absurd: Paradoxes in Leadership.* New York, NY: Touchstone.

Freedman, Jill, & Combs, Gene. (1996). *Narrative Therapy: The Social Construction of Preferred Realities.* New York, NY: W.W. Norton & Company.

Freire, Paulo. (1999). *Pedagogy of the Oppressed.* New York, NY: Continuum Publishing Company.

Fussell, Paul. (1983). *Class: A Guide Through the American Status System.* New York, NY: Touchstone.

Galeano, Eduardo. (1998). *Upside Down: A Primer for the Looking-Glass World.* New York, NY: Metropolitan Books.

Gans, Herbert J. (1995). *The War Against the Poor.* New York, NY: Basic Books.

Harrison, Lawrence E., & Huntington, Samuel P. (Eds.). (2000). *Culture Matters: How Values Shape Human Progress.* New York, NY: Basic Books.

Henderson, Nan. (1996). *Resiliency in Schools: Making It Happen for Students and Educators.* Thousand Oaks, CA: Corwin Press.

Jaworski, Joseph. (1996). *Synchronicity: The Inner Path of Leadership.* San Francisco, CA: Berrett-Koehler Publishers.

Kahlenberg, Richard, D. (2001). Learning from James Coleman. *Public Interest.* Summer.

Kretzmann, John, & McKnight, John. (1993). *Building Communities From the Inside Out: A Path Toward Finding and Mobilizing a Community's Assets.* Chicago, IL: ACTA Publications.

Lewis, Oscar. (1966). The Culture of Poverty. *Scientific American.* Volume 215. Number 4. pp. 19–25.

Mattaini, Mark A. (1993). *More Than a Thousand Words: Graphics for Clinical Practice.* Washington, DC: NASW Press.

McKnight, John. (1995). *The Careless Society: Community and Its Counterfeits.* New York, NY: Basic Books.

Miller, William R., & Rollnick, Stephen. (2002). *Motivational Interviewing: Preparing People for Change,* Second Edition. New York, NY: Guilford Press.

O'Connor, Alice. (2001). *Poverty Knowledge: Social Science, Social Policy, and the Poor in Twentieth-Century U.S. History.* Princeton, NJ: Princeton University Press.

Payne, Ruby K., DeVol, Philip, & Dreussi Smith, Terie. (2001). *Bridges Out of Poverty: Strategies for Professionals and Communities.* Highlands, TX: aha! Process.

Phillips, Kevin. (2002). *Wealth and Democracy: A Political History of the American Rich.* New York, NY: Broadway Books.

Pransky, Jack. (1998). *Modello: A Story of Hope for the Inner-City and Beyond.* Cabot, VT: NEHRI Publications.

Putnam, Robert D. (2000). *Bowling Alone: The Collapse and Revival of American Community.* New York, NY: Simon & Schuster.

Sapolsky, Robert M. (1998). *Why Zebras Don't Get Ulcers: An Updated Guide to Stress, Stress-Related Diseases, and Coping.* New York, NY: W.H. Freeman & Company.

Sautter, Craig. (2005). Who Are Today's City Kids? Beyond the "Deficit Model." North Central Regional Educational Laboratory, a subsidiary of Learning Points Associates. http://www.ncrel.org/sdrs/cityschl/ city1_1a.htm

Senge, Peter M. (1994). *The Fifth Discipline: The Art & Practice of The Learning Organization.* New York, NY: Currency Doubleday.

Sharron, Howard, & Coulter, Martha. (1996). *Changing Children's Minds: Feuerstein's Revolution in the Teaching of Intelligence.* Birmingham, England: Imaginative Minds.

Shipler, David K. (2004). *The Working Poor: Invisible in America.* New York, NY: Alfred A. Knopf.

Sowell, Thomas. (1998). Race, Culture and Equality. *Forbes*. October 5.

Sowell, Thomas. (1997). *Migrations and Cultures: A World View*. New York, NY: HarperCollins.

Taylor-Ide, Daniel, & Taylor, Carl, E. (2002). *Just and Lasting Change: When Communities Own Their Futures*. Baltimore, MD: Johns Hopkins University Press.

Washburne, Chandler. (1958). Conflicts Between Educational Theory and Structure. *Educational Theory*. Volume 8. Number 2. April.

Bibliography

Alexie, Sherman. (1993). *The Lone Ranger and Tonto Fistfight in Heaven.* New York, NY: HarperPerennial.

Axelrod, Robert. (1997). *The Complexity of Cooperation: Agent-Based Models of Competition and Collaboration.* Princeton, NJ: Princeton University Press.

Bluestein, Jane. (1995). *Mentors, Masters, and Mrs. MacGregor: Stories of Teachers Making a Difference.* Deerfield Beach, FL: Health Communications.

Bradshaw, John. (1988). *Bradshaw on: The Family.* Deerfield Beach, FL: Health Communications.

Bragg, Rick. (1998). *All Over but the Shoutin'.* New York, NY: Vintage Books.

Carnevale, Anthony P., & Desrochers, Donna M. (1999). *Getting Down to Business: Matching Welfare Recipients' Skills to Jobs That Train.* Policy & Practice of Public Human Services. March.

Champy, James. (1995). *Reengineering Management.* New York, NY: HarperCollins Publishers.

Clark, Richard. (1992). *Building Coalitions.* Columbus, OH: The Ohio Center for Action on Coalitions for Families and High Risk Youth, Ohio State University.

Cooper, J. California. (1991). *The Matter Is Life.* New York, NY: Bantam Doubleday.

Covey, Stephen R. (1989). *The Seven Habits of Highly Effective People: Powerful Lessons in Personal Change.* New York, NY: Simon & Schuster.

Danziger, Sheldon H., Sandefur, Gary D., & Weinberg, Daniel H. (Eds.). (1994). *Confronting Poverty: Prescriptions for Change.* Cambridge, MA: Harvard University Press.

Dash, Leon. (1997). *Rosa Lee: A Mother and Her Family in Urban America.* New York, NY: Plume.

Davidson, Osha G. (1996). *Broken Heartland: the Rise of America's Rural Ghetto.* Iowa City, IA: University of Iowa Press.

Dean, Christiann. (1991). *Empowering Partnerships with Families.* Innovations in Community and Rural Development, Cornell Community and Rural Development Institute. Internet Website: www.cals.cornell.edu/dept/cardi/publications/innov/in1093-2.html. September.

Deavers, Kenneth L., & Hattiangadi, Anita U. (1998). Welfare to work: building a better path to private employment opportunities. *Journal of Labor Research.* Volume 19. Number 2. Spring.

Drucker, Peter F. (1990). *Managing the Non-profit Organization.* New York, NY: HarperCollins Publishers.

Drucker, Peter F. (1993). *Post-Capitalist Society.* New York, NY: HarperCollins Publishers.

Drucker, Peter F. (1995). *Managing in a Time of Great Change.* New York, NY: Truman Talley Books/Dutton.

Feuerstein, Reuven, et al. (1980). *Instrumental Enrichment: An Intervention Program for Cognitive Modifiability.* Glenview, IL: Scott, Foresman & Co.

Fisher, Roger, & Ury, William. (1983). *Getting to YES: Negotiating Agreement Without Giving In.* New York, NY: Penguin Books.

Fox, Matthew. (1994). *The Reinvention of Work.* New York, NY: HarperCollins Publishers.

Frank, Robert H., & Cook, Philip J. (1995). *The Winner-Take-All Society: Why the Few at the Top Get So Much More Than the Rest of Us.* New York, NY: Penguin Books.

Gans, Herbert J. (1995). *The War Against the Poor.* New York, NY: Basic Books.

Garmezy, Norman. (1991). Resiliency and vulnerability to adverse developmental outcomes associated with poverty. *American Behavioral Scientist.* Volume 34. Number 4. March/April.

Gee, James Paul. (1987). What is literacy? *Teaching and Learning: The Journal of Natural Inquiry.* Volume 2. Number 1. Fall.

Goad, Jim. (1997). *The Redneck Manifesto.* New York, NY: Simon & Schuster.

Gordon Rouse, Kimberly. (1998). Resilience from poverty and stress. *Human Development Bulletin.* Columbus, OH: Ohio State University Extension. Spring.

Greenspan, Stanley I., & Benderly, Beryl L. (1997). *The Growth of the Mind and the Endangered Origins of Intelligence.* Reading, MA: Perseus Books.

Gurian, Michael. (1997). *The Wonder of Boys: What Parents, Mentors and Educators Can Do to Shape Boys into Exceptional Men.* New York, NY: Jeremy P. Tarcher/Putnam.

Hart, Betty, & Risley, Todd R. (1999). *Meaningful Differences in the Everyday Experience of Young American Children.* Baltimore, MD: Paul H. Brookes Publishing Co.

Heider, John. (1985). *The Tao of Leadership.* Atlanta, GA: Humanics Limited.

Helmreich, William. (1995). *Holocaust Survivors and the Successful Lives They Made in America.* Somerset, NJ: Transaction Publishers.

Henderson, Nan. (1996). *Resiliency in Schools: Making It Happen for Students and Educators.* Thousand Oaks, CA: Corwin Press.

Hijuelos, Oscar. (1999). *Empress of the Splendid Season.* New York, NY: HarperFlamingo.

Howard, Philip K. (1994). *The Death of Common Sense.* New York, NY: Random House.

Huang, Chungliang Al, & Lynch, Jerry. (1995). *Mentoring: The TAO of Giving and Receiving Wisdom.* San Francisco, CA: HarperSanFrancisco.

Jaworski, Joseph. (1996). *Synchronicity: The Inner Path of Leadership.* San Francisco, CA: Berrett-Koehler.

Johnson, Vernon E. (1973). *I'll Quit Tomorrow.* New York, NY: Harper & Row Publishers.

Joos, Martin. (1967). The styles of the five clocks. *Language and Cultural Diversity in American Education.* 1972. Abrahams, R.D., & Troike, R.C. (Eds.). Englewood Cliffs, NJ: Prentice-Hall, Inc.

Kelly, Kevin. (1998). *New Rules for the New Economy: 10 Radical Strategies for a Connected World.* New York, NY: Viking.

Kingsolver, Barbara. (1993). *Pigs in Heaven.* New York, NY: HarperCollins Publishers.

Kissler, Gary D. (1991). *The Change Riders.* Reading, MA: Addison-Wesley Publishing Company.

Kiyosaki, Robert T., & Lechter, Sharon L. (1998). *Rich Dad, Poor Dad.* Paradise Valley, AZ: TechPress.

Kohm, Amelia. (1998). Cooperating to survive and thrive: innovative enterprises among nonprofit organizations. *Nonprofit World.* Volume 16. Number 3. May/June.

Kurtz, Ernest. (1979). *Not-God: A History of Alcoholics Anonymous.* Center City, MN: Hazelden.

Kurtz, Ernest, & Ketcham, Katherine. (1992). *The Spirituality of Imperfection.* New York, NY: Bantam Books.

Kutchins, Herb, & Kirk, Stuart A. (1997). *Making Us Crazy: DSM: The Psychiatric Bible and the Creation of Mental Disorders.* New York, NY: The Free Press, Simon & Schuster.

Laabs, Jennifer J. (1998). Welfare law: HR's role in employment. *Workforce.* Volume 77. January.

Lee, Chang-Rae. (1995). *Native Speaker.* New York, NY: Riverhead Books.

Making Welfare Reform Work: Tools for Confronting Alcohol and Drug Problems Among Welfare Recipients. (1997). New York, NY: Legal Action Center. September.

Martini, Alberto, & Wiseman, Michael. (1997). *Explaining the Recent Decline in Welfare Caseloads: Is the Council of Economic Advisors Right?* Washington, DC: The Urban Insititute. July.

Martz, Linda. (1999). Community Health Access Project. *Mansfield News Journal.* July 8.

Mattessich, Paul W., & Monsey, Barbara R. (1992). *Collaboration: What Makes It Work.* St. Paul, MN: Amherst H. Wilder Foundation.

McCall, Nathan. (1994). *Makes Me Wanna Holler.* New York, NY: Vintage Books.

McCourt, Frank. (1996). *Angela's Ashes: A Memoir.* New York, NY: A Touchstone Book, Simon & Schuster.

Merton, Thomas. (1965). *The Way of Chuang Tzu.* New York, NY: New Directions.

Mitchell, Stephen. (1988). *Tao Te Ching.* New York, NY: HarperCollins Publishers.

Montano-Harmon, Maria Rosario. (1991). Discourse features of written Mexican Spanish: current research in contrastive rhetoric and its implications. *Hispania.* Volume 74. Number 2. May. pp. 417–425.

Morrison, Toni. (1982). *Sula.* New York, NY: Plume.

Naylor, Gloria. (1992). *Bailey's Cafe.* New York, NY: Vintage.

Newman, Katherine S. (1999). *No Shame in My Game: The Working Poor in the Inner City.* New York, NY: A Borzoi Book, Alfred A. Knopf.

Ng, Fae M. (1993). *Bone.* New York, NY: HarperCollins Publishers.

O'Brien, Charles P., et al. (1996). Myths about the treatment of addiction. *Lancet.* Volume 347. Number 896. January.

O'Connell Higgins, Gina. (1994). *Resilient Adults: Overcoming a Cruel Past.* San Francisco, CA: Jossey-Bass.

Oliver, Caroline (Ed.). (1999). *The Policy Governance Fieldbook: Practical Lessons, Tips, and Tools from the Experience of Real-World Boards.* San Francisco, CA: Jossey-Bass.

Olson, Krista, & Pavetti, LaDonna. (1996). *Personal and Family Challenges to the Successful Transition from Welfare to Work.* Washington, DC: The Urban Institute. May 17.

Oshry, Barry. (1996). *Seeing Systems: Unlocking the Mysteries of Organizational Life.* San Francisco, CA: Berrett-Koehler Publishers.

Palincsar, A.S., & Brown, A.L. (1984). The reciprocal teaching of comprehension-fostering and comprehension-monitoring activities. *Cognition and Instruction.* Volume 1. Number 2. pp. 117–175.

Pavetti, LaDonna. (1997). *Against the Odds: Steady Employment Among Low-Skilled Women.* Washington, DC: The Urban Institute. July.

Pavetti, LaDonna. (1997). *Moving Up, Moving Out or Going Nowhere? A Study of the Employment Patterns of Young Women.* Washington, DC: The Urban Institute. July.

Payne, Ruby K. (2003). *A Framework for Understanding Poverty* (Third Revised Edition). Highlands, TX: aha! Process.

Quinn, Daniel. (1999). *Beyond Civilization: Humanity's Next Great Adventure.* New York, NY: Harmony Books.

Rubin, Lillian. (1996). *The Transcendent Child.* New York, NY: HarperCollins Publishers.

Schaefer, Dick. (1987). *Choices & Consequences.* Minneapolis, MN: Johnson Institute.

Sennett, Richard, & Cobb, Jonathan. (1972). *The Hidden Injuries of Class.* New York, NY: W.W. Norton & Company.

Sharron, Howard, & Coulter, Martha. (1996). *Changing Children's Minds: Feuerstein's Revolution in the Teaching of Intelligence.* (Third Edition). Birmingham, England: Imaginative Minds.

Shenk, David. (1997). *Data Smog.* New York, NY: HarperCollins Publishers.

Steinberg, Stephen. (1981, 1989). *The Ethnic Myth: Race, Ethnicity, and Class in America.* Boston, MA: Beacon Press.

Tribe, Deana L. (1993). Contemporary images of Appalachian Ohio: a view from within. *Journal of the Appalachian Studies Association.* Volume 5.

Underhill, Paco. (1999). *Why We Buy: The Science of Shopping.* New York, NY: Simon & Schuster.

Upchurch, Carl. (1996). *Convicted in the Womb.* New York, NY: Bantam Books.

Washburne, Chandler. (1958). Conflicts between educational theory and structure. *Educational Theory.* Volume 8. Number 2. April.

Wasserman, Harvey. (1972). *Harvey Wasserman's History of the United States.* New York, NY: Harper Colophon Books.

Werner, Emmy. (1995). *Pioneer Children on the Journey West.* Boulder, CO: Westview Press.

Wheatley, Margaret J. (1992). *Leadership and the New Science: Learning about Organization from an Orderly Universe.* San Francisco, CA: Berrett-Koehler Publishers.

Whitman, Linda Hall. (1997). Welfare-to-work management. *HR Focus.* Volume 74. October.

Whitmyer, Claude. (Ed.). (1994). *Mindfulness and Meaningful Work: Explorations in Right Livelihood.* Berkeley, CA: Parallax Press.

Eye-openers at ...
www.ahaprocess.com

■ Join our **aha!** news list

  Receive our free newsletter with periodic news, updates, recent articles by Dr. Ruby K. Payne, and more! And get a free book, *Understanding Learning,* when you join!

■ Register online for Bridges Out of Poverty U.S. National Tour and Dr. Payne's U.S. National Tour

■ Visit our online store

  Books, videos, workshops

■ Learn about our Training Certification programs

  A Framework for Understanding Poverty

  Bridges Out of Poverty

  Meeting Standards & Raising Test Scores

■ If you liked *Bridges Out of Poverty,* look for *Getting Ahead in a Just-Gettin'-By World: Building Your Resources for a Better Life.* It's DeVol's latest publication—a step-by-step life-planning workbook for individuals in poverty working in groups with a facilitator.

Resources for communities from aha! Process

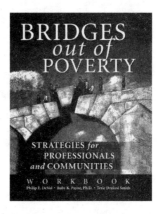

Workbook: *Getting Ahead in a Just-Gettin'-By World: Building Your Resources for a Better Life*

Getting Ahead by Philip E. DeVol is a step-by-step, life-planning workbook for people in poverty that brings together three primary influences: (1) Dr. Ruby K. Payne's work on the hidden rules of class, (2) research on knowledge transfer, and (3) the knowledge of participants who live in poverty.

The workbook is designed to be used as an investigation tool by people working in groups with a trained facilitator. The participants explore the impact that poverty has had on them, investigate economic realities, complete a self-assessment of their own resources, make plans to build their own resources, and develop a mental model of community prosperity.

Bridges Out of Poverty Workbook

This workbook is used in conjunction with "Bridges Out of Poverty" workshops and the book. It contains highlights covered in the training.

Five pages are provided at no charge on the downloads page on our website.

Workbook: *Getting Ahead in a Just-Gettin'-By World: Facilitator Notes*

If you are considering using this program, the first 20 pages of the *Facilitator Notes* provide an good way to get an understanding of the work. These pages include the program's philosophy, theory, motivation, and incentive, and it gives background for teaching each of the modules in *Getting Ahead in a Just-Gettin'-By World*.

Visit our website at www.ahaprocess.com for a complete listing of products.

Order Form

Please send me _____ copy/copies of *Bridges Out of Poverty* at $22 per book (or $15 each for 5 or more books). Enclosed is payment for:

Books	$ _____	
Shipping	$ _____	($4.50 first book + $2.00 each additional book)
Subtotal	$ _____	
Sales tax	$ _____	(Only residents of Alabama, Florida, Georgia, Kentucky, Nebraska, New Mexico, Tennessee, and Texas)
Total	$ _____	

UPS Ship-to Address (no post office boxes, please)

Name_____

Organization _____

Address _____

_____

Phone _____

E-mail _____

Method of Payment

PO # _____

Credit card type_____ Exp. _____

Credit card # _____

Check $ _____ Check # _____

Thanks for your order!

www.ahaprocess.com

PO Box 727 • Highlands, TX 77562-0727
(800) 424-9484 • fax (281) 426-5600